Ethics for Civil Services

अ अक्षर
प्रतियोगी पुस्तकें

Ethics for Civil Services

Alok Ranjan
(Retd. IAS)
Ex. Chief Secretary Govt. of Uttar Pradesh

RADHAKRISHNA

ISBN: 978-93-91950-57-6

Ethics for Civil Services

First Edition: 2022

Price: ₹290

Published by
Radhakrishna Prakashan Pvt. Ltd.
G-17, Jagatpuri
Delhi-110 051

Branches: Ashok Rajpath, Near Science College, Patna-800 006
Ist Floor, Darbari Building, Mahatama Gandhi Marg, Prayagraj-211 001
36 A, Shekspear Sarni, Kolkata-700 017

Website: www.radhakrishnaprakashan.com
Email: info@radhakrishnaprakashan.com

Printed at
B.K. Offset
Naveen Shahadara, Delhi-32

ETHICS FOR CIVIL SERVICES
by Alok Ranjan

CONTENT

Chapter 1

Concept of Ethics

Ethics and Human Interface

Essence of Ethics

Ethics are the standards by which human actions can be judged as being right or wrong. Morality defines which action can be termed as right or wrong while ethics goes forward to propose standards to judge better a particular action as right or wrong. The great value of this is in decision-making both in the personal life of an individual as well as in his professional life. The important questions of life are how one should live life; what is the meaning of happiness in life; how would you call a particular action as being virtuous? What do we understand by duty and justice? How do we relate to other human beings, living creatures and the environment? These questions have been a major concern of human society right from the beginning of civilization and human beings have always endeavored to live a moral and ethical life cherishing values which bind the society together and take it forward on the path of progress through right living. In simple language the essence of ethics is a right way to live.

The concern of religions has been similar to that of ethics but ethics is not religion. A person can be non-religious but ethical. However, a religion has no meaning if it does not propagate ethics though not all human beings who swear by religion live an ethical and moral life. However, if you look at this historically then you find that ethics has been the fundamental concern of all religions. The Vedic philosophy and its quintessence the *Upanishads* have clearly defined the right way to live. It says that to penetrate through illusion and understand the ultimate truth of human existence is to understand what is right. Similarly, all the great religions of the world propound moral codes. For instance, Jesus Christ advocated

"Love your neighbor as thyself". Buddha advocated truthfulness, right living, right motives, right speech and right action. Confucius, the great Chinese philosopher, said that a superior man is one who is humane, thoughtful and motivated by a desire to do what is good rather than by personal profit. Another Chinese philosopher Lao-Tzu talked about the virtues of simplicity and sincerity.

Human beings govern themselves by expressing the general will of the people in the form of a law but ethics is not synonymous to following a law. A good system of law does incorporate many ethical standards but law cannot be different from that which is ethical. Ethics is also not the same thing as following culturally accepted norms. For example, discrimination on caste basis was accepted in the Indian society but was ethically wrong.

The terms values, ethics, morals and character are often used in an interchangeable manner but there are subtle differences between them though each reinforces the other. Values are the accepted principles or standards of an individual or a group and affect their attitudes and aspirations. Values can be said to be like the anchor of a ship. Ethics is a study of moral standards and how they affect conduct. Morals relate to issues of right or wrong and prescribe how individuals should behave and has as its basis the personal conscience of an individual. Character is an extension of values and focuses on qualities of mind and feeling which is reflected by the action of an individual or a group. Character expresses itself in conduct. We can say that morality is an individual set of commitments even when they are not accepted by others but one cannot be ethical alone. Ethics brings other people for the realization of the self. A person can be moral, listening to the voice of his conscience without demanding that others also follow his moral code.

Public servants have to carry out their duties in an ethical manner and very often a code of ethical conduct is prescribed for them. They must realize that they hold public office as a trust and use it only to further public interests rather than personal gain. Openness, efficiency, transparency, integrity, fairness, responsiveness and accessibility are the foundations of public service ethics. The Nolan committee has enunciated seven principles of ethics in public life namely selflessness, objectivity, accountability, openness, honesty and leadership.

The SARC (Second Administrative Reform Commission) has defined ethics as a set of standards that society places on itself which helps guide behavior, choices and actions and is expressed in action.

For example, indulging in corruption and abuse of public office are examples of unethical behaviors. SARC goes on to say that both values and institutions matter. Values are needed to serve as guiding stars and they exist in abundance in our society for a sense of right or wrong are intrinsic to our culture and civilization. It goes on to say that creation of institutions and designing of incentives are of utmost importance in promoting ethical conduct of public servants. However, to promote desirable behavior the State comes up with the system of laws, the compliance of which promotes desirable behavior. Enforcement of rule of law and deterrent punishment against corruption are critical to build an ethically sound society.

It has been found that a discussion on ethics often evokes more emotion than reason and very often professional bodies display an ethics aversion syndrome. Very often we hear even public servants say that they know their job and do not need to be lectured on ethics. Often people find ethical standards as being impractical and unrealistic. It is also true that if an organization is ethically flawed then its members will not behave in a fully ethical manner. It is thus important for ethics to be the foundation stone of all organizations if a culture of ethical conduct is to be ensured amongst its members. It is important to understand that ethical conduct ultimately leads to the progress of an individual and organizations. Ethics goes along with better performance and is not the opposite of it. For example, a public servant has to maintain total integrity if he wants to do justice to his job and bring about quality delivery of public service.

Ethics in Private and Public Relationships

Ethics governs both private and public relationships. There is also no clear demarcation between the two as it would not be proper to call a person ethical on the basis of his public conduct if in his private life he carries out unethical activities. For example, a public servant may be honest and sincere and competent in his public or professional life but could be illtreating his wife at home which means that in his private life he is not ethical. A moral agent must be ethical both in private and public relationships.

Private relationships are those which an individual has with his family members like wife, parents, siblings and other relatives and friends. It also includes the relationships that an individual may have with other members of the society at a personal level like going to a shop to buy some products and relationship that you may have with the shopkeeper. It is the culture of the family which decides the ethical norms of the behaviour of an individual. For instance, we are taught to be respectful to our parents and be obedient. The basic value of love, trust, helping each other, selflessness, caring kindness, truthfulness and other aspects of moral behaviour are learned in the family by either following the example set by the parents or the values inculcated through the teachings imparted by them. Then it is friends through whom we imbibe morals and values and finally at schools and college it is a teacher who sets the ethical or moral standards for us. Our religious practices are also the source of personal values. It is through rewards or punishment or other incentives or disincentives that a human being acquires his ethics and values. Most of these values are universal in nature like always telling the truth, not injuring anybody, not stealing, being kind and generous and to be loyal and faithful to one's relations. Every religion talks about moral conduct and impresses upon its followers to abide by the prescribed moral code.

Public relationships refer to the role of an individual in his job, as a professional, and as a member of the society, for example, the relationship between the doctor and his patients. There is a code of ethics for doctors and medical professionals which guides their behaviour towards patients and their jobs and every doctor is expected to follow the ethical code. Similarly every profession whether it is law, journalism, teaching or government service has its own code of ethics which defines their public ethical conduct. For example, a public servant is expected to be honest, sincere, open, transparent, impartial, objective, efficient and committed to act as per the law and the constitution.

Every organization or institution has its own work culture which governs the relationships between its members and with the outside world. For example, government servants are often accused of being more concerned with procedures than delivering actual results. However, public servants are also expected to be concerned about the poor and the marginalized sections of the society. A public servant is supposed to function in a manner that he serves the people. In private sector organizations the main purpose often is making profits and very often their behaviour is governed accordingly. For example, many industries violate environmental norms just to generate more profits without being concerned about the negative impact on the health of the society. However, all this is now changing because of the pressure of society. In India also, the company law act has been amended and SEBI has given detailed guidelines of the compliances that a company has to ensure and this provides the basis for the ethical conduct expected of a company. Similarly, investors are now investing more in companies which follow norms of environmental, social and corporate governance ethics. Along with profits commitment to society is now defining the ethics of private organizations also.

Ideally there should be no difference between the conduct of a person in his private or public relationships. In both, he has to follow the ethical standards and moral code. However, as pointed out in the first paragraph very often there are cases where a person may be ethical in his public life but not so in his private relationships with his or her family members. Such a person cannot be called an ethical person. A commitment to ethics is essential in private as well as public relationships.

Branches of Ethics

1. Descriptive ethics—This branch of ethics is concerned with the history and evolution of ethics and tries to find out the reason behind the choices made by moral agents in their behaviour and how this is linked to the belief system of the people. In other words, it is an effort to empirically understand the moral belief system of people.
2. Normative ethics—This branch of ethics tries to search and find out the correct standards of moral behaviour and makes an effort to prescribe how people should act. It also suggests punishment when a person deviates from the moral path. The theory of Aristotle, Kant, Mill and even the *Bhagvat Gita* are theories of normative ethics and shall be discussed in another chapter.
3. Meta ethics—This branch of ethics studies, its origin and meaning of ethical concepts. It studies ethical terms and theories and also tries to understand the meaning of moral terms and moral judgments.
4. Applied ethics—This relates to application of ethics to real life problems e.g. the taking of dowry or reservation for the weaker sections in Government jobs.

Determinants of Ethics

The determinants of whether an act is ethical or not are—

1. Object of the act;

2. The circumstances in which the act was performed; and
3. The end or intention in the mind of the person performing the act.

Every action performed by human beings has a good, bad or indifferent object which defines it. For example, stealing is by nature bad while honesty is good. It means that the essential nature of an act could be either good or bad or indifferent and shall remain so irrespective of the circumstances of purpose. The second determinant of an act being ethical is the circumstances in which it has been performed. The circumstances determine how good or bad an action is. The third determinant is the purpose or end of the action for example, if a public servant commits an irregularity with the intention of making undue personal gains then his purpose is wrong and he will be liable for criminal action. However, if his intention is to complete a project on time in public interest and he bypasses some procedures then his intention is right and his action cannot be called unethical. Thus, it is clear that these three factors determine the ethics or morality of an action.

How would we decide the extent of accountability of a person for a wrong action done by him? He would be fully responsible if the action is voluntary, meaning that he has full knowledge of the situation and has taken the action willfully. However, it could be that he has taken this action under pressure or duress or threat to his family or himself and such action even though performed with knowledge of its consequences cannot be termed as unethical. There are times when a person is overcome by emotions and acts in anger and his action at such times is involuntary as they have been provoked by some action of the others. Even though a person is supposed to keep his passions in check, these actions are less unethical or immoral then those performed with deliberate intent.

A question can be asked what determines the ethical behaviour of an individual. There can be many factors behind this with the most important being the individual value system and beliefs of a person. Every person has his own ethical code which influences him in taking decision in personal as well as professional life. The culture and ethics of an organization also influences the conduct of its members. Most professional bodies and organization have a code of ethics which sets the standards for their ethical conduct. The ethos and value system of a country or society also has a direct influence on the ethical conduct of its members.

Consequences of Ethics

It is the individual who takes a decision or carries out an action which could be described as ethical or unethical. There is a doctrine of determinism which believes that the decisions and actions of human beings are caused or determined by external forces which means that human beings are not autonomous or free agents to decide things on their own. If we go by this theory then human beings cannot be judged morally on the basis of their actions as it is the external forces which are making them act in a particular manner. This is opposed to the other theory that human beings have a free will and so it is they who decide what action they should take and so are responsible for the morality or ethics of their actions. The philosophy opposed to determinism is called libertinism which says that human actions are derived from the human mind and reason over which they have a large degree of control and as such they would be responsible for the morality of their actions. If you take the case of civil servants, you will find that they are not entirely free to decide issues as they have to take decisions as per rules, laws, regulations, guidelines as well as under the prevailing political, economic and social circumstances. Yet despite all this there is always the element of discretion in decision-making and it is this which will decide whether a civil servant is acting ethically or not. For example, if there is an external pressure on a civil servant to do something which he does not believe to be correct he has the discretion to refuse and put forward his views with justification. Also, in matters related to integrity, the position is absolutely clear and it is the free will of the civil servant which decides whether he will work with honesty and integrity, or not. A corrupt civil servant can never take the excuse that he acted in this manner due to some external pressure. The ethics of a public servant is always choosing public interest over personal gain and this is a guiding factor for all his conduct.

Every action has a consequence and the same applies to human actions. Every thought of a human being is expressed in the form of words or actions which have a consequence for which the person is himself responsible. The consequences of an action can be good as well as bad and this is often known as a double effect. If we choose wrong means to achieve a desirable end we can say that this is not acceptable as the bad effect of the means used is greater than the good effect of the outcome. Violence or use of force is bad but if a person resorts to force in self-defence it is considered correct or good. An army when fighting the enemy kills the soldiers of the other country but here its actions are considered good as they are in the interest of his country, thus, we see that the consequences of an action can be termed as good or bad depending upon the situation in which it has been undertaken and the intention behind it. The opponents of this double effect doctrine are of the view that moral agents are fully responsible for the consequences of their actions and intention or situation.

It is true that human beings are responsible for their moral actions. It is up to the moral agent to decide whether he wants to tell the truth, steal, injure others or kill anybody or covet the other person's property and he should be responsible for the consequences of this action. The same applies to public servants who are responsible to observe ethical conduct and will be responsible for anything unethical that they do. However, even criminal law recognizes the necessity of criminal intention for taking action against an individual. Thus, intention of doing an act is important and if the intention is not bad then the consequences should also not be as harmful as they would be if the intention was bad.

Human beings live their lives in pursuit of happiness and act accordingly but some of their actions give them pleasure while others give pain. Human beings would always try to do that, the consequence of which gives them pleasure. However, it is also a fact that when we look around in the real world we find that those who always act ethically or morally sometimes have to face a lot of pain and unhappiness while those who are unethical or immoral evidently seem to enjoy a happy life. This question always poses a dilemma before individuals and you can hear people ask why do bad things happen to good people? For example, a corrupt officer enjoys a high quality of life and also reaches the top of his career while an honest officer sometimes does not reach the top or even faces false allegations. However, by and large ethical actions lead to good consequences and it is important for an individual or a public servant to behave in an ethical manner even if, for some time, he does not get the desired results.

Role of Family in Values

We have already defined ethics as a set of standards that determine the moral behavior of an individual. Values are principles which a person has and which influences his attitude and his behaviour. Values are related to the thought-process of the individual and his sense of right and wrong. They are associated with the personal rather than the professional aspects of a person and can be categorized as moral values, social values, religious values, political values and others. Values are determined by the experiences that a person has in interaction with others. Though there are certain values like telling the truth which are universal, there are others which vary from person to person. The family, teacher, friends and other members of the society play a large role in determining the value system of an individual.

Family is by far the most important source of the value system of an individual. A person learns values by looking at the example of his parents, other relatives and siblings. Many of these values are learnt unconsciously by simply observing the seniors and the family and imitating them. For instance, if the father of the child imbibes alcohol and does not consider it wrong then the child would also have a similar belief. A child also notices how his parents behave with each other and others in the society and develops similar values in his attitude and behavior. Parents and elders in the family also consciously impart values to their children and constantly reinforce them by giving example and also by use of reward and punishment. For example, parents impress upon their children to be hard-working and sincere in their study and these values remain with the child when he grows up. The family always impresses upon a person the importance of sharing, caring, sacrifice, selflessness, kindness, generosity, politeness, courtesy and other important values which are the essential aspects of the value system of an individual. Generally it is the positive values that are passed down from the elders to a person in a family. It is the family which teaches the person to have faith in God, to observe religious practices, to be obedient and respectful to elders and never cheat, tell lies or do anything illegal or wrong.

However, often a person inculcates negative values from his family also. For instance, if women are nor respected in his family he would also not be able to have the right attitude towards women in his personality. Moreover, often social values have come down from generations and the family believes in them and passes them on to its members. A classic example is the belief in the caste system in India with a sense of there being a hierarchy amongst the castes leading to wrong behaviour with castes which a person considers to be of a lower origin than him. Similarly, very often communal feelings in a person also develop while being members of a family which has a communal thinking. Further, if the father of a person is dishonest or corrupt then the person is likely to absorb the same personality traits as he would not be considering them to be wrong.

There is no doubt that the family is the cradle of values that enters into the subconscious mind of an individual and determines his mindset and attitude and behavior.

Role of Society in Values

Every individual is a member of the community and society around him and is influenced by the societal values. For instance, if in a society people feel that it is not wrong to pay bribes to get your job done then members of the society imbibe this value. In India we find that at the time of marriage a large dowry is demanded by the family of the bridegroom. This practice has wide acceptance in the society and permeates the value system of its members. Most young boys are not averse to taking dowry in their marriage even though it cannot be justified as a moral or ethical act. Similarly members of a particular caste, especially in a rural area, do not want to sit and eat with members of lower castes and this reprehensible value remains with the individual throughout his life. In a similar way there are some societies which put a high premium on the value of charity and helping the poor. The society makes its members follow the value system, even though it may not be ethical, by reward or punishment which forces people to conform to a particular behaviour pattern just because it is the accepted norm in a society. Family is nothing but the microcosm of the society and it absorbs the value system sanctioned by the society.

Role of Educational Institutions in Values

Next to the family, it is the educational institutions that play a major role in the formation of the value system of an individual. The role of the teachers is next only to the parents. A child always respects his teachers and follows their directions. It is in the school or college that a person inculcates values like punctuality, obedience, respect for others, how to behave with other children, how to be a member of a team and how to work hard with sincerity to achieve your goals. A person learns discipline in the educational institutions. It is here that he imbibes values necessary to be a good citizen and develops a rational, logical, analytical and scientific manner of looking at things and solving probles. It is in schools and colleges that the mind of a person is broadened and he learns about both success and failure and how to handle them.

The family, the educational institutions, the teachers, friends and society all contribute to the development of the personality of the individual and his basic value system. If you want to change the values of a person it is through these institutions that it is possible to do so.

Chapter 2

Human Values— Lessons from the Lives and Teachings of Great Leaders, Reformers and Administrators

Introduction

The great leaders, reformers and administrators shed a lot of light on how to live a life based on human values by the example of their lives and their teachings. They become icons of the society whom people admire and respect and desire to follow in their footsteps. We have already discussed that values are the guiding principles for an individual, organization, society or the nation. There are universal values which hold true in all conditions, for all peoples at all times like the value of being truthful. There are other values which are specific to a family, community, society or nation and are a reflection of the thinking at a particular time. An example of this is the attitude towards women which has undergone great change overtime but still varies from person to person.

Human Values

All great leaders and reformers share certain basic human values. They all are committed to serve the people and the society and to take it forward in the right direction. They are people of integrity with empathy and compassion for the under privileged. They all are truthful and correct in their behavior and actions. They work for benefit of the people or humanity and not for their personal gains. They work towards making the quality of life of the people better. Their work is guided by truth, love, care, concern, kindness, compassion, selflessness and commitment to justice.

Leaders have the personality traits of decision-making and commitment to the people and their organizations. They iron out the differences between the followers and bring them together to work as a team for the fulfillment of a larger goal. They are full of idealism and are also people of action. They work for others and not for themselves and wield power with humility and kindness and a sense of justice. The administrators specifically focus on the qualities of fairness, impartiality, objectivity, transparency and integrity. The reformers are those who are deeply concerned and disturbed by the wrong practices that they find as being prevalent in the society. They have a lot of respect for humanity and want to change the quality of the life of the people for the better.

Though the syllabus of the UPSC does not give the names of these leaders who should be studied we will take a few examples to illustrate the learning that we can get from the life of great people.

Gandhi

Mahatma Gandhi is revered as the father of the nation. He was a saint as well as a political leader and a reformer and his life is perhaps the greatest example of the attributes that a leader must possess. He gave India freedom from the oppressive British rule but was always committed to truth and non- violence. He resorted to non-violent methods to continuously apply pressure on the British Government to give freedom to India. He never cared about personal power and did not want any post for himself.

Gandhi believed that the means to achieve a goal are as important as the goal itself. He suspended the non-cooperation movement as soon as he heard of violence being indulged in. This is a great lesson for all as we so often try to justify our actions by saying that the end result is good or moral. Gandhi was concerned about the morality of the means used. For instance, today many politicians feel that they have to somehow win the election and gain political power and resort to all kinds of immoral or unethical means to achieve these goals. Similarly administrators sacrifice their integrity and bow down to political pressure justifying their action by saying that the result achieved is for the good of the society. Gandhi's value system would not accept the use of such methods to achieve a goal no matter how desirable it may be. Gandhi was sad when India got freedom as there were communal riots. The horrors of the partition were against the basic values that Gandhi believed in.

Gandhi's life was an example of a life based on the philosophy espoused in the *Ramayana, Bhagwad Gita* and the *Upanishads* and the highest ethical standards propounded by these texts. Gandhi believed in the oneness of mankind and had equal respect for all religions though he was a practicing Hindu. He wanted all communities and people to live together in peace, friendship, brotherhood and love. He had no hatred for anybody. He fought against the British imperialist system but did not hate the British. His life teaches us to have a universal vision of humanity in human life. There could be no discrimination between one human being and another in Gandhi's world.

Gandhi believed in the dignity of an individual and was not in the favor of a coercive state. He was also a great social reformer who fought against the curse of untouchability and discrimination against the lower castes. He treated human beings as equal.

Gandhi regarded God as being the source of all light and life and for him God was truth-knowledge-bliss (*Sat-Chit-Anand*). He saw God in every human being and so emphasized service to humanity. Non-violence for Gandhi was a creed of fearlessness in the face of injustice which must be resisted. Non-violence was not the policy of a coward but that of a man with great inner strength.

Gandhi was open to the good principles of all religions and societies. He believed in continuously evolving towards realization of the higher truth.

The residents of the Ashrams of Sabarmati and Kochrab observed 11 vows which are an indication of the thinking of Gandhi and along with truth and non-violence included celibacy, control of the palate, no stealing, not having personal possessions, fearlessness and respect for all religions.

Gandhi also identified seven social sins which are—

1. Politics without principles: According to Gandhi politicians should follow ethical principles in politics if the politics has to be moral and serve the interest of the people. Gandhi would never have appreciated the immense use of money and muscle power in politics and the desire of political parties to get votes without any concern for morality.
2. Wealth without work: It is important to work for a living and acquire wealth through honest work. Gandhi was in favor of manual labour.
3. Commerce without morality: Business should not only focus on maximizing profits but also pay attention to the development and welfare of the society and the community. All business should be based on morality and such business would ultimately lead to welfare of all including the businessman.

4. Education without character: Any education which does not build the character of a person is imperfect and harmful and will not lead to social welfare.
5. Science without humanity: Gandhi was not against science but for him science and technology must have a purpose which is human welfare and betterment of quality of life of the people. Technology should not lead to dehumanization of the human society.
6. Pleasure without conscience: Gandhi, true to the Indian culture and ethos, was against a life of sensual pleasure. He advocated a life devoted to individual and social welfare.
7. Worship without sacrifice: There can be no worship of God without any sacrifice. The sacrifice could be that of bad habits, bad companions or vices. No worship can be perfect without sacrifice which may be in the form of any kind of fasting or suffering at the altar of God.

There can be no greater prescription for living a good life than following the above principles and avoiding the seven deadly sins.

Gandhi saw a positive correlation which between the rights and duties of citizens in a state and to enjoy rights one must perform one's duties. Gandhi was of the view that every man has an equal right to the necessities of life. Today we see so many people talking of their rights but are not conscious of their duties. Gandhi would term such behavior as unethical.

Gandhi's concept of democracy was based on morality, justice, truth and individual freedom. For him a perfect democracy is one in which the welfare of the maximum is ensured and there is no exploitation of the weak by the strong. He wanted to spiritualize politics and endow the state with a moral basis. As regards public policy Gandhi was clear that the biggest test of a right policy was to see how it would be effect the poorest and weakest person and whether such a person's quality of life would be improved by it.

Gandhi had a clear concept of justice which had six main constituents—

- Pure Justice: This comes from kindness, compassion, care and love.
- Satanic Justice: This is wicked in nature motivated by the selfishness of man.
- Claim to Natural Rights: The basic rights given by nature to be available to all.

- Social Justice: Equal treatment of all in society and no exploitation.
- Absence of Duress: No use of force or compulsion.
- No harm to the opponent party: Gandhi did not believe in hating even one's own enemies. For example, he felt no hatred towards the British but was against the British colonial system.

Gandhian ethics is based on four axioms—truth, non-violence, non-attachment to worldly wealth and *sarvodaya* (welfare of all). He wanted to achieve the goal of an ideal society through institutional changes like bread labour, trusteeship and spiritualization of politics. For him the means of achieving of goal was as important at the end. His goal was to build a moral society and bring about all round development of the human being.

As far as his economic philosophy is concerned he believed in sustainable and balanced development consisting of self sufficiency and self reliance and leading to human development. For him an economic system should cater to the needs of all and not to their greed. He focused on village as the primary organization which needed to be developed as most of India lived in villages. He advocated the development of Khadi or Village Cottage Industries and he was in favor of technological improvement through appropriate technology to make village industries more efficient. He was in favor of decentralization of political and economic power as according to him this would lead to the holistic development and welfare of all.

There is no doubt that Gandhi was one of the greatest human beings ever born and there is no wonder that the great physicist Albert Einstein observed that generations to come would wonder whether such a person actually lived in "life and blood".

Nelson Mandela

Just like Gandhi, Nelson Mandela fought against injustice and discrimination and his life is a saga of the fight against apartheid in South Africa – inhuman treatment of the black by the whites. He was imprisoned for more than 30 years before he succeeded in achieving dignity and equality for his people. Mandela was of the view that the brave man is not one who is not afraid but who conquers his fear. For him every man had a duty towards his country and the community. Just like Gandhi, Nelson Mandela used non-violence as a method to fight for truth and justice. He believed in universal values of love and brotherhood. The greatest moment came when he was released from prison, contested and won the elections and became the President of South Africa. He forgave the whites for oppressing the blacks and treated all men equally as South Africans and human beings. His life is a great example of persistent fight against an unjust system and the qualities of always believing in one self and never giving up. There was no hatred in Mandela against the whites but he opposed the system of discrimination. He believed in the oneness of mankind.

Martin Luther King Jr.

Martin Luther King was a great black leader who gave his life fighting for a just and equal inclusive society. He fought non-violently for the rights of the black people of the United States of America and it was through his effort that the civil rights acts of 1964 and the Voting rights Act 1965 was passed to give equal rights and dignity to the blacks. His philosophy was best expressed in the most famous speech made by him which was as follows "I have a dream. It is a dream deeply rooted in the American Dream that one day this nation will rise up and live out the true meaning of its creed—that all men are created equal". He was opposed to racial injustice and dreamt of a world of brotherhood. He wanted to achieve his ends by love and not hatred and he famously said that "Not to satisfy the thirst of freedom by drinking from the cup of bitterness and hatred".

Abraham Lincoln

Lincoln was the President of USA from 1860 to 1864 and is remembered for ending slavery in America by signing the emancipation proclamation. He courageously fought the civil war and saved the nation from getting fragmented. He stood up for justice and equality despite the opposition and even sacrificed his life for the cause and the nation. His life is an amazing story of how he contested and lost the elections at various levels but continued to believe in himself and finally was elected the President of United States of America. We learn from him how to stand up for the values, principles you believe in irrespective of the consequences.

Bal Ganga Dhar Tilak, Jawahar Lal Nehru, Sardar Vallabhai Patel, Rajendra Prasad, Jai Prakash Narayan and Subhash Chandra Bose

The above is the list of those people who gave up lucrative careers and worked tirelessly for the freedom of the Indian nation. This is only an indicative list because there were so many others like Bhagat Singh who gave their life for the country. We learn from such great people the importance of standing up for what you believe in even though the adversary may be extremely powerful. We learn that it is not a life of comfort but a life of idealism which is important and that the nation is above us all.

The example of these great leaders tells us that you have to have ideals, you have to stand-up for truth and justice, you have to put others before yourself and stand firm courageously in the face of any adversity or opposition. Civil servants must learn that they are entering the service not for personal profit or power but to serve the people and they should be committed to ethics, morality and values.

Lessons from Administrators

It would be difficult to list out the names of administrators as there have been many who have contributed to the Indian nation. Jawahar Lal Nehru stablised the new Indian nation and made sure that democracy took deep roots in India. He ushered in an era of socialist planning, inclusiveness, scientific temper and non-alignment in international relations. Similarly, Sardar Vallabhai Patel was firm and determined and made sure that the Indian nation did not breakup into smaller nations. He united India and was responsible for maintaining the civil services in the same way. We can talk of the achievements of TN Seshan who made sure that elections in India were free and fair and APJ Abdul Kalam who worked tirelessly to inculcate values, scientific thinking and self belief in the youth of India. There have been great civil servants who came up with innovation to transform the society. We can learn from the lives of great administrators about their complete commitment to public service and integrity. They worked for the development of the nation and to make sure that the constitution and the rule of law was followed in letter and spirit. They were transparent, impartial and neutral and their concern was not for their personal gains but for the benefit of the society. They worked for the citizens and believed in prompt and affective action, building teams and delivering results. Above all was their commitment to human values and public service values. Nobody who became great could have done so without being an example of ethical and moral behavior.

Lessons from the Lives and Teachings of Great Reformers

India has been blessed to have great saints and spiritual thinkers whose lives and teachings give numerous learnings with respect to human values, ethics and morals.

Swami Vivekananda

This is the first name which comes to mind when you think of great reformers. He gave back self confidence to all Indians who had lost belief in themselves and their culture due to thousands of years of subjugation. He awakened the suppressed soul of India as he made Indians realize that they are heirs to a great religion, a great culture and a great civilization. He asked them to "Arise and Awake and stop not till the goal is reached." He was committed to serve the poor and the sick through the Ram Krishna Mission. He believed in the potential divinity of the soul and the universality of all religions. He said that India is an example of not only universal tolerance but universal acceptance. He took the message of Hindu religion and Indian civilization to the west and tried to harmonize Indian Spiritualism with western science and technology. He wanted people to have faith in themselves and live a life of idealism and service. He advocated practical Vedanta which is a humanistic philosophy of a way of life.

Swami Ram Krishna Paramhansa

He was the God and Guru of Swami Vivekananda and believed that the God is present in all human being in entire creation. His life and teachings were a testimony to the harmony and oneness in all religions and the human race. He advocated human beings to lift their consciousness above lust, greed and all such immoral thinking and actions. For him *jeeva* was Shiva and therefore, the highest value for a human being was to serve others.

Raja Ram Mohan Roy

He was a great social, educational and religious reformer who established the Brahmo Samaaj in India which was an organization committed to reform the Indian Society from within. He worked against social injustice and unfair, unequal and inhuman social practices prevalent in the society. He worked hard to abolish the practice of Sati which used to force widows to immolate themselves on their husband's funeral pyre. He also opposes child marriage. He felt that these reforms will strengthen the Hindu society. In addition, he carried out religious reforms like not worshiping any images or idols, not sacrificing any animal as part of worship and there being no need to perform rituals. He had extremely liberal religious views. He also founded educational institutions for the development of the country. He believed that India had a bright future.

Dayanand Saraswati

He was another powerful social and religious reformer who founded the Arya Samaj. He believed that *Vedas* were the supreme truth as they were the revealed word of God. He was against the caste system and stood for giving equal status to all men and women. He was against all obscurantist religious practices and simplified many of the elaborate Hindu rituals.

Tiruvalluvar

He was a great poet, preacher and thinker. His works bring out the deep commitment to humane and universal moral values. His great work *Thirukkural* elaborates on virtues, worldliness and love. He emphasized gratitude, self-control, right conduct, faithfulness and forgiving one's enemies.

There are many great reformers about whom we can talk. However, the learning from their lives and teachings are similar. They talk about the oneness of humanity and no distinction between various religions. They advocated universal human values like love, forgiveness, telling the truth and other aspects of right conduct. They took up issues about practices and customs which according to them were not correct even though most of the society followed them. They wanted to remove all evils from the society and make human beings good, noble and happy.

Thus we find that we learn about a commitment to ethics, morals and human values from lives and teachings of great reformers, leaders and administrators.

References

Ethics for Governance – Reinventing Public Services by B. P. Mathur.
Business Ethics & Corporate Governance by B. N. Ghosh.
Ethics, Integrity & Aptitude by G. Subba Rao & P. N. Roy Chowdhury.
Lexicon edited by N. N. Ojha.

Chapter 3

Attitude

Introduction

Attitudes determine how a person will behave in real life situations. The success or failure of a person in career or relationships depends upon his attitudinal makeup. In fact Jeff Keller in his eponymous famous book says that attitude is everything. There is no doubt whether a person is happy or sad or is a winner or loser depends entirely upon his attitude. One cannot control all that takes place in one's life but it is up to the individual how he responds and this is determined by his attitude.

Context and Structure

Perception, values and attitudes are interrelated terms. Our values and attitudes are shaped by a perceptual process and in turn determine how we perceive things. Different people see the same phenomenon differently due to difference in values and attitudes. For instance, in a law and order situation often the officers and the citizens and members of political parties perceive the same incident in a different manner. The three important related terms are beliefs, attitudes and values. Beliefs are primarily cognitive in nature. Cognitive means the process of acquiring knowledge through reason, intuition and perception. Attitudes are essentially affective (emotional) in nature. Attitudes have referents which are the objects for which there are feelings. For example, if I say I like a particular job I am expressing my attitude towards the job and liking—it means that my attitude is favorable. Values are judgmental in nature which means that we find something more desirable than others.

Attitudes and values develop through the perceptual process. It is through perception we have our knowledge about the world. The process involves receiving, selecting, organizing, interpreting, checking and reacting to sensory stimuli or data. The stimuli are an external factor but the characteristics of a perceiver are internal factors like psychological needs, experience, background and personality. After receiving the data the perceiver interprets it. Various factors contribute to this interpretation.

a. Perceptual set – Previously held beliefs about the behaviour of a particular group.
b. Stereotyping – Favorable or unfavorable opinion about a group. Gender stereotyping is a classic example of it.
c. Halo effect – Opinion or attitude towards a single person. For instance, an officer can have a very good impression about an employee and so would tend to overlook any mistakes made by him. This is known as positive halo effect.
d. Perceptual defence – If a person gets data which threatens his beliefs then he tries to deny it or justify or look for modification of data which are illustration of perceptual defence.
e. Interpersonal context – This is about the relationship between the perceiver and the others present in a particular situation.
f. Organizational context – The climate of an organization influences perceptions.

We have thus seen that different people perceive same situation in a different manner which has an obvious impact on his behaviour.

Attitude is generally used to describe the behaviour of a person. There are three aspects of attitude—Affective (emotional), Cognitive (knowledge based) and Conative (action). The cognitive component means that you form your opinion on the basis of knowledge available to you. Affective refers to feelings and their impact on attitude. While conative refers to attitude being determined by a certain predisposition or tendency.

Attitude can be understood as a mental filter through which a person experiences the world. A person may be optimistic and have a positive attitude towards life or he may be a pessimist and have a negative attitude. A person with a positive attitude always thinks "I can" while one with a negative attitude thinks "I can't". A person with a negative attitude focuses on problems and always finds fault with others while a person with positive attitude looks for solutions and good qualities in others. A person with a negative attitude looks at limitations while one with a positive attitude always concentrates on possibilities.

Factors Influencing Attitudes

There are a number of theories about what leads to formation and maintenance of attitudes.

1. Classical or Pavlovian conditioning – This is a process by which a person is made to respond in a desired manner by exposing him to a stimuli. Conditioning is done by pairing to stimuli. A classic example is the famous Pavlov experiment in which a bell was rung and it was followed by food being given to dogs. The food led to salivation in the dogs. After some time just ringing of the bell would lead to salivation even if food was not produced. This is known as Pavlovian conditioning where the stimulus of ringing a bell produced a conditional response from the dogs. This kind of conditioning plays an important role in the development of attitude. This is also known as the learning theory of attitude. Another example of this is that a child may observe that parents enjoy watching and cheering a game of cricket. As he grows up he will find that a cricket match evokes the same response in him.
2. Instrumental Conditioning – Any behavior which has a favorable outcome is reinforced while one with a negative outcome is suppressed. Parents and teachers play a crucial role in this kind of conditioning.
3. Observational learning – A person starts behaving in a particular manner by observing the rewards or punishment that a person exhibiting such behaviour gets. He learns from the experience of others. For example, a child may hear his parents make unfavorable comments about civil servants. He is likely to repeat similar comments when talking to his friend as he has learned this observing his parents.

Functional Theory of Attitude (Daniel Katz)

Attitudes perform various functions for a human being and meet their physical, social and emotional needs. Theories of attitude say that attitude has the following functions:

1. It has a knowledge function which means that an individual tries to understand his environment and see if it is consistent with his ideas and thinking. In this way he makes sense of the world around him and tries to organize his response accordingly. He acquires basic knowledge to interpret the world

around him and respond. In this way an individual brings order and clarity to the complexities of human life and provides a meaningful and structured environment.

2. Attitude has utilitarian function which means that an individual would develop that attitude which would help him to maximize returns and benefits and minimize the disadvantages. This is why we see people developing positive attitude towards objects or things which gives them tangible benefits. For example, a civil servant would bend down to every wish of the political executive because he knows that he will gain in terms of his career by being close to him. In essence it means that we tend to develop favorable attitude towards things that aid or rewards us. We are likely to change our attitude if by doing so we are able to meet our goals or avoid negative consequences.
3. Attitude has a social role also and this is known as the social identity function of attitude. This determines how an individual would express himself in social interaction and try to establish his own identity.
4. Attitudes promote self esteem of a person. This attitude means a person protects himself from the truth about himself or about life and acts as a defence mechanism to handle mental and emotional conflicts. This is known as ego defensive function of attitude which serves to protect us from the harsh reality of life and acts as a defense mechanism. For example, people having feeling of inferiority develop an attitude of superiority.
5. Another function of attitudes is to express a value which means that a person shows what he stands for and this is an expression of his own self image with the intensions of reinforcing it. An officer may have a self image of being democratic and so will cultivate attitude and behaviour patterns which reinforce this opinion that he has about himself.

The functionalist theory of "Katz" explains why attitudes change. According to him an attitude changes when it is no longer serving its purpose. A change in attitudes towards personal relationships with time is an example of this theory.

Cognitive Dissonance Theory

This theory shows that a person's behaviour affects his attitude. It may happen that there is dissonance or disharmony between the beliefs and attitudes of a person and this leads to a feeling of discomfort. The individual then makes an effort to reduce the dissonance through change in his behaviour. It happens when we take a decision favoring one alternative even though we have reasons for favoring another. Dissonancy theory says relationship among two cognitions can be consonant, dissonant or irrelevant. Cognitive dissonance is an unpleasant state which an individual always tries to reduce or eliminate. This can be done by adding new cognitions and changing existing ones. For example, we can decide that we were wrong and change our mind or we may seek more information to restore consonance or discredit source of dissonance by seeking counter evidence.

The sources of dissonance could be—

1. Information inconsistency – we receive information that contradicts what we already know or believe.
2. Disconfirmed expectations – people prepare themselves for that which does not occur or opposite takes place. For instance, you expect to succeed in the civil service exam but fail to do so.
3. Insufficient justification for behaviour – people doing things that they lack justification for.
4. Post decision dissonance – after taking a decision you feel dissonance because you have rejected some good thing and accepted something as not good.
5. However, not all inconsistencies lead to dissonance. It may be that cognitions are not important to the individual and do not produce discomfort or contradictions can go unnoticed and if a person feel that he is not personally responsible then he is not likely to feel dissonance.

Bem's Self-Perception Theory

This theory says that we infer our attitude from our behaviour and is a commonly proposed alternative to dissonance theory. We observe our behaviour, there is no tension and calmly draw reasonable inferences. For example, a person may infer that he does not like other person just because he had behaved rudely with him. Both self-perception and cognitive dissonance theory make the same predictions but self-perception theory can explain things that dissonance cannot, like people are suddenly rewarded for something they did earlier because they liked to do it but now after the reward they come to like it less.

Dissonance theory successfully explains what happens when we act contrary to our clearly defined attitudes. We change our attitude to reduce the dissonance. However, when attitudes are not well formed self-perception theory explains the attitude formation that occurs as we act and reflect.

Relationship between Attitude and Behaviour

As we have seen attitude is a person's mental outlook which defines the way he thinks and feels and is influenced by his education, experience and environment. The attitude of the person can be positive, negative or neutral. Behaviour is the reaction of an individual to a particular person, action or environment. It is the way we control our actions towards other people. An attitude is the mindset of the person and behavior is the outward expression of the attitude. Attitude shows how you think or feel while behaviour is what you do. Attitude defines the way we perceive things while behaviour corresponds to social norms. Attitude can influence behaviour in many ways. Social norms determine what kind of an attitude is acceptable in the particular social group and situational constraints can block the attitudes being expressed as overt behaviour. Many policy makers feel that behaviour should be changed first and the change in attitude will follow. A classic example of this has been the implementation of Swatch Bharat Programme. There was widespread open defecation in India not only because of shortage of toilets but because of general attitude towards sanitation and hygiene. This programme constructed toilets in every household and motivated the people to use the toilets making them aware of the health risks of open defecation. Anybody not using toilets was shamed in the village and as a result of social pressure the behaviour of people changed and they started using toilets. Gradually this has led to a change in the overall attitude of the people towards sanitation. In a similar way there was a negative attitude prevalent in rural areas towards sending girls to school or college. The government started awareness campaigns like "Beti Bachao Beti Padhao" and started enrolment campaigns for girls in schools so that it became a socially accepted behaviour to send girls to schools. Gradually the attitude of those opposing it has also changed. The decision of an individual or a group to adopt a particular behaviour is determined by the positive or negative consequences of behaviour, approval or otherwise behaviour by those who matter and other factors that facilitate or impedes behaviour like cultural, personal or situational factors.

Attitude can be consistent with behaviour when the attitude is strong and occupies an important position in the attitude system of a person and also the person is very well aware of his/her attitude. If there is no strong external pressure or group pressure on the person then also attitude corresponds to behaviour. If a person feels that his behaviour is not being watched or evaluated by others then his attitude or behaviour are consistent. The same is true when a person feels that the behaviour has a high positive result. In people with high level of integrity the attitude is the same as behaviour, for example, Mahatma Gandhi.

Social Influence and Persuasion

Social influence basically means our behaviour is influenced by outside social factors like social influences. An individual who is subjected to social influences can comply with it which means that his behaviour will show that he is in agreement but inwardly he is not fully convinced. He is conforming to the social influence but without conviction. Secondly, people tend to identify with an influential person whom they respect and know intimately. Thirdly, people may internalize belief systems of others. The behaviour of a person is influenced by his family, their values and beliefs and the peer whom he relates to. Social influence can be normative or informative. The former means that an individual goes along with the crowd in order to gain acceptance while the latter means that the individual follows the behaviour of the crowd because he feels that they have more knowledge of the situation than him. This is particularly true in a crisis situation. Thus, social influence can be described as a change in person's behaviour, thoughts, feelings and attitude that results from interaction with other individual or groups in society. In this way an individual makes real changes to his outlook and behaviour as a result of communication with others who are perceived to be similar, desirable or expert.

"French and Raven" have presented a formalization of the notion of social influence as the outcome of application of social power from one of the five basis of such power such as reward power, coercive power, legitimate power, expert power or referent power. An individual can change his attitude and views as a response to these aspects of social power. Reward power means that benefiting individuals change their views on the basis of social rewards. Coercive power implies that individuals are forced to change their views due to external force. Legitimate power means that people feel that they are following just and fair rules while expert power is promoting respect for higher level of knowledge or ability while referent power means expression of solidarity with peer social group.

Human beings are social animals and as such their behaviour and attitude is influenced by social influences with or without their being aware of it. Individuals are governed by social norms and usually accepted ways of thinking, feeling or behaviour that are shared in social groups. Thus social influences bring about change in behaviour or actions in response to a stimulus. Several studies have pointed towards the social influence that the majority has in a group. At the same time research has shown often there is a strong social influence on a minority in a group setting.

Dynamic Social Impact Theory

This theory has three basic rules which consider how individuals can be sources or targets in social influences. Social impact is a result of social forces including the strength of the source of impact, the immediacy of the event and the number of sources exerting the impact. This theory means that conforming to social influences depends on the strength of the group, its importance, its immediacy and the number of people in the group and it implies that conformity will increase as the strength and proximity increases. This theory envisages individuals in the society interact and influence behaviour of one and another.

According to this dynamic theory, force determines social influence, immediacy, and the number of sources, as in the previous theory. However, these groups are complex systems that change constantly and are never static. The dynamic social impact theory reorganized the groups into four basic patterns: consolidation, clustering, correlation, and continuing diversity. These patterns allow group dynamics to operate and ideas to spread throughout the group.

- Consolidation: When people interact with each other, their actions, attitudes, and opinions become standardized to one another over time.
- Clustering: People tend to interact with group members with similar opinions.
- Correlation: Over time, the individual group members' opinions on a variety of topics begin to converge and correlate with one another.
- Continuing diversity: If members of a minority group communicate with the members of a majority group but resist their influence, there may be some degree of adversity.

These theories help us understand the influence that other people or groups can have on each other. Social impact theory states that sources can affect us in our daily lives. Thanks to this theory, we can measure just how much they impact us. We can know what factors are going to affect us the most and how to avoid social impact, if necessary.

These days all of you are aware of the tremendous social influence of social media. Members of Whatsapp groups begin to agree with the views expressed in their group even if they hold a different view. This is because of desire to conform with others and also the fear of being criticized if you voice a different opinion. Today social media through Youtube, Whatsapp group, Facebook and Twitter play a great role in influencing the attitude and behaviour of a person. Political parties use this to get votes whereas companies use this to create a positive feeling towards their product.

Persuasion

Persuasion is the way in which we try to change the attitude and also the behaviour of a person. The force of persuasion depends upon who is the source of persuasion, what is the message and who is the audience. For instance, the Honorable Prime Minister, senior leaders and doctors of repute have been constantly giving the message of social distancing, wearing masks and washing hands in a bid to persuade the people to change their behaviour in order to fight against Corona. The source of persuasion must be someone whom you trust or respect, like and find attractive. For instance, so many companies advertise their products using a brand ambassador like a cricketer or a film star and people are persuaded to have a positive attitude towards this product leading to their purchasing it. Here, the attractive personality of the celebrity is being used to persuade buying behaviour. In fact, the entire concept of advertising and sales promotion is a classic example of persuading the consumer to behave in a particular manner. Politicians use the content of the speeches and speak to people in the language they understand and make promises to influence their voting behaviour. Often a person may not have been keen to vote for a particular party but is persuaded to do so by repeated messaging by people whom he respects and admires.

Persuasion is not always successful and often people resist persuasion. Sometimes people have been exposed to counter arguments and are resistant to change their attitude and behaviour due to persuasion. This is known as attitude inoculation. For instance, a person may have been fully convinced by the ideology of a particular party and hence inoculated against effort to change his thinking. Also, if a person is forewarned that an effort is being made to change his behaviour through persuasion he resists this and thinks up all the possible ways of refuting the arguments before him. For example, a friend may forewarn that a particular car salesman will try and persuade you to buy a particular car even though there are certain problems with the engine of the car. You would then not be persuaded by this car salesman when he tries to influence you. Then there is the boomerang effect which means that a person strongly reacts to an effort to change his attitude when he feels that the other person is trying to impose his will on him. This leads to a situation of confrontation. This often happens when insurance companies try to market their product in a very aggressive manner trying not to give the consumer any room to think or analyze. Finally a person who is intelligent and knowledgeable is likely to resist persuasion. This is known as stockpile effect.

Advertising companies have to be careful that they persuade a person in a manner that he does not start resisting the persuasion. The message has to be subtle, refined and presented in a manner that the recipient develops a positive frame of mind towards it.

From the above it is clear that persuasion can be explained as a symbolic process in which communicators try to persuade other people to change their attitude or behaviour regarding an issue through the transmission of a message in an atmosphere of free choice. The prime elements of persuasion are—

1. Persuasion is symbolic, utilizing words, images and sounds.
2. It involves a deliberate attempt to influence one another.
3. People are not coerced but are free to choose.
4. Persuasive messages can be conveyed verbally and non-verbally. Television, radio, internet or face to face communication can be the methods used.

Theories of Persuasion

There are two types of theories about persuasion. One is elaboration likelihood model (ELM) which is used in counseling. This model believes that if a person thinks a lot about a particular message then he is likely to be persuaded and more so if he feels that the message is of relevance to him for instance the persuasion to make a person give up smoking. In this model the processing route is central meaning that the person receiving the message is an active partner in the process of persuasion. The other theory is known as the Heuristic systemic theory (HSM) which suggests that persuasion will take place through peripheral processing route which is indirect and uses non verbal communication. This theory holds the view that the people are lazy and tend to minimize the use of their cognitive resources. The ELM theory is more likely to have a lasting impact than the HSM model.

Thus, we see that persuasion has the effect of shaping, reinforcing and changing responses. It is an effective technique to change a person's attitude, intention, motivation or behaviour. These days all of you are aware of how there are influencers in social media who influence and persuade people to adopt a particular behaviour.

Moral Attitude

Moral attitude relates to what we consider as being right or wrong. In fact, most of the human actions try to find a moral justification for them. Nobody in this world would like to be called immoral or amoral. The basis of all religions has been morality. The ten commandments of Christianity are nothing else but moral principles. Similar precepts are found in all religions of the world. Basically a moral attitude determines how an individual will react in a particular situation and how he would make a choice. Humans are blessed with a free will which means that it is up to them to decide how they would think, speak or act. This is also known as the ability to discriminate between different choices and select that which is morally correct. Your conscience always guides you in making a moral choice. Moral values or attitudes are the basis of a code of ethics. Most of the moral values are universal and are the highest amongst all values. Speaking the truth, being good, being faithful, respectful, humble and pure are examples of such moral values. A person with a moral attitude will not be lustful, greedy, proud and envious and would never covet the property of others. We can say that human civilization has survived and evolved because of this emphasis on moral values. All Indian and Western philosophers have brought out importance of a moral attitude in the growth of an individual and rise of a civilization.

There are, however, certain moral values which are specific to a particular society or nation. For instance, the respect for elders and teachers is a hallmark of the Indian civilization but may not be so prominent in other societies. Similarly in some societies eating non-vegetarian food and drinking alcohol is considered immoral whereas in others it is accepted. Similar is a difference in attitude towards women or other races in various societies.

It would not been an exaggeration to say that the difference between human beings and others is the existence of a strong moral code which directs their action.

Political Attitude

It was Aristotle who said that man is a political animal. Human beings collaborate and work in groups where there is always a struggle for power which is the essence of politics. In any group there are people who try to dominate and influence the thinking of a group and take it in a particular direction. You would find that there is always a lot of competition for people wanting to become chairperson, secretary or other office bearers of any social, religious, voluntary, economic or political organization. The political attitude of a people determines how they would behave in the struggle for power within the group.

Normally, the term 'political attitude' is understood by people to describe how political parties have different ideologies and contest for power to govern a state or a country. The political attitude of an individual will determine which political party he will support. This could be based on the ideology of the party or specific promises that a party makes about what it would do if it comes in power. For example, in USA there are only two main parties—the Republicans and the Democrats. The former is in favour of reduction in taxes or open liberal economy and have a conservative attitude towards schemes like health care but the Democrats may be more inclined towards a greater role of the state in issues like health and education. In India also, people may vote for BJP or Congress or Left parties depending upon their political attitudes. The political attitude of a person can be broadly categorized as "Left" which implies a socialist inclination or "Right" which means an attitude in favour of free market economy. Within this brought distinction the political attitude can oscillate from radical to liberal to moderate to conservative and finally reactionary. This is a complete spectrum of political attitude.

Political attitude begins to form at a very early age. An individual is likely to get influenced by the political thinking of his parents. Thereafter the teachers in school and college also play an important role in forming political attitudes. The kind of friends one has and the social groups in which he moves also is an important factor in creating or affirming political attitudes. Then, very often, the political attitude is determined by the leadership qualities of a political leader whom people admire and so follow. We have seen during elections how the election manifesto of political parties and the kind of speeches that are given determines the voting patterns. Oratory and rhetoric have an important role to play in influencing political behaviour as also the concern for economic issues and assessment of the performance of the political parties.

We have witnessed, in the recent history, the struggle between authoritarian governments and democracies. After the Russian revolution, the last century saw the political ideology of capitalism along with a liberal democracy and communism with state power competing with each other. Russia has changed but China continues as a bastion of communism but with an open economy. Rest of the world is at different levels of a liberal democracy. This is related to the history, culture, economic development and social values of a country.

Except for hard line members of political parties we find that the political attitude keeps changing. Politicians switch from one party to another in the quest for holding positions of power. Similarly, the voter also changes his political attitude depending upon his assessment of the leadership and ideology of a political party to deliver results and solve the problems of the citizens. Of course, the values of a person, his age, economic status, personality attributes and perception determines his political attitude. In India, especially in states like UP and Bihar, caste and community factors along with religion play a major role in voting for a particular party and the political parties also pander to this by making pronouncements along these lines and also selecting candidates to contest election on this basis.

Today the social media and electronic as well as a print media play a major role in influencing the political attitude of a person. The political parties realise this and make full use of media specially the social media which has a tremendous reach.

Attitude of a Winner

Jeff Keller has a written two remarkable books—*Attitude is Everything* and *Winning Attitude*. Attitude has a clear relationship with success and a person with a positive and right attitude always comes out a winner. Attitudes are determined by what we think because thoughts decide what we will become. A winner always takes responsibility for his actions and continuously visualizes success. Such a person sets goals for himself and makes a commitment to achieve them and does not quit under any circumstances. With an attitude of perseverance all things are attainable. A winner always turns his problems into opportunities—he converts tragedy into triumph. Adversity does not dishearten him and he uses it to bring out his hidden potential and learns valuable lessons from it which lead to opening of a new door. A winner is always positive in his thoughts, words or action. Whatever the circumstances, he never complains. He confronts his fears and makes an effort to perform even when out of his comfort zone. A winner is never afraid to fail and has the ability to handle both success and failure.

Attitude of a Civil Servant

The success of a civil servant also depends entirely on his attitude. He must have a positive attitude and always desire to give results and deliver outcomes. The general perception is that the civil servants always say "no" to everything and are more concerned about following procedures than delivering service. In fact the attitude of a civil servant should be to see how he can help any citizen who comes to him and also provide good governance to ensure effective public service delivery. So many times I have noticed in my career that officers instantly reject any new idea or innovation and are always comfortable in maintaining status quo. This is why there is a negative perception about civil servants in society. This attitude must be changed. Also the civil servant should have the attitude and behaviour of a public servant and not of a monarch. He has to inculcate an attitude of humility rather than arrogance. His attitude should be citizen friendly, transparent, open and objective. He should have an attitude of total commitment to financial and intellectual integrity.

Chapter 4

Aptitude and Values for Civil Services

Introduction

We have seen the importance of values in human beings which govern their actions, thoughts, speech and behaviour. Values are closely linked to morals and ethics. Each is a part of the other and closely intertwined. There are universal values which have been propounded by all religions and hold true for all societies at all times. *The Gita*, the *Ten Commandments*, the tenets of Islam, Sikhism, Buddhism, Jainism and all religions prescribe the same set of values in order to become a good human being. The universal values include attributes like truth, non-violence, not stealing or cheating, not coveting another woman or property of other person, kindness, generosity, charity, concern for the poor and others Human civilization has existed and thrived on the foundation of these values. Today, we are worried at the loss of values in the society as this would certainly lead to the demise of the human race. In addition, there are values which are specific to a particular culture, country or people and these would include things like how to treat the elders, modes of social behaviour, eating habits, dress, form of greeting and approach to work and duty. We can say that the universal values are the foundation of every society whereas there are other values which are determined by the particular circumstances, history and geography of a nation or society.

Foundational Values for Civil Services

Every profession or organization has its own set of values to guide the behaviour and action of its members. The civil service also has certain foundational values which enables its members to carry out their responsibilities as civil servants and deliver public services and good governance to the people. It is true that a civil servant works according to rules, systems and procedures but there are large areas of discretion where it is the values which will determines how a civil servant behaves. Civil servants are also human beings and so are guided by the universal values. For instance no civil servant should take bribes as this is like stealing from the society. However, there are certain values which form the very base of the action system of a civil servant.

- **Honesty and Integrity**

The first such value is honesty and integrity. A civil servant uses public funds for the benefit of the citizens and he is expected to do so with utmost honesty and integrity. Today, the rising incidence of corruption has corroded the basic value system of civil servants and unfortunately this has become a wide spread phenomenon. Civil servants use the position and power to enrich themselves at the cost of the citizens which amounts to breach of trust. Integrity means that public office shall not be used for private gain. A civil servant should never accept any kind of illegal gratification from any person in exchange of doing his work. He has to work impartially regardless of any pressure or situation and always enforce the rule of law. He should not bend down to illegal requests or directions from superiors or politicians. He should be transparent and open in all his actions and should do nothing which is against the code of ethics or conduct expected of civil servants. Apart from financial honesty and integrity, about which I have written in detail in the chapter on Corruption, intellectual integrity is also very vital. An officer should set an example of conduct by his own behaviour and be consistent in his actions. For example, if he wants his team members to be objective he should set an example for them by his behaviour.

- **Impartiality**

This means that a civil servant should always act on the basis of the merits of a case and not on other subjective factors or with a desire to unduly favor or benefit anyone. So often it is noticed that civil servants favor certain groups on grounds of caste, community, political affiliation or personal relationship. This is against the basic tenets of impartiality which is essential for a civil servant to carry out his duties. For example, in Uttar Pradesh I have seen many officers supporting members of their caste above others irrespective of merit. Whenever any matter comes for a decision it should be examined without any personal prejudice and according to the rules, law and regulations and a decision taken in the best interests of citizens. I have seen many officers bending the rule of law to suit the political party in power. This is not correct and it erodes the very base of good governance.

Impartiality and non-partisanship are closely linked concepts. The latter means the civil servant does not have any kind of bias when he deals with matters that are put up before him. Civil servants can be efficient and effective only if they are impartial and non-partisan. It is the duty of the civil servants to advise the political executive in matters of policy formulation and administration. The civil servant must render his free and frank advice using all the knowledge at his command and put up a comprehensive and balanced picture before the political executive. This advice should never be coloured by personal prejudices or biases. Once a decision is taken the civil servant should implement it accordingly. The public services should also be delivered in a non-partisan manner with the benefits reaching the intended beneficiaries.

The concept of objectivity is also an extension of impartiality and non-partisanship. The officer should take decisions and act on the basis of observable phenomena and should never allow any personal prejudice, bias or emotion to come in the way. An objective person always follows the objective truth which means he is fair and not likely to be under any external influence. In fact you may have observed that when ministers take oath they say that they will discharge their duties without any fear or favor. This oath is essentially about objectivity in public affairs. It is true that political parties tend to take decisions to favor their own party workers or supporters but a civil servant is expected to treat all citizens equally and be absolutely impartial and objective. For example, very often the party in power interferes in the selection of candidates for government posts and puts pressure on the civil servants to do so. However, it is the duty of a civil servant to design a selection process which is purely based on merit and he should also resist any pressure to unduly or illegally favor any individual or group. This is the essence of impartiality and objectivity.

Very often when government schemes are evaluated you find a lot of shortcomings. The politicians may like to hide unpleasant information but the civil servant must be truthful and objective and then use this information to design strategies to improve the delivery of the schemes. The important point is that the civil servant can only be affective if he is truly objective and this also creates a positive perception in the eyes of the people about the administration.

Closely linked to these concepts is the principle of neutrality which is also considered an essential attribute for a civil servant. In fact, neutrality, impartiality and objectivity all mean that the civil servants should be totally unbiased and without prejudice in their work. They are committed to the constitution, rule of law and answerable to the citizens. Unfortunately for the last several years civil servants have started to become politically aligned. This is not proper and a civil servant must remain politically neutral. The civil servant has to give his objective advice to the government but is also expected to implement the decisions once they are taken. This does not mean that he gets aligned with the party in power. The civil servant, in a democracy has to work with whichever political party forms the government. Civil servants should never start speaking the language of the party in power nor should they go out of their way to support representatives of the party in power to the detriment of the opposition. Recently in many states like UP, officers have openly come out as supporters of a particular party. This is against the ethics of a civil servant. No civil servant can become a member of any political party or organization or assist or aid or help in any manner any political activity. His family also has to behave in a manner that is not against the law or the government. Though a member of the service is qualified to vote he should not make his political preference open. A civil servant is not entitled to criticize the government in power.

- **Devotion to Work and Public Service**

A civil servant must be extremely hard working and sincere in whatever he does. There should be a spirit of complete devotion and dedication to public service. He should realise that he is a public servant and he is accountable to the public for his actions. He should work hard to understand the problems of the people and do his best to resolve them. He has to see that basic minimum services reach the people and through his effort improve the quality of life of the citizens. He handles public money and so he must do so with integrity and dedication so that each rupee spent is directed towards improving the welfare of the people. He should make sure that all government schemes and projects are implemented correctly and the money spent on them actually reaches the intended beneficiary. His commitment is towards the nation and its people and so he must ensure effective public service delivery. He should not do his work mechanically but should be inspired by high ideals. He should have a sense of mission and should take pride in the fact that through his work he is serving a national cause. He should work with focus and a sense of direction so that he is productive and result oriented. He should work in a spirit of service and sacrifice and never put personal needs or gains above public service.

- **Empathy**

We have discussed this concept in detail in the chapter on Emotional Intelligence. Empathy simply means that you put yourself in the shoes of the other person to fully understand his feelings, desires, concerns and actions. This is only possible if an officer understands and is able to regulate himself. Thereafter, he has to listen to the other person and understand his emotions and feelings. Empathy is necessary to deal with people and one can never be a true leader if one does not have empathy. A public servant needs empathy to understand the problem of the people especially the under privileged class in order to resolve them and give them satisfaction.

- **Tolerance and Compassion Towards the Weaker Sections**

We are a democracy and in democracy decisions are always subject to debate and dissent is its soul. This means that we have to be tolerant to the views and behaviour of others. A public servant will find that often people oppose a particular action of his. He should not respond in anger but be open to discuss and either be able to convince or be flexible to modify his decision. I would go a step further to say that a civil servant has to go beyond tolerance to acceptance of a different view point. India is a pluralistic society where there are differences of religion, language and culture. The civil servant should accept these differences and never impose his views by force or by using the power of his office. He should have respect for human rights. However, there are things which a civil servant should never tolerate. He should have zero tolerance towards offences against women, social injustice or corruption in public life. He should not allow anything to be done which is against the rule of law and the values and enshrined in the constitutions.

Compassion is a noble quality advocated by all major religions of the world. One should be sensitive towards all human beings and all living beings. Compassionate people have empathy and active desire to alleviate the suffering of the people. A civil servant is expected to work towards the welfare of the weaker sections of the society. He has to be compassionate towards the needs of the marginalized and the disadvantaged people and take affirmative action in their favor. Wherever, he has the discretion he should use it in favor of the weaker sections. Though the civil servant is expected to be impartial he must show a bias in favor of the poor and the weak. In India we still have a large number of people who are poor and do not have access to proper health care and educational opportunities making them ineligible for proper employment. There are also cases of exploitation of the lower castes by the upper castes and of the poor by the rich and the civil servant must act in favor of the weak with compassion. Similarly a civil servant must see that women are not discriminated against in any manner.

Conclusion

Any civil servant who has the above foundational values of civil service discussed in the chapter can be said to have the right attitude for a civil servant. Some people question whether the selection process for the civil service is able to gauge the aptitude of the candidate. I would say that except for the ethics and to some extent the essay paper the exam does not directly test aptitude. Of course, it is possible in the interview to understand the aptitude that an individual may have for the civil service. However, the very process of the exam is such that only a person, who works very hard, is intelligent, determined, willing to accept failure, has the grasping power to understand different issues and has good oral and written communication skills can succeed. These are essential qualities for a civil servant. However, in real life it is the aptitude that an officer has to deal with people which is most important. A civil servant has to lead a team and he must have the ability to motivate and inspire his team members to work towards a common goal. Moreover, he has to listen to the grievances of the people, especially the weaker sections and resolve them with sensitivity. This is the reason why very often candidates who secure a very high rank in the civil service entrance exam do not do very well in their service career. I have seen many toppers failing in their career because they could not relate to people or handle the continuous pressure of the job. At the same time I have seen cases of officers who were low in merit at the time of selection but had an aptitude for the job and so became immensely popular and successful. Even in the IAS, I found that not all officers have the aptitude for all kinds of jobs. Some are good at running a district while others are good at handling files in the Secretariat. Some officers are good for regulatory departments like home, transport, and tax collection while others are creative, innovative and flexible and so most suited for development departments like education, health or agriculture. Unfortunately in government the postings are not done as per the aptitude of an officer leading to right kind of outcomes not being achieved. Even in the British days the ICS officers who were not comfortable with an administrative job were diverted to become judges where they became hugely successful.

Aptitude for the civil service cannot be evident at an early age but if the training programmes after selection are properly organized they can develop the aptitude for civil service in most candidates. Qualities like leadership can be developed through training and this is essential for a civil servant. The basic value system and the foundational values must be ingrained fully in the selected civil servants during the course of their training and orientation before they take up the job.

Chapter 5

Emotional Intelligence

Introduction

Emotions refer to feelings or a state of consciousness in which we experience, love, joy, sorrow, hatred or anger. The personality of every individual has a rational as well as an emotional aspect. A human being can be fully understood only if he is aware of his intellectual as well as emotional makeup.

According to Goleman we have two brains, two minds and two different kinds of intelligences—rational and emotional. Success in life is determined by both emotional as well as rational intelligence which is often measured as IQ. We are all aware of the entrance exams like SAT, CAT, GMAT and GRE. These test the verbal, analytical, logical and mathematical skills of a student. On the basis of the score achieved in these exams which are a test of IQ the future career of a student is determined. However, IQ alone is not sufficient to ensure success in life which depends upon the emotional intelligence of the individual also. In fact, psychological research has shown that IQ contributes only about 20 percent of the factors that determine success in life while emotional intelligence covers the balance 80 percent. In a similar manner a successful civil servant has to have a balance of IQ and emotional intelligence to be successful. A major part of the job of a civil servant is to deal with people and for this he requires the quality of understanding their feelings and behaviour patterns to adequately respond to them, satisfy them, motivate them and bring about overall harmony in the system.

Concept of Emotional Intelligence

Emotional intelligence is an ability to understand one's own feelings as well as that of others. It is an ability to perceive the emotion of others from their verbal and non-verbal communications as well as accurately assess one's own emotions.

Intelligence is not a one dimensional skill. Howard Gardner came out with the theory of multiple intelligences which are the essence of success in life. He identified seven types of intelligences—mathematical (logical), linguistic, spatial, kinesthetic, musical, interpersonal and intrapersonal. The last two would constitute emotional intelligence which has been defined by Daniel Goleman as "Abilities such as being able to motivate one self and persist in the face of frustrations, to control impulse and delay gratification, to regulate one's mood and keep distress from swamping the ability to think, to empathize and hope." These are positive qualities which lead to realization of goals and fulfillment in life. Gardener himself has described interpersonal intelligence as the capacity to understand people—what motivates them, how they work and also the ability to respond to their moods, temperaments, motivations and desires. Intrapersonal intelligence according to him is the ability to understand one self—knowledge about self and one's own feelings and to discern the guiding factors of your own behaviour.

Mayer and Salovey describe emotional intelligence as having four attributes—

1. Perceiving emotions: Two understand emotion you have to first accurately perceive them.
2. Reasoning with emotions: This involves the link between the emotion and thinking and cognitive activity.
3. Understanding emotions: The ability to interpret the behaviour of others.
4. Managing emotions: The ability to regulate self and respond to the emotions of others.

The most prominent proponent of emotional intelligence has been Daniel Goleman according to whom emotional intelligence has five main attributes—

1. Self-awareness: This is the ability to understand one self, your own feelings and what motivates you as well as discerning your strengths and weaknesses and have a realistic assessment of your capability.
2. Self-regulation: This is about being in control of your emotions. For example, you are able to control your anger and remain

calm in all situations. It also means that you do not lose faith in case of failure and have the capacity to bounce back. Such a person always exhibits controlled and mature behaviour which is essential for a leader.

3. Motivation: This is about your understanding about what motivates you to perform better. Self motivation makes a leader optimistic and he is able to create an atmosphere of faith and hope amongst his team members.
4. Empathy: This is perhaps the single most important attribute of emotional intelligence. You should be able to understand how the person you are dealing with is feeling. It is like imagining what you would expect if you were in the position of the other person. You respond to the feelings of other persons and this helps you in developing a rapport with them and makes you an affective team leader.
5. Social skills: This enables you to handle emotions in social relationships. This helps in negotiation, networking, conflict resolution and encouraging cooperation.

Emotional Intelligence for the Civil Servant

Almost all civil servants who qualify the difficult civil service examination have a high level of intellectual ability but in real life their performances are very different. I have seen many candidates who have topped the civil service exam but have not been at all successful in their professional life. Actually the most important quality in your job is ability to deal with people and so it is the emotional intelligence of an officer which determines his success.

Today in the corporate world successful organizations are looking for leaders rather than managers. Similar is the requirement in civil services. The civil servant of today does not have to be one who merely regulates and maintains status quo but one who can provide effective leadership and bring about a positive change in society. Emotional intelligence is the basic pre-requisite of being a leader. A leader has to be able to motivate his team towards fulfillment of a goal. He has to lead by example if he is honest and a person of integrity then his team members would also be having similar qualities. A true leader should work in a participative manner allowing people to put forward their views, then arriving at a decision through consensus and then having the ability to inspire and motivate his team members to implement the decision in letter and spirit. It is thus clear that a civil servant can be a true leader and effectively deliver public services if he has the emotional intelligence to inspire and motivate his team to achieve results and outcomes.

A very important quality required of a civil servant is to communicate his views and ideas to people and to understand their grievances. Communication is a two-way process. A civil servant must have the ability to communicate effectively. He must be adept at both written and oral communication. However, the most important aspect of communication is to have the ability to listen to others and understand their feelings and viewpoints. This is the essence of empathy which is an essential attribute of emotional intelligence. As an officer one has to meet people who have their grievances which you would be able to respond properly only if you have developed emotional intelligence. For the person with a grievance the problem is very serious for her and she expects you to listen to her properly, pay attention to the problem, assure her that action would be taken and do your best to resolve the issue. An officer can do this only if he is self-aware and has empathy. I recall an incident when I was Secretary to the Chief Minister and an old man came to meet me. I recognized him as the Office Superintendent of collectorate in one of my earlier district postings. He was looking extremely upset and nearly in tears. He told me that he had retired several years ago and not got his pension as the office clerks were raising unnecessary objections one after another. He was in dire financial straits. I immediately rang up the concerned officer and asked him to resolve the matter within a week. After one week the old Office Superintendent came to me smiling and thanked me. He had started getting his pension and all issues had been resolved. I remembered that during his service career this Office Superintendent also had a reputation putting a lot of objections on every file and many citizens used to complain about him. I told him that he had no need to thank me but he should sit down and think how many people he had treated in the same way as he had been treated and try to feel the sense of frustration and helplessness they must have felt. He realized and felt genuinely sorry. Emotional intelligence means to put yourself in the shoes of the others and behave as you would like the other persons to behave towards you. Grievance redressal is one of the most important aspects of the work of a civil servant and only those with high emotional intelligence are able to satisfy the people.

A civil servant should be able to control his anger and never give the impression that he is under stress. This requires a high degree of self awareness and self regulation. So many officers lose their temper easily and shout at subordinates with the result that they lose the respect of their team and are not able to achieve their goals. It is important for a civil servant to remain calm and composed under all conditions. For example, a District Magistrate or Superintendent of Police have to face several law and order situations and confront violent mobs where if they become tense or lose their temper then they would further complicate the situation and never be able to resolve a law and order situation successfully. A person with high emotional intelligence would remain calm and thus be able to take the right decision in such crisis situations and also be able to motivate his team to perform better. The team members always look towards the leader and behave accordingly. I recall a law and order situation in which my Additional District Magistrate and Rural Superintendent of Police had ordered firing on a mob killing a few people. They were very apprehensive that when the SP and I (DM) reach the spot they will pull them up for not being able to resolve the situation with tact and creating a law and order problem by opening fire. When we reached the spot I could read from their body language that they were low on confidence. They had been outstanding officers and I knew that they must have acted in good faith. I patted them on the back and said that I have full confidence in them and I am sure that they had taken the right decision and that they have my total support. I then asked them to mobilise the entire team and ensure that no further violence in reaction took place. Their entire body language changed and they worked day and night for the next week to bring about peace in the area. This is an example of use of emotional intelligence to get the best out of your team.

So many officers who lack emotional intelligence are insecure and so always blame the subordinates if anything goes wrong. I have seen in meetings that senior officers start blaming their team members in front of everybody if the meeting starts going against them. Even otherwise one should never scold or pull down a subordinate in front of others. It is best to talk to him alone even if you want to say something about his performance. This is the way to build a team to perform and this is a hallmark of emotional intelligence.

Civil servants are often perceived by the public as being arrogant, proud, insensitive and rude. These are all negative qualities and indicate low emotional intelligence on the part of the civil servants. A civil servant should always behave with humility, politeness and sensitivity. He has to behave like a public servant and not like a monarch. This requires self-awareness, self-regulation and empathy which are all attributes of emotional intelligence.

A civil servant with high emotional intelligence is always quick to praise others and never feels jealous of other officers. So many officers are ready to criticise others but a word of praise never reaches their lips. Jealousy or envy are the worst possible emotions to have as they lead to stress, make you unpopular and ultimately affect your performance on the job.

A civil servant, especially in the IAS and IPS has to constantly deal with politicians and ministers. They need a lot of emotional maturity to handle these interactions properly. They should give full respect to a representative of the people but at the same time maintain their allegiance to the rule of law and the constitution. A high degree of emotional intelligence is required in these situations. You should not have an attitude of contempt towards public representatives and carry the impression that they are always wrong. In fact they are not and have full knowledge of the real problems of the people and so a civil servant must give attention to what they say. At the same time a civil servant should never commit a wrong act under pressure.

A civil servant is expected to handle conflict situations on a regular basis and he has to do it without attachment and with a positive frame of mind which are the attributes of emotional intelligence. Also a civil servant has to regularly deal with change and often bring about change with his leadership. He should be comfortable to work in such an environment and also be able to convince and lead others on the path of change. A person with emotional intelligence can achieve this.

It is the duty of a civil servant to work in the interest of the marginalized sections of society—the poor, minorities and the scheduled castes and scheduled tribes. This requires a high degree of sensitivity and empathy. Also a civil servant has to be sensitive towards gender issues. Almost daily we hear of cases where women have been molested and the local police station or officers have not taken action on time and have behaved in a highly insensitive and unacceptable manner. These are all indicators of a low level of emotional intelligence. In fact it is unfortunate that generally the administration displays low emotional intelligence. Qualities like empathy and compassion are absent in the behaviour of most civil servants. Fortunately unlike IQ emotional quotient (EQ) can be developed in a person through training and should become a regular feature in the training module of a civil servant.

The need of the hour is to make administration citizen friendly and to decentralise the process of decision-making. Civil servants are also required to work with civil society groups, NGO's, Panchayati Raj Institutions and voluntary organizations. An officer with low emotional intelligence will not be able to do this properly as he would view this as a dilution of his powers. It requires a high level of emotional intelligence to be transparent and to work in participation with citizen groups without holding on to the halo of power. Good governance is not possible without the civil servant having high emotional intelligence.

Conclusion

Emotional intelligence is the quality which makes a real difference between a good and a poor leader. Those with high EQ are able to understand, regulate and motivate themselves. They have a genuine interest in resolving the problems of the people and have the sensitivity to understand what the person on the other side of the table expects from them. They are mature, calm, confident and caring in their behaviour. Such officers are remembered for a long time by their team members and citizens who interact with them. It is only the civil servants with emotional intelligence who can make a genuine contribution to the society.

Chapter 6

Moral Thinkers and Philosophers—Contribution

Western Philosophers

Introduction

Greece is a small nation on the Mediterranean Sea but it was the cradle of the western civilization. Trade gave wealth, leisure and security to the people of Greece which led to speculation about the nature of man and riddles of the universe. Science, mathematics and astronomy developed and philosophy began. Philosophy started with trying to understand the material world and Democritus (460-360 BC) was the first materialist thinker who opined that there was nothing in the universe but atoms and space. This line of thinking was carried forward by Epicurus (342-270 BC). However, the most fertile development of Greek philosophy took form with the sophists who were like travelling teachers of wisdom. They discussed all aspects of life and asked questions without being afraid of any religious or political taboo. They were men of reason and some argued that by nature all men are equal but civilizations and manmade institutions make them unequal. Another school was of the view that by nature all men are equal and morality is an invention of the weak to control the strong. For this school the supreme virtue was power and best form of government was aristocracy. For the sophists man was at the centre of the world. After Sparta defeated Athens in the Peloponnesian war (430-400 BC) the aristocratic government of Sparta was praised and the democracy of Athens was said to be the main reason for its losing the war. It is in this context that Greek moral philosophers and thinkers emerged.

THEORIES OF ETHICS (Dimensions of Ethics)

Relativism

There are several theories related to ethics. The first theory can be called theory of ethical relativism which is often publicly espoused by people who really do not believe in it. This theory says that there is no single ethical standard that applies to all people or societies. The ethical relativist does not believe in the existence of a universal standard that applies to all. Some people may be in favor of capital punishment while others may oppose it. This theory says that everyone should apply and be judged by his or her own standards and thus the approach of the relativist is open minded, non-judgmental, virtuous and correct. However, it would be difficult to think of a society based on a concept of ethical relativism for instance, one person may consider paying taxes a moral duty while the other may have a different opinion. The society has to agree on one point and cannot have different standards for different people even though it is a fact that people differ in their beliefs and moral judgments. Relativism is not a very practical concept.

Ethical Absolutism

On the opposite spectrum of relativism is the concept of ethical absolutism which in itself can be divided into four sub-groups—

1. Teleology

Everybody wants to be happy and so should also desire happiness for others and the greatest good is to promote greatest happiness. This is the basis of utilitarianism which is the predominant teleological ethical theory. According to this theory the morality of an action is determined on the basis of its consequences. This means that the end would justify the means. This could have a negative connotation but here the end is happiness of all so it has a positive meaning. For example, happiness for a public servant could come from remuneration, good working conditions and enriching job content. The famous utilitarian philosophers were Jeremy Bentham and JS Mill. In essence, promoting the greatest happiness is the most ethical principle for the advocates of this theory.

2. Deontology

The deontological theorist is of the view that the ethics of an action does not depend upon consequences but upon the important features of the act itself. Immanuel Kant is the most notable philosopher of this school. For Kant, the most important aspect of ethics is consistency and the golden rule for this is "Do unto others as you would have them do unto you".

3. Intuitionism

This is the belief that human beings have a moral sense that recognizes the moral character of an act. For instance, our moral sense will tell us that it is always better to help people in the stress. This theory is of the view that moral judgments depend upon feelings more than theories and arguments.

4. Virtue Theory

The fourth major group is the virtue theory associated with Aristotle. This theory considers an act to be good on the basis of the character, trait or virtue that the act evidences, for example, giving money to poor is an act of kindness and generosity is an ethical action while cheating or telling lies is an unethical action.

If we want to compare these theories we can say in simple language that teleology says that one should act in order to produce the greatest happiness as a consequence; deontology says that one should act according to the proper principle and be consistent in applying it; intuitionism is of the view that we should act according to our inner sense of right or wrong while virtue theory propounds that a person should act as being one of good character and set a good moral of example for others to follow. According to this we can compare the questions that followers of each theory would like to discuss:

Teleology

A. What are the consequences of my action?
B. What are the long term effects of my action?
C. Does my action promote the greatest happiness?

Deontology

A. What principle applies in this case?
B. Can this principle be applied consistently in all similar cases?
C. Can this principle be considered as a possible universal principle of behavior?

D. Which course of action best exemplifies the ideal of treating all people as ends in themselves?
E. Which course of action best exemplifies and most fully promotes ideal of a society where people promote each other rather than have a conflict?

Intuitionism

A. What does my conscience tells me about this action?
B. Do I feel good about this action?

Virtue Theory

A. What character state does this action express?
B. What effect will this action have on my character?
C. What will be the effect on the character of other people?
D. Is this the action of a person whose character I would admire?

All these theories have their relevance and are applicable to human beings. However, there may be situations where there could be ambiguity or conflict between them.

SOCRATES

Every study of western moral philosophy starts with Socrates. He travelled around the city gathering people of all ages and professions around him and discussed with them various issues related to man and society. His method was that of debate and asking questions. He did not claim to have all wisdom but considered himself to be a seeker of wisdom and the starting point of his philosophy was that he did not know anything and wanted to know. It was for this reason that he started with doubting all prevalent beliefs, dogmas and axioms. He wanted to know the answer to the important question of what man is and what can he become. He dealt with moral and physiological questions and his interests were ethical rather than scientific. He practiced what he preached and stood for his beliefs even when he was tried for corrupting the youth and showing irreverence towards God and condemned to death. For Socrates ethics has a purpose and belief that a moral and ethical life would lead to human happiness. He was an advocate of the view that the only worthwhile pursuit for man is virtue and man must work towards self improvement which is far more important and pleasurable then indulgence in worldly success like wealth and glory. Virtue for Socrates was always to be preferred to material good.

Socrates believed in God and was always critical of unjust or immoral acts like adultery, ill-treating parents, stealing or betraying friends. He was of the view that men desired what is virtuous or good for them but are ignorant and so do not know how to go about it. Questions may be asked of this view of Socrates that men only desire good things and only moral knowledge is required to make them fulfill their desires. He advocated a simple life concerned with the soul and not focus only on the needs of the body. For Socrates body could be an obstacle in the path of acquiring true knowledge. Basically the Socratic view was that the unexamined life was not worth living and therefore, one should keep asking questions to arrive at an interpretation of the good and the virtuous.

Socrates was ahead of his time and so the people in democratic Athens wanted him to be punished and accordingly he was asked to drink the hemlock. He went about doing so quietly and with dignity without making any effort to ask forgiveness or try to bribe his way through prison.

PLATO

Plato was a follower of Socrates and always delighted to see his master questioning dogmas and beliefs which sharp questions. Plato enjoyed the debate and joined them and became passionate about wisdom. The death of his master filled him with a scorn for democracy. Since he was a student of Socrates the democratic leaders of Athens looked at him with suspicion and so he left Athens and travelled for several years after which he returned to Athens and founded an academy based on his thinking and wrote the famous dialogue titled 'Republic'. He was the founder of the Platonist school of thought and his academy was perhaps the first institution of higher learning in Europe. His philosophy maintained that virtue was the most important element of ethics and that the objective of any moral action was the well-being and happiness of human beings. Plato's moral ideals appear to be austere and self abnegating and that the soul for Plato was expected to remain aloof from pleasures of the body and be always involved in pursuit of higher knowledge while communal life demanded the subordination of the individual wishes to the common good.

During his life Plato's ethical thoughts kept changing. Plato does not at any stage give an organized or systematic treatment of the basic principles of ethics governing human behavior. He is concerned with the qualities that a good soul must have which for him is necessary to have a good life. Plato was an ardent admirer and follower of the Socratic method and Socrates and engaged in a comprehensive examination of the nature of knowledge and reality and he presented his investigations as dialogues between Socrates and others. He began by questioning traditional virtues like courage, justice, moderation and piety and then widened the scope of his enquiry.

Plato was of the view that knowledge is what is required to lead a good life. His view of happiness and virtue are elaborated in his thinking that there are three parts of the soul, each having its own object of desire. The first is reason which desires truth and the good of the whole individual; the second is spirit which is pre-occupied with honor and competitive values and the third is appetite which is about the low taste for food, drink and sex. These three parts can pull in different directions and harmony comes only when all these part do their jobs properly. Plato examines the concept of justice and just like the three parts of the soul in the individual he finds three classes in the well functioning state—rulers, guardians and producers. The wise state is one where the rulers understand the good; the courageous state is one in which guardians retain in the heat of the battle the judgments handed down by the rulers about what is to be feared; temperate state are those is that in which all citizens agree about who is to rule; and in a just state all just three classes do their assigned work properly and if a city has to be a virtuous then each citizen must contribute appropriately. Plato takes an extremely comprehensive view of the concept of justice in which a person who possesses this virtue is in the possession of all other virtues and thereby achieves health of the soul.

A famous doctrine of Plato is that reason cannot fully understand the human good without grasping the form of the good itself and this leads to a highly ambitious education programme put forward by Plato. It starts with exposure to stories, poetry and music from childhood and then continues to training in mathematical principles. This education would lead to a person to understand the first principle of the Good.

Plato is known for his theory of FORMS. When a philosopher attains intellectual perception of the soul he gains knowledge of the forms and those philosophers who have an insight into forms should be the rulers of a state or alternatively rulers should becomes philosophers. Plato regarded the idea of the good and god as identical. He considered good as an idea and an individual virtue which described the ethical world in the political state. In the *Republic* Plato considers that individual virtue is possible only for citizens of a moral state and solutions to the political ills of the states can be handled only if philosophers are made kings. Plato may have been led to believe this because of the role mobs can play in a democracy exemplified by the sentence awarded to Socrates. We can see that Plato is not talking about equality in the society and expecting the citizens to accept the status as guardians, soldiers, farmers or others. This conception allows for the existence of injustice but Plato does not see anything wrong in the concept of the rule by hereditary guardians since they have been imparted the required knowledge and training to carry out their job. Plato's *Republic* is not democratic by any means and appears totalitarian. It is based on the principles of aristocracy as power is vested in the guardians while others are excluded. Plato is neither in favor of private property nor that of the family system. He also is in favor of censorship so it is clear that Plato is subordinating the individual to the state in the belief that a state run by philosophers would automatically ensure the good of all.

ARISTOTLE

Aristotle was born at Stagira, a Macedonian city some 200 miles to the north of Athens in the year 384 BC. He went to Athens and was a student of Plato for 20 years where his intelligence was greatly praised by Plato. King Phillip of Macedonia called Aristotle to undertake the education of Alexander. He taught the Alexander for a couple of years before Alexander moved out to conquer the world and Aristotle returned to Athens where he founded his own school of philosophy called Lyceum. Aristotle was 53 years old when he established the school. He was already very famous and many students flocked to his school. This school was different from the academy founded by Plato and was more inclined towards biology and the natural sciences. Aristotle was a person of a very great sense of observation with which he tried to make sense of the universe around him even though at that time there was hardly any scientific equipment to assist him. He gathered a vast body of data around him to understand the working of the material world. Aristotle's writings ran into hundreds which included works on logic, science, aesthetics and philosophy. Aristotle concerned himself with almost all problems under the sun and presented a great synthesis of knowledge.

The Foundation of Logic

Aristotle created a new science of logic through which he disciplined the Greek intellect to think in a particular manner. It is this logic which provide the basis for training the mind in reasoning and also instrumental in the development of science. Logic was simply the art and method of correct thinking and Aristotle believed that the process of correct thinking can be reduced to rules like in science in mathematics. This means that any important discourse is subjected to a scrutiny and definition. Aristotle said that every good definition has two parts—first, it assigns the object in question to a class or group whose general characteristics are also its own, for example, man is first of all an animal and secondly, it indicates where the objects differs from all other members in its class. For Aristotle man was a rational animal. Linked to this the other great contribution of Aristotle to philosophy is the doctrine of the syllogism. A syllogism is a trio of propositions of which the conclusion follows the truth of the other two premises for example, man is a rational animal; but Ashok is a man; therefore Ashok is a rational animal. In mathematical terms if A is B and C is A then C is B.

Aristotle and Science

It has been said that it is Aristotle who gave science to mankind. There was scientific thinking in Greece before Aristotle but it was not very exact. Aristotle caught the thread of scientific development in Greece and carried it forward by going into great details and making varied observations and then bringing it all together in a single body of organized thought. However, his physics was almost like metaphysics in which through observation he analyzed matter, motion, space, time, infinity, cause and other such concepts. He analyzed the thinkers before him and refuted them. He rejected the view of Pythagoras that the sun is the center of our system and he felt that it was the earth which was the centre. He created zoological gardens and tried to arrange it in a continuous series the infinite variety of life. His observations did not lead him to the theory of evolution. Not many of his observations in biology have stood the test of time, for instance, he believed that women have fewer teeth than men and that a man has only eight ribs on each side. However, he also made some very relevant observations like birds and reptiles being very closely allied in structure and his declaration that man belongs to one group of animals. He was also of the view that the more highly developed and specialized a specie or an individual happens to be, the smaller would be the number of its offspring. He also established the science of embryology. Before Aristotle there was no organized science of biology and as such despite the errors this is a great contribution of Aristotle to the discipline.

Metaphysics and God

Aristotle said that everything in the world is moved by an inner urge to become something greater than it is and everything is both the form and reality which has grown out of something which was its raw material or matter. For example, man is the form of which the child was the matter. Matter would mean possibility of form while form is the finished reality of matter. Nature is the conquest of matter by form which means a constant progression of life. Development in this world is not accidental but everything is guided in a certain direction. Aristotle believes that there is a God though not the simple and human God conceived by others. God is pure energy and is a final cause of nature, the drive and purpose of things, the form of the world and the sum total of its vital processes and powers. Aristotle's theory of the soul says that the soul is the sum of the powers of the body and cannot exist without it. A particular soul can exist only in its own body.

Aristotle created the study of esthetics, the theory of beauty and art. Art was nothing but an imitation of reality. The noblest appeal to the intellect as well as to the feelings.

Ethics and Happiness

Aristotle was concerned with the important question of what is the best life? What is virtue? How shall we find happiness and fulfillment? Aristotle said that the aim of life is not goodness for its own sake but happiness. The basic attribute of man is his ability to think and it is the development of this faculty which would give him fulfillment and happiness. A life of reason was the road to happiness. virtue will depend on clear judgment, self control, symmetry of desire and artistry of means. There was a road to guide a person to virtue and this is the middle way or the golden mean. Aristotle advocated avoidance of extreme positions and virtue for him was moderation which was the mean between two extremes which could be called the two vices, for example, humility and vanity are extreme vices but proper pride is the golden mean and a virtue. Similarly, between cowardice and rashness is courage; between stinginess and extravagance is liberality; between sloth and greed is ambition and between indecisiveness and impulsiveness is self-control.

Golden mean is not the exact average of the two extremes and fluctuates as per the circumstances of each situation. This doctrine of the mean is an important part of Greek philosophy. Aristotle says that the golden mean is not the only secret of happiness. We must have a fair degree of worldly goods. The noblest of the external aids to happiness is friendship and friendship requires equality. However, the essence of happiness remains within us, in rounded knowledge and clarity of soul. The pleasure of senses is not the way. Happiness has to be a pleasure of the mind. The ideal man of Aristotle is one who does not expose himself to danger needlessly but in a great crises is willing to even give his life; he is open in his dislikes and preferences and talks and acts frankly; he never feels malice and always forgets and passes over injuries; he does not speak evil of others and is measured in his speech; he bears the accidents of life with dignity and grace making the best of his circumstances. He is a man of virtue, full of valour, generosity, loyalty and dignity. He is a magnanimous individual though the virtues of such an individual depend to a large extent on his having an exceptional social position thereby associating virtues of nobility with hereditary privilege and inequality.

Justice for Aristotle is the virtue of the state and not of the individual. He talks about two kinds of justice—distributive and corrective. Distributive justice is rewarding people according to merit while corrective justice deals with inflicting punishment for a wrong doing.

The freedom of the human will is important for Aristotle and right action is the outcome of the human will choosing between good and evil using reason to make their choice unlike Socrates who believed that virtuous actions are involuntary. Aristotle said that human choices are voluntary except in extreme circumstances.

Ethical virtues for Aristotle consisted in controlling of emotion by reason. It is difficult to control human passions but if they are brought under the control of reason then this leads to discipline which is the essence of self control. Repeated practice makes this virtuous conduct a habit.

Politics and States

For Aristotle politics was a division of ethics and welfare of citizens was the only objective of the states and people could be happy and virtuous only in a state. Man according to the Aristotle was a political animal. Aristotle was not in favor of monarchy but said that the best practicable polity was aristocracy, the rule of the informed and capable few. Government was too complex to have issues decided by numbers. He was thus not in favor of democracy for it was based on a false assumption of equality.

Criticism

Aristotle accepted inequality and preferred aristocracy to democracy. He also accepted slavery and the superiority of men over women. He was too moderate and does not realize that feelings and emotions play a vital part in human life and the great philosopher Bertrand Russell called his ethics conventional and smug. Aristotle's ethics was called Nicomachean Ethics. In essence it says that the highest good in life is Eudemonia which can be achieved in accordance with virtues in a sustainable way so that it permeates the human psyche throughout the life. It shows how it is possible to be a virtuous man through right actions, right habits and right character. In a way this is very similar to a philosophy of Buddhism. To conclude we can say that Aristotle was easily the greatest philosopher and thinker of all times who spoke about all aspects of life in this world. His was a marvelous mind and his thoughts have greatly influenced philosophy over the ages.

EPICUREANISM AND STOICISM

Greek philosophy after Aristotle concerned itself with issues relating to ethics and Epicureanism and Stoicism were two main schools which held different views about the purpose of life. Epicurus was of the view that the main purpose of life is to constantly strive for happiness. Happiness is an end to be achieved while pain has to be avoided. Happiness comes when an individual is mentally serene and calm. One should not have excessive desire as this would lead to happiness. It is better to live a simple life of moderation to attain happiness. Epicurus felt that religion and superstitions were the chief obstacles to happiness. Pleasures of the mind were superior to that of the body and, therefore, a person must aim to be mentally calm and serene. This philosophy was criticized on the grounds that it led to human beings becoming satisfied with what they have and not taking steps to improve their lot in life and this could lead to problems and troubles and consequently unhappiness.

Stoicism did not agree with the idealism of Plato. The Stoics were of the view that sense impressions get imprinted on the mind and this is what constitutes knowledge as opposed to Plato who felt that mind is the source of knowledge and senses led to error and illusions. God for them was an absolute governing the universe and this world is marked by purpose and harmony and governed by cause and effect. The essential attribute of man is reason and this universe is governed by absolute laws. A good or virtuous life is one which is a life of reason and morality comes from rational action. The Stoics had no place for emotions in their thinking which meant that they subscribe to asceticism as a way of life. From their faith and knowledge emerged their belief in equating knowledge with materialism and they denied the existence of non-material entities and the universe was a unity. For them virtue alone was good and vice was evil and everything else was a matter of absolute indifference. A wise man is a virtuous man. They were criticized for being extreme in their views but definitely had a noble view of life.

UTILITARIANISM

We have discussed in an earlier chapter regarding theories of ethics and utilitarianism is a part of teleological theory which prescribes what a human being ought to do. It judges the right or wrong of a human action on the basis of ethical principles. Its basic tenet is that we should do only those things which lead to the greatest happiness of the greatest number of people. This thinking believes that the worldly happiness of man is the only good and all policies and actions of individuals and institutions should work to bring about this happiness. The main proponent of this philosophy was Jeremy Bentham while other prominent members of this school are David Hume and John Stuart Mill. The Neoclassical School of Economics was based on this concept of utility maximization. Welfare economics has also emerged from this philosophy. Utilitarianism believes in maximization of pleasure, minimization of pain, maximization of happiness and satisfaction of desire to bring about the greatest good of the greatest number. The focus is on minimizing harm to affected individuals and maximizing their gains or utility. If there are alternatives to be chosen from in a particular situation, the utilitarian will choose that course of action which would promote greater utility.

One criticism of theory is that it neglects the rights and needs of the minorities. Secondly, if corruption was to lead to maximization of net utility then this philosophy would find it acceptable. In a way unethical or immoral conduct can be accepted if in some way it leads to maximizing the happiness of the greatest number of people. Utilitarianism is not Altruistic meaning thereby that it does not say that you put the interests of others above your own interest. It is concerned with happiness in general and the happiness of oneself is as important as that of anyone else. Many critics feel that Bentham was supporting egoism or human selfishness but this is not true as the utilitarian's treated the welfare of everyone as equal and argued that human beings are not utterly selfish and indifferent with happiness of others. There are others who criticize this doctrine by saying there are higher ends in life than just pleasure which is what this philosophy is concerned with. Then again there is an issue of distinction between higher pleasures and lower pleasures. It also does not explain the selfless action of people like the sacrifice of soldiers. Many writers also criticize utilitarianism on the grounds that it ignores distributional aspects of happiness or utility meaning thereby that it is not concerned with distribution of happiness amongst members of a society. This theory believes that any action which leads to the maximum benefits and happiness of the greatest number of people in a society is a just action. It takes into consideration the well-being of most people but not all people.

IMMANUEL KANT

Kant was the foremost philosopher of the deontology theory of ethics. We have seen that this theory says that ethical behaviour is based on rights and duties and it is the motive that matters rather than the consequences of an overt action. It is the means which are more important than the ends. Kant advised that we should do unto others which we want them to do to us. For Kant universal ethical principles are based on justice, rights, fairness, honesty, respect. He says that morality is impartial and applies equally to all and that it is concerned with our intentions rather than with the consequences of our actions. There are two types of deontologists—act deontologists and rule deontologists. The former believe that ethicalness of a person is determined by his overt actions, while the latter believe that there are certain rules of moralities which people follow in their actions. According to the rule deontologists the ethicalness of a person is based on rules guiding his behaviour. Kant's categorical imperatives provides some of these rules and has two building blocks—a person should choose to act in a way which is acceptable to him if another person acts in the same manner in a same situation; secondly, in the event of an ethical dilemma a person should act in a way that respects and treats all the others involved as ends as well as means. These imperatives are guidelines for decision makers to do their duties in a responsible manner.

Right is the entitlement to do certain things, for instance, a priest is entitled to worship. Rights can be legal, constitutional, fundamental or moral and they give us the liberty, choice and empowerment. For examples, right to life is given to citizens of India by our Constitution. Kant argues that rights are based on intrinsic value which lies in your ability to make rational decision and to do what is morally good.

Duties are moral obligations like duty to self, others and to God which include duties like respect for truth, respect for law or respect for life. Kant is clear that you have to act ethically irrespective of the need of the others. There are four principles of Kantian theory of duty–

1. Morality of your actions depends upon what you intend to do and not on the consequences.
2. Moral rules are impartial and apply equally to everyone.
3. An action is moral if you can justify the rule that everyone can follow.
4. People are not merely means to ends. They should be treated as human beings with infinite value.

Kant's moral law comes from man's rationality or reason. For him human reason is autonomous not depending on any external sources and moral law is located within this reason. Kant was of the view that a man is a rational animal and men should not be treated as means but as ends in themselves.

Kant has been criticized on the grounds that his ethics rest on abstract laws without regards to results which may follow from rigid adherence to principles. He wants ethical laws to be followed unconditionally regardless about what the outcome may be. A man has to do his duty without needing to know the outcome of their morality. Morality is its own rewards and it is necessary for one to always do what he should.

THOMAS HOBBES

Egoism is the ethical philosophy of ethical interest and ethical egoism which claims that it is necessary and sufficient for an action to be morally right that it maximizes its own self interests. American thinker Ayn-Rand was an advocate of this theory. Thomas Hobbes was an advocate of psychological egoism which claims that each person has but one ultimate aim which is his own welfare. Hobbes argues that society originates from out of self interests and fear and not out of any natural feeling for one's fellow men. He finds it natural and reasonable that each person should take interest in his own welfare and happiness and that the only rule of life is self-protection. Hobbes was of the view that laws of nature are immutable and eternal. There are moral laws based on reason which determines the behaviour of one person with another. For him morality requires social authority in the form of sovereign. Morality is based upon law and the law of the absolute sovereign. Only the institution of government can give reward or punishment. Only in this situation is moral conduct possible. For Hobbes it is not possible to follow the precepts of morality without the existence of civil authority.

JOHN LOCKE

Lock is known for his contribution to political theory and in contradiction to Hobbes. He believed that original state of nature is happy and characterized by reason and tolerance. In that state every one is equal and independent and none had the right to harm another's life, health, liberty and possessions. The state was formed by social contract and guided by natural law. The ethical theory of laws was based on the belief in the natural goodness of humanity. The pursuit of happiness and pleasure when conducted rationally leads to private happiness and general welfare.

JEAN-JACQUES ROUSSEAU

Rousseau was a moralist and a political theorist. He believed that man was by nature good. An ideal social order is one where individuals submit to general will which is what rational people would choose for common good. General will was not identical with the will majority or even with the will of the entire citizen. It was conceived as a will belonging to the body politics. The general will is always right and to the public advantage. Rousseau is of the view that full development takes place when the advantages of a state of nature are combined with the advantages of social life. He had total faith in the existence of the common good in the rightness of the general will. Rousseau rejected reason in favor of the heart. For him reason was abstruse and difficult. Rousseau's noble savage was a good husband and a kind father; he was not greedy and believed in natural kindness.

Concept and Theories of Justice

According to the western philosophers there were three worthwhile things in this universe—Truth, Beauty and Justice. Justice has several definitions but we can safely say that if a person gets treatment in proportion to what he deserves this can be called justice. There is no absolute justice in this world and what we see is relative justice.

There are many types of justice. The first type can be called Procedural Justice which says that it is important to see whether action has been performed using the correct procedure or law. This is quiet important for a public servant who has to administer as per the rule of law and always follow the procedures prescribe by the government. The second type is often called Commutative Justice where all people are treated equally irrespective of their background and given equal opportunities for development. This is a goal towards which all governments strive for as they want to have a system where there is equality of opportunity for all and this principle is also enshrined in a constitution. A third type of justice is Compensatory Justice which sets right the injustice done through unequal treatment in the past by compensating for this it is important that the compensation is fair. An example of this is the benefits which are given to the poor and the under-privileged to compensate them for their status and life. Fourthly, there is Retributive Justice which comes in the form of punishment to a defaulter like imposition of fine on those who violate rules or laws to prevent the person from repeating such acts in the future. This type of justice also takes into account the motive of a person committing an act. Fifthly, there is a Communitarian Justice which is justice to a particular community suffering injustice in the past. The reservation for Scheduled Castes and Scheduled Tribes will form in this category. Finally there is a Distributive Justice which says that the benefits and burdens in a society should be distributive equally among its members.

The basic principle of justice is the principle of fairness.

Theories of Justice

1. Utilitarian Theory: This theory believes in justice leading to maximum happiness of the maximum people. It provides justice to majority but can be criticized for working against the interest of the minority.

2. Egalitarian Theory: This is the form of distributive justice which says that burdens and benefits to be distributive equally. However, it is criticized on the grounds that all human being are not equal, they have different needs and that if they are all treated equally there is no incentive for intelligent people to work harder. Also many feel that the concept of equity which means equality in terms of capability, need and resource endowment is more meaningful than equality. However, as far as political rights are concerned it is important for every government to ensure equality in this respect.
3. Capitalist Theory of Justice: This is the basis of the economic doctrine of capitalism which says that everybody should receive according to his contribution this means that a worker with higher productivity will earn more than one with less productivity. Thus inequality is accepted in this concept of justice and it is criticized on the ground that it does not take into account that people have different abilities and opportunities and also that often productivity is difficult to measure.
4. Karl Marx and Theory of Justice: Marx was of the view that capitalism was not a just system as it led to the exploitation of the labour by the capitalist class which was basically unjust. His labour theory of surplus value said that the capitalist does not pay a laborer according to his productivity and each worker creates a surplus value for which he is not paid. He was of the view that capitalism believes only in concentration of capital which was often monopoly capitalism and the proletariat is exploited. A reserve army of labour is created by displacement of labour by machinery leading to greater poverty. According to Marx, capitalist system led to distributive injustice and alienation of worker. He believed that communism was the ultimate system and it was through violent class conflict that communism would replace capitalism as a system. However, his theory has not been proved right by subsequent events where capitalism has been able to modify itself according to the times and the interest of the workers have also been taken care of. The communist system has failed to deliver in Soviet Union and east European countries and even China has adopted the open market system though continuing with a totalitarian political system.

John Rawls' A Theory of Justice

A landmark Theory of Justice (1971) which is regarded as an alternative to the theory of utilitarianism has been regarded has a landmark. Rawls was not happy with the idea that political theory till that time was moving between two dominant ideas of utilitarianism and intuitionism. He attempted to explain the structures of intuition and explain the principles governing distributive justice. His theory was based on three principles—

1. Equal liberty for all citizens: For instance in India our constitution gives us fundamental rights like freedom of speech, expression and freedom to own private property. Rawls felt that these goods are essential for every citizen to live a meaningful life and should be equally distributed. This principle is very much enshrined in our constitution and is the basis for a democratic form of government. In India, it is through democracy that we govern our country and each person has an equal right to vote or participate in the democratic process.
2. Equality of Opportunity for everybody: This is essential to have a just society where every person can maximize his inner talents and potential and grow in life. The Indian Constitution specifically provides for equality of opportunity and all government schemes and policies are geared towards this principle. In fact, wherever it is felt that some people have less opportunities than others the government intervenes by providing special benefits for them. All the poverty alleviation schemes and employment generating schemes fall under this category. The reservation for schedule castes and schedule tribes is also an example of this. The belief is that there is a difference in the conditions of the people which should be attended to.

Rawls talks about the original position which is the starting neutral position and should be such that the principles of the justice chosen must be equally applicable to everyone. This is called the Principle of Universalizability. Rawls is concerned with two basic questions of distributive justice which are how can we find the principles of justice and what are these principles. He is of the view that it is important to have a set of principles to determine that division of advantages among the participants. His conception of social justice is to provide a standard whereby the distributive aspects of the basic structure of society are to be assessed. Rawls rejects the importance of merit and talent and no benefit should flow to a person exclusively on this basis to the disadvantage of the less fortunate.

According to Rawls, justice can be achieved on the basis of a hypothetical social contract which determines the principles of justice which emerged from a concept of equality. In this way Rawls is talking about commutative justice with an equal start and fairness to everyone. The claim of people to social goods should not depend on natural endowments. He applies the different principles which say that people may receive extra rewards for their talents only if that leads to the benefit of less well off. In this way Rawls tackles the issues of inequality in his theory of justice. Rawls also assumes that rational individuals would agree to two other different principles—equality in the assignment of basic rights and duties and socio-economic inequalities are permitted only if these result in compensating benefits for everyone. Justice is an outcome of fair agreement as per the social contract. John Rawls holds rationality as the most effective means to achieve the given ends.

His theory is criticized on the grounds that the different principles may not be accepted by the rich who would not sacrifice their money for the betterment of the poor. However, in reality, in countries like India the government imposes taxes on the rich and uses them to come out with schemes and projects for the development of the poor. Thus, we see that the different principles are used by the government to bring about fairness and justice in the society.

Libertarian Theory

The most important proponent of this thinking is Robert Nozick (1974) according to him the transfer of income and wealth from rich to the poor is unjust. He believes that only if the exchange is voluntary only then it can be called just. It will depend upon the free will of the individual and not on any external pressure on him. Justice emerges from true freedom based on the free choice of individuals, thus, this theory is not in favor of the government intervening to benefit the poor and the needy. If we believe this theory then it could imply that inequalities continue and the society and the poor remain poor. For a just society it is also important to provide freedom from poverty, disease and illiteracy. Only freedom from coercion is not important for justice but freedom from socio-economic conditions leading to some sections of the society lagging far behind is also of vital importance.

CONTRIBUTION OF INDIAN ETHOS AND ETHICAL THINKING

India is one of the oldest civilization and its culture and ethos is full of ethical and moral precepts about meaning of life and the right way of living. Religion has been of foremost importance in the Hindu culture where it was believed that human happiness is not possible without religion. However, Indian ethics is vast and there are many schools of philosophy which define the nature of God and the right conduct for human beings. At one end are scriptures like the *Gita* which talk about everything coming from God and God realization as the aim of life but there are also others schools especially Buddhism and Jainism who are either silent about the existence of God or deny it.

Buddhism

In the 6th century B.C. Buddhism evolved as a system of ethical ideals as an attempt to answer the questions relating to the purpose of life. Buddha was silent about the existence of God and his teachings are based on the "Four Noble Truths" taught by him. According to Buddha the Four Noble Truths are—

1. The world is full of suffering and people suffer from pain, poverty, disease and old age. Suffering leads to sorrow and sadness.
2. Suffering has a cause which is desire. It is desire which creates suffering. In essence there is a cause and an effect.
3. There can be cessation of suffering if we can remove the cause.
4. If a person follows the ethical path and does not run after needless desires he will be able to put an end to all sufferings and miseries and also liberate himself from the vicious cycle of birth and death (attain nirvana).

The ethical path to achieve this is the noble eightfold path—

1. Right understanding
2. Right thought
3. Right speech
4. Right action
5. Right living
6. Right effort
7. Right mindfulness
8. Right concentration

If people follow this eightfold path they will be able to free themselves from the bondage of desire which is the root cause of suffering. The paths are connected to each other and prescribe the right way of living if one has to overcome suffering. The first three paths help in understanding the nature of suffering while the fourth path is about the way to end it.

Buddha advocated the middle path to be followed to get the best results. This means that neither should a person follow a rigid path of extreme austerity nor a path of total indulgence. Self mortification and self indulgence are both to be avoided and it is through the middle path that one would attain nirvana and enlightenment. Nirvana was a state of perfect desirelessness.

Lord Buddha advocated Ahimsa (non-violence) and a life full of love and compassion towards all. He was of the view that men should overcome hatred with love and evil with good and his life is an example of this kind of living. He wanted human beings to be considerate, selfless and put a lot of emphasis on inner purification. Human beings are caught in a vicious cycle of birth and death leading to continuation of suffering and it is only through right kind of knowledge that the cycle can be broken. A central idea of teaching of Buddha is that our past *Karmas* (actions) determine our present station and status of life.

Buddha's approach has been rational where it is up to the human being to follow a way of life whereby he can get over pain and suffering in this world.

Jainism

The 6th century B.C. also gave rise to Jainism and Mahavira Jain was the last and most important of the 24 Tirthankaras who contributed to the development of this religion. Jainism does not believe in the existence of God but is of the view that our sorrow is due to our being caught in a cycle of birth and death and the main cause of this is our ignorance. This ignorance can be overcome by true knowledge which leads to enlightenment and liberation (*Moksha*). To achieve this, five ethical principles need to be followed:

1. Non-violence and non-injury to any man or animal.
2. Truthfulness
3. Non stealing
4. Non possession (*aprigraha*)
5. Celibacy (*brahmacharya*)

Human beings are different and work in different environments and therefore observance of these five principles would be different—it would be very strict and rigorous for monks but relaxed for house-holders.

Jainism regards every living creature as potentially divine and nobody should harm them. Non-violence is the path to self-consciousness. The true nature of our soul is realized when we become free from the duty-bound obligations and attain divine consciousness. A soul has to make an effort to conquer the inner enemies by constant practice. Jainism is an extremely ethical religion of self development. Jainism also prescribes three commandments to guide human behaviour

1. Right perception (faith)
2. Right knowledge
3. Right conduct

Jainism aims to attain perfection and for this it advises restraints of the body, speech and mind. Every Jain should cultivate virtues like humility, purity, truthfulness, forgiveness and simplicity.

Hinduism

Before Buddhism and Jainism was the period of *Dharma Sutras* which came out with ethical principles and commandments for the Hindu way of life. The moral standards and norms of ethical behaviour are discussed in these *Dharma Sutras*. The most important of these is the *Manu Smriti* which gives details of duties and responsibilities of various social classes of people. According to *Manu Smriti* there are four stages in human life:

1. *Bramhacharya* (celibacy)
2. *Grihastha* (family life)
3. *Vanprastha* (retired life)
4. *Sanyas* (life of renunciation)

The life span of a human being was expected to be 100 years and each of these stages was of 25 years each. The first stage was about learning and character building; the second was about living the life of a house-holder and earning a living and looking after one's family; the third stage was about moving away from active life and devoting oneself to spiritual activity and the fourth stage was about completely moving away from family life. In this way a man was supposed to live a balanced life. Hinduism carries this system of balance further by giving four objectives of life.

1. *Dharma* (religion)
2. *Artha* (wealth)
3. *Kama* (sensual pleasure)
4. *Moksha* (salvation)

Thus one can see from the above that the Hindu view of life was very comprehensive and a man was expected to concern himself with the material as well as spiritual aspects of life. Sensual pleasure was not frowned upon but access of all forms was to be avoided. One was allowed to one's wealth but in a righteous way without cheating or corruption or immorality. Religious ideals should guide all activities of human beings and salvation has to be the ultimate objective. One has to be God-fearing and always conduct himself in the right manner.

Varna Ashram

Hinduism devised a caste-based social system assigning social duties of each caste. The four castes were:

1. Brahmana (teachers and priests)
2. Kshatriya (administrators and the army)
3. Vaysha (traders and farmers)
4. Shudra (servants and manual labor)

This social stratification was to be on the basis of ability and not on birth but overtime this gave way to the Jati System which became hereditary and exploitation of lower castes by the upper became a social evil.

Ramayana

Ramayana is a great epic which narrates the story of Lord Ram and his victory over Ravana which symbolizes the victory of good over evil. This scripture has been internalized by generations of Indians over thousands of years and has become the guiding source of all ethical and moral conduct expected of a human being. The central message is that good ultimately triumphs over evil even though it has to face many obstacles on the way which should not dissuade a person from the moral path. Ram is an ideal person and his personality is endowed with all the qualities that a human being should possess, elevating him to the level of divinity and being worshipped as an incarnation of God. Ram was an ideal and obedient son who left the palace just a day before his proposed coronation and went to the forest for 14 years to honor the commitment that his father Dushrath had given to one of his queens, Kaikeyi. He did so with equanimity without any rancour even towards Queen Kaikeyi. He was a loving husband and brother and gave love and respect to all. After defeating Ravan he took over as King of Ayodhya and his rule was perfect and ideal and is called Ram Rajya. He devoted his life for welfare of all his citizens. He did not rule for personal gain or comfort but to serve the people and give them justice and good governance. Public servants can learn a lot from this approach of Ram towards governing his kingdom. Ram was perfect in his conduct, in his personal as well as public life and set the high ideals towards which all human beings should aspire.

Mahabharata

Mahabharata is the other major epic of Hindu civilization. It is the story of a devastating war between Pandavas who represented truth and justice and Kauravas who were symbols of injustice and immorality. This epic also signifies the victory of just over the unjust and good over evil. This victory would not have been possible without the blessings and support of Lord Krishna to the Pandavas signifying that being good alone is not enough but one has to devote to God to get victory over the forces of evil. *Mahabharata* is an epic which portrays both ethical and unethical conduct and brings out the entire noble and the profane qualities in human beings personified by the various characters of the epic. There are issues relating to ethical dilemmas which have been brought out in this epic like Bhishma, Drona and all the elders remaining silent as Queen Draupadi is attempted to be forcibly disrobed in front of everybody on the directions of unethical Duryodhana. The most significant part of *Mahabhrata* is the *Bhagwat Gita* which is narrated by Lord Krishna to Arjuna in the battle field of Kurukshetra and this scripture is a complete document of ethics and morality that is expected of a human being.

Bhagvad Gita

Gita is the essence of all the *Upanishads* which are the treasure-house of all philosophical wisdom of ancient India. Shri Krishna counseled a despondent Arjuna just before the battle of Mahabharata started. It was Sankaracharya who discovered the importance of *Gita* and preached the people by writing a commentary on it. The science of the *Gita* is the collection of all the essential teachings of the *Vedas* and is aimed at acquiring knowledge about the ultimate truth which is God or Brahma. *Gita* as narrated by Shri Krishna makes Arjuna aware of his duties and that he has to fight a war against injustice and he should not be deluded from his goal by any weakness or ignorance of thinking. The most significant words of the *Gita* is the one which elucidates the all important philosophy of *Karma* or detached action. It says that the right of a person is to work only and he should not be concerned about the fruits of his actions nor should he be attached to inaction. This theory emphasizes that man should constantly act renouncing the fruits of his actions. It is when the actions of the men are motivated by material or sensual desires that unhappiness and pain is caused. Only by detached action can a man acquire wisdom and come out of ignorance. Action is always superior to inaction but it is important to control the senses by the mind. A sensual life is a life of sin and not worthwhile. Lord Krishna says that man should free himself from attachment, lust and anger and take refuge in him (God) and by doing so be purified by the fire of knowledge. One should be calm, serene, peaceful and treat happiness and sorrow equally. *Gita* advocates living a life of higher consciousness which is *sattvic* as opposed to *rajasic* or *tamsik* which is a life of ignorance and inaction. The purpose of life is to evolve towards a *sattvic* way of living which is possible only when one is not attached to action. That person is the highest, frèe from all delusions worships God with one's heart.

Gita outlines the qualities that are required of a divine human being. The qualities mentioned are fearlessness, purity of heart, steadfastness in knowledge, almsgiving, control of the senses, study of the *Shastras*, austerity and uprightness. It goes on that energy, fortitude, purity, absence of hatred and pride are divine qualities which should be cultivated by human beings for it is only in this manner that they shall be able to liberate themselves from the bondage of delusion. *Gita* also points out the qualities which should be avoided which include ostentation, arrogance, self-conceit, anger, harshness, lust and greed. Any human being who is filled with insatiable sensory desires is deluded and impure. Such a person is given to lust, greed and anger and destroys his self and opens the gateway to hell for himself. It is only with supreme knowledge and wisdom as brought out in the *Gita* that man can free himself from darkness and live a meaningful life. *Gita* wants a human being to be like a yogi who is always constant and steady and striving for union with God.

Gita emphasizes the philosophy of *karma* (action) which is based on *jnana* (knowledge) and supported by *bhakti* and its meaning to life and aspires to move from a lower to a higher level of consciousness. Control over the senses is the foundation of a virtuous life. Human beings have been given free will to choose their course of action and therefore are responsible for their actions (*karma*) and have to face the consequences for the same in this life or the next. *Gita* believes that the soul is permanent and does not die but only changes body from one life to another. *Gita* is not in favor of ritualism or ceremonialism and advocates equanimity of mind which means that a person is not perturbed by unhappiness or happiness and is free from attachment, fear and anger. Such a person attains true wisdom.

Bhagvad Gita is a gospel for action and concerned with realization of God. Action is the basis of human life and inaction has to be avoided at all cost but this action has to be selfless and based on noble motives. The message of *Gita* is the essence of Indian philosophy and is universal and timeless.

Advaita Vedant (Sankaracharya)

This philosophy put forward by Sankaracharya has been enunciated in the *Upanishads* and says that *Brahm* (universal soul) and *Atma* (the individual soul) are one and it is only because of ignorance that man sees them as being different. This ignorance is called *avidya* which needs to be eliminated by right knowledge if a person has to attain liberation from the cycle from birth and death. The right path to achieve this is that of *bhakti* (devotion) and *jnana* (knowledge). *Brahm* is the only reality while this world of the senses is an illusion. Sankaracharya says that *pravritti* is a tendency in human being to live a life of pleasure and enjoyment and is a lower path of morality while the higher path of transcendental morality is called nivritti or the tendency of the mind to refrain from empirical pleasure and enjoyment. *Nivritti* is attained when one renounces the fruits of all actions and all desires. The performance of one's duty is the path to freedom from bondage and ignorance. Attainment of Brahma (God) gives us the highest bliss and complete happiness. The essence of the theory of the Sankaracharya is non-dualism meaning that the atma and brahma are one.

Visishtadvaita (Ramanuja)

Ramanuja was critical of the *advaita* philosophy of Sankaracharya and modified it as *Visishtadvaita*. He believed in oneness of God but also said that all visible things in the world are His manifestations or attributes. He gave special importance to devotion or *bhakti* to God. He himself worshipped Vishnu and Narayan and believed that devotion has an enormous power that can eliminate bad effects of past *Karma* and help in attaining *Moksh*. One must live a moral and ethical life in order to get the blessings of God.

Yoga—Eightfold Path of Patanjali

Yoga means union with God and Patanjali advocated an eightfold path to achieve this. In common parlance we often associate yoga only with yogic exercises or *asanas* which is only one part of the eightfold path. The eightfold path of yoga that consists of the following:

- *Yama* – The right actions a person should indulge in like non-violence, truth, honesty, non-stealing and non-passiveness.
- *Niyam* – This includes purity in thoughts and deeds, containment, regular study of scriptures and constant awareness of the divine power.
- *Asana* – This refers to the yogic exercises.
- *Pranayam* – This refers to control of breath.
- *Pratyahara* – This is about taking the mind away from the senses and controlling the senses.
- *Dharana* – Pure concentration.
- *Dhyan* – This is about meditation on God.
- *Samadhi* – Final stage where union with the divine is achieved.

Guru Nanak

Guru Nanak was a great spiritual leader and founder of Sikh religion. He believed in one God and said that there is no difference between a Hindu and a Muslim. He was not in favor of idol worship and ritualism. He believed in continuous remembering of the name of the Lord. Three main tenets of his teachings were—

1. *Vag Chakk* – Helping those who are in need.
2. *Kirat kar* – Working to make a living honestly.
3. *Naam Japna* – Meditating on the name of God.

Guru Nanak was a great teacher and philosopher whose teachings comprehensively bring about the essential qualities of a ethical or moral way of living.

Charvaka Ethics

This system of philosophy does not believe in God and says that there is no life after death and this world is an outcome of natural evolution. Religion was invented by man and does not flow from any divine authority and the soul is nothing but a part of the conscious body. Consciousness arises out of matter and death alone is liberation. All religious ceremonies are unnecessary and enjoyment or happiness is aim of life. Charvaka is of the view that a man is happy only through the gratification of his senses and the purpose of life is to maximize pleasure and minimize pain. This ethic of sensual pleasure of Charvaka has been criticized by other schools of Indian Philosophy which talk of a higher purpose of life and a life of virtue which alone can lead to genuine happiness.

Kautilya

So far we have talked about the spiritual heritage of Indian culture in ethics. However, we need to talk about Kautilya or Chanakya who was the famous political philosopher and his teachings enunciated in his book *Arthshastra* influenced the way kings ruled or handled administration or governance

According to Kautilya the elements of a state are:

- The king.
- The ministers and other officials.
- Territory of the states and its populations.
- Fortified towns and cities.
- Treasury and wealth.
- Forces and defense, law and order.
- The allies.

He was of the view that it is the people who constitute a kingdom and there can be no country without people and the protection of the people is the duty of the king. He advocated *Dandaniti* which is the use of punishment to maintain law and order. The welfare of the people was the prime function of an ideal king who exhibited the highest qualities of leadership, intelligence and energy. The king was expected to have self control and self discipline and led the people by his example. The *Arthshastra* prescribes a detailed code of conduct for the king which included the quality of accessibility to people and prompt resolution of grievances.

The advisors to the king should be people of talent and knowledge on whose good judgments the king can depend. They should be people of integrity and the king must appoint them after testing their qualities. Similarly, the high level public officials should be competent, responsible and honest and should be accountable for their work and give the right kind of advice to the king. Kautilya emphasises the importance of civil services and providing good administration which should consist of persons of unimpeachable character, and possessing highest qualities of leadership. They should follow a strict code of conduct and work with efficiency. To maintain efficiency he advocated periodic rotation of powers. He suggested strong actions against corrupt and inefficient officers. Kautilya has gone in to great detail about accounting, audit and management of state money so that money is spent properly. He desires that the king should always be active in the management of the economy to bring about economic growth and generate wealth.

An essential duty of the king was to provide justice and maintain law and order. He also suggested the creation of a secret service with spies and secret agents to brief the king about every activity in his kingdom. Kautilya also gave a theory of foreign policy and how to build relations with neighboring states and handle enemies. He also talked about building up of the army and control over them. He advocated a highly effective taxation structure and system of financial management. He was a strong advocate of character, discipline and self-control on the part of the king and high public officials. He has contributed significantly to Indian thinking about politics and economics.

References

1. *Business Ethics and Corporate Governance* by B.N. Ghosh
2. *Ethics for Governance – Reinventing Public Services* by B.P. Mathur
3. *Universal Message of Bhagwad Gita* (3 Volumes) by Swami Ranganathnanda
4. *Story of Philosophy* by Will Durant
5. *History of Philosophy* by Bertrand Russell
6. *Ethics Integrity & Aptitude* by G Subba Rao and P. N. Roy Chowdhury
7. *Lexicon* (Chronicle) Edited by N.N. Ojha

Chapter 7

Civil Service Values and Ethics

Public/Civil Service Values and Ethics in Public Administration Status and Problems

Public service is a public trust. Civil servants have to realize that their job is to serve the people and not act as their masters. Public interest has to be of paramount importance and the public servant must be fair in his dealings, always responsive to public interest and should manage public resources properly and efficiently. This is the basis of good governance. A public servant has to be impartial, non-partisan, objective, efficient, transparent and honest. He has to be accountable to the people and should always act as per the rule of law and the principles laid down in the constitution and in all his actions, respect and honor democratic principles. Above all he has to display complete financial and intellectual integrity.

A civil servant has to demonstrate the highest standards of professional competence, efficiency and effectiveness. He has to, at all times, uphold the constitution and the law. The basic values of public service and ethics of public administration are transparency, integrity, legitimacy, fairness, responsiveness and efficiency and effectiveness. A civil servant must get the best value for public assets deployed in public management and should avoid waste and extravagance and the use of public assets.

The American society of public administration has laid down the code for the public servant. This code says at all times the public servant should put public interest above self interest and subordinate institutional loyalties to the public good. Discretion should be exercised to promote public interest. They should promote affirmative action but oppose any kind of discrimination and harassment. The public servant should encourage people to participate in the affairs of the government. The public servant should respect the constitution and the law and promote constitutional principles of equality, fairness, representativeness, responsiveness and due process in protecting the rights of the citizens. He should be honest in his duties and fair in his conduct. He should serve the people in an efficient and effective manner and should always strive for professional excellence.

One of the standard principles of public life have been laid down by the Nolan Committee in UK. They have given seven principle—

1. Selflessness – Holders of public office should not do anything for personal gain but only for public interest.
2. Objectivity – All decisions should be taken on merit.
3. Accountability – Public servants are accountable for their decisions to the public and are open to any appropriate scrutiny.
4. Openness – Holders of public offices should be transparent and open in all their decisions and actions.
5. Honesty – They should work with total honesty and integrity.
6. Leadership – They should set an example by their leadership for others to promote these principles and deliver public services to the people.

It is on the basis of the above recommendations that UK has drawn up a code of values and ethics for ministers, parliamentarians and public servants.

A study by the OECD (Organization for Economic Cooperation and Development) which has a membership of 37 countries has agreed on eight core values for public management. They are impartiality, legality, integrity, transparency, efficiency, equality, responsibility and justice. All over the world governments are concerned about the need for high standards of conduct in public life. The OECD has issued 12 principles for "Managing ethics in public service" to help countries review the institutions, systems and mechanisms. They have been promoting public service ethics with the idea to integrate them with the broader public management environment. These principles are:

1. Ethical standards for public service should be clear.
2. Ethical standards should be reflected in the legal framework-laws and regulations.
3. Ethical guidance should be available to public servants.
4. Public servants should be aware of their rights and obligations in terms of exposing actual or suspected wrong doing within the public service.

5. Political commitment to ethics should reinforce the ethical conduct of public servants.
6. The decision-making process should be transparent and open to scrutiny.
7. Clear rules defining ethical standards should guide the behaviour of public servants.
8. Administrators should demonstrate and promote ethical conduct.
9. The policies and practices of an organization should demonstrate their commitment to ethical standards.
10. Public service conditions of human resource should promote ethical conduct.
11. Adequate accountability mechanism should be in place within the public service.
12. Appropriate procedures and sanctions should exist to deal with misconduct.

The current status about public service values and ethics in administration calls for a lot of improvement. The public is not satisfied that the structure of public administration is working in their interests and you often hear people complaining about the poor quality of public services or lack of response from public servants.

There are various reasons for the above perception of the people and can only be addressed by a commitment to the core values and ethics of public service. Some of the main problem areas have been discussed in the other chapters of the book but I would reiterate them here for emphasis. Corruption in public life is on the increase. It starts from the use of money power in elections and then continues with the ministers and the civil servants colluding to make illegal personal gains at the cost of the public exchequer. There is far too much political interference in government and too much pressure on the civil servant not allowing him to do his duty fairly and honestly. There has also been a general decline in the value system of public servants who are more interested in pleasing their political bosses and amassing wealth than in delivering public service to the people with honesty, dedication and professionalism. It is the duty of all the three wings of governance—the legislature, executive and the judiciary to work together to create a culture of commitment to the ethical conduct of public service. An environment needs to be created where ethical working is rewarded and the opposite punished. The civil servants face various ethical issues like—corrupt officers getting away with no action against them and also reaching the top posts. A system has to be put in place where career advancement is linked to professional and ethical conduct of civil servants.

Ethical Concern and Dilemmas in Government and Private Institutions

An ethical dilemma is a situation where an individual or a public servant has to choose between two alternatives both of which are ethically correct. If he chooses one it might go against the other or be at the cost of the other. Here the individual has to exercise his discretion to which course of action is ethically more correct or appropriate. This often depends upon the context of the situation and also on what an individual values most. Ethical dilemmas confront a person working in a government or private institution or in his personal life also. The response may vary from person to person.

Some of the biggest examples of ethical dilemmas that come to my mind are related to the great epic *Mahabharat*. Let me just give a few illustrations. Draupadi is forcibly brought into the chamber where the game of dice is being played between the Pandavas and the Kauravas. Yudhistra has lost his kingdom, his brothers and his wife Draupadi in the game of dice. Duryodhan, the leader of the Kauravas, orders the public disrobing of Draupadi who cries for help towards all the seniors and gurus. Bhishma is the oldest member of the family and highly respected for his bravery, courage and values. He is extremely upset by what is going on and is aware that ethically he should stand up and stop this evil act of disrobing Draupadi but he has taken a vow to always support the Hastinapur king and is ethically committed to support him and not oppose him in any way. This is a classic ethical dilemma. Unfortunately Bhisma chose to honor his oath to always support the Hastinapur king and did not get up to stop the disrobing of Draupadi. We could question his decision. Had he spoken up the unpleasant situation could have been avoided and even helped in not escalating the bitterness between the Kauravas and the Pandavas. However, he chose the option of loyalty to the king. In a similar way we find Arjun confronted with an ethical dilemma in the battle field. He has to fight a war because the other side is being unjust to him and his brothers. At the same time he sees his old relatives and gurus on the other side and cannot possibly think of killing them in a war. Lord Krishna recites the *Gita* to help Arjun get over his ethical dilemma and fight the war for justice and for the victory of good over evil.

In personal life also, we come across several similar situations. There is the story of a saint who never used to tell a lie and is one day sitting under the tree and meditating when he sees a man running and this man tells him that dacoits are chasing him to kill him. After sometime the dacoits reach the spot and ask the saint whether he has seen a man go by and which way has he gone. The saint agrees that he has seen the man but points in the wrong direction thereby saving the life of the man. Now the saint has told a lie which amounts to being an unethical practice but he has done this to save the life of a man which is a very ethical and moral act. I am sure we will agree with the decision of the saint. This is the essence of an ethical dilemma where you make conscience choices from alternatives which are both ethically correct. A public servant faces a lot of situations where there are conflicts of interest and ethical dilemmas. Sometimes he has to decide between a professional action which is mandated by the government and personal values which are not in favor of that action. There are also situations where if a person acts ethically he suffers professionally and these are called personal cost ethical dilemmas.

A civil servant has to give his views fairly and frankly to the political executive who has to take a decision. It may happen that the civil servant is overruled by his political boss and has to take action according to decisions even though he does not believe in it. This is a typical ethical dilemma. However, it is the duty of the civil servant to put forward his views giving all reasons but he has to carry out whatever decision is taken by the competent authority. Similarly, a civil servant can face a situation where he finds that if he does the right thing and exposes corruption his bosses, who may be involved, are likely to be annoyed but here it is clear that he must take action against corruption at the cost of annoying his superiors. A civil servant can be confronted with a situation where a private corporation is offering an excellent job to his son and not asking for any favor in return but he also knows that it is unethical to take favors from private parties who can then cash it later on. His duty towards his son is in conflict with the code of conduct of a civil servant. This kind of situation was best illustrated in the famous Hindi movie Shakti in which Dilip Kumar is an honest and a strict police officer whose son (Amitabh Bachchan) is kidnapped by criminals and they ask him to release some big criminals in exchange for the custody of his son. His wife and other relatives put pressure on him but he is committed to his duty as a civil servant and in public interest he does not do so. He manages to rescue his son. What would have happened if he had not succeeded and the son had been harmed? In the movie itself Amitabh Bachchan grows up resenting that his father preferred his duty over his love for the child. He becomes a criminal and ultimately the movie shows that Dilip Kumar as a police officer has to arrest or kill him. This is an extreme case but brings to life the conflict between public duty and personal issues and these kinds of ethical dilemmas have to be tackled by public servants very often in their career.

A civil servant has to often support a corrupt officer just because he is politically strong. He has to also carry out illegal orders if he wants to maintain good relations with his superiors. The answer to these ethical dilemmas is clear—he has to choose the ethical path and not allow corrupt officers to thrive or do illegal things just because there is pressure from the top. There may be short term problems but ethics and values always triumph in the end. A very typical ethical dilemma before a public servant is when he has to choose between two officers—one of them is extremely competent but dishonest and the other is honest but does not work. The civil servant has to work efficiently and effectively and deliver results and at the same time not allow any dishonest practices. A way out could be to select the competent officer but warn him that he should not indulge in dishonest practices and also not delegate too many financial powers to him and curtail his discretion.

A civil servant has to follow rules and procedures and deliver results also. Sometimes these rules and regulations and the procedures are so complicated and detailed that they obstruct the path of efficient delivery of public services and giving of results. A civil servant has to ensure that he gives results though if he ignores the rules then he can be punished for committing irregularities. The civil servant has to find a way out of the red tape to give results. If required he should simplify the rules and processes and also change them wherever required. The Government of India has done so as part of its governance reforms.

Very often a civil servant has to take up a major project like construction of a dam which is required to improve the agriculture productivity and economic status of the farmers of the area. However, such large projects also mean dislocation of a large number of people from their villages and loss of their traditional employment as well as having an adverse effect on the environment and wild life. This is once again an ethical dilemma. The solution would be to construct a dam but fully provide relief and rehabilitation to the displaced people, destroy minimum number of trees and vegetation and see that the wild life is not unduly disturbed. In fact, the conflict between environment and growth is a very common ethical dilemma in all projects and the civil servant has to balance both sides.

While designing macro-economic policies the public servant is faced with the ethical dilemma of focusing only on economic growth or on distributive justice. The former would often raise the standard of living for all but lead to widening of inequalities while the latter could lead to slowing down of the growth process. Once again the public servant has to resolve the dilemma by focusing on inclusive growth.

Principle of Constitutional Morality

A civil servant has to be loyal to the constitution. There are specific provisions in the constitution to which a civil servant is bound by oath to follow. However, there is the Principle of Constitutional morality which guides the ethical conduct of a civil servant. This principle is the very basis of a democratic form of government and people in power should be guided by this morality in all their actions. The legislature, executive and the judiciary have all to follow the principle of constitutional morality which is the soul of the constitution and declares its ideals and inspiration. Part-3 of the Constitution has provision dealing with the dignity of the individual and it is also a part of this concept. It is the moral basis on which the constitution has been drafted and visualizes the kind of society we want our country to be and the kind of governance that is desirable. At any time if any of the wings of government are faced with the problem of decision-making then it is the constitutional morality which should guide them. The power of the government has to be exercised in public interest. Our constitution recognizes the plurality of our culture and diversity. The preamble of the constitution says that India is a sovereign, socialist, secular, democratic republic and aims to secure to all its citizens justice which is social, economic, political and liberty of thought, expression, belief, faith and worship. It also assures its citizens of equality of status and opportunity and strives to promote among all fraternity assuring the dignity of the individual and unity of nation. Each word of the preamble is an expression of constitutional morality and should guide the conduct of all involved in governance in the country.

Ethical Concerns

There are a lot of ethical concerns which may lead to an ethical dilemma and are often the cause for poor governance. Good governance and ethical conduct are linked to each other. The various ethical issues faced by civil servants are those relating to increasing corruption among officers and lack of action against them, political interference, lack of accountability, lack of transparency, political alignment, nepotism and lack of concern towards the poor and the under privileged.

The SARC has listed out some of these major ethical concerns. They are—

1. Corruption especially at the cutting edge level of the bureaucracy.
2. Perceptible lack of commitment in public servants towards the grievances of the citizens.
3. Red tapism and unnecessary complex procedures causing hardship to the citizens.
4. Government servants rarely being held accountable for poor performance or lack of integrity.
5. Lack of accessibility of public functionaries and attitude of arrogance and indifference.
6. Frequent transfers of officers reducing their effectiveness.
7. Unholy nexus between corrupt politicians and bureaucrats.

Ethical Concerns and Dilemmas in Private Institutions

Just as in government there are ethical concerns and dilemmas in private sector and non-government organizations. The private corporate sector is primarily concerned with making profits as they would not exist if they do not earn returns on the money invested. However, there are a lot of ethical concerns which have to be taken into account. For instance, a private sector industry can not damage the environment through air, water or noise pollution as these would lead to adversely impacting the health of the citizens and also unsustainable growth. Further they should look after their labour and ensure that it is not exploited. There should be no safety hazards for the workers and the management has to arrange for the safety and protection of its workers by providing protective gear. The private sector has also to ensure that they do not make profits through corrupt, immoral or unethical practices. They owe taxes to the government and should not make an effort to evade taxes which are required for the development of the people. Many corporations bribe the lower level officers to get their power bills reduced or indulge in unfair labour practices. These have to be avoided as it is as important to be ethical as it is to be profitable. The private sector has a duty to the community also and should try to provide basic minimum services to the people around them. This is a part of corporate social responsibility which they should follow with full sincerity. Many private sector corporations take loans from banks and utilize them for personal glory and developing personal assets and became defaulters. This is an example of gross misuse of public money and is a criminal act. Currently people like Vijay Mallya of Kingfisher and Nirav Modi have been accused of this crime. It is the duty of the private sector organization to present a true and fair picture of their accounts and not siphon off the funds of the share holders. The case of Satyam computers comes to mind in this connection. There are also cases of wrong facts being advertised about their products and substandard products being produced.

Laws, Rules, Regulations and Conscience and Ethical Guidance

Human beings are guided internally by their functions which tell them which action is moral and should be followed and so is a very important source of ethical guidance. However, as a member of the society the government frames laws, regulations and rules which can be termed as the external factors of ethical guidance for a human being. No human being is expected to break the law. If he does so he has to face the punishment for the same. Public servants in their actions are governed by rules, regulations and laws but they also have a conscience which is always acting as the source of ethical guidance. In fact, whenever there is any doubt about any decision it is the voice of the conscience to which a public servant should listen.

Laws

In our democratic system the laws are debated and enacted by the legislature. The executive has to act as per these laws and implement them while the role of the judiciary is to interpret the laws and also see whether they are unconstitutional in anyway. Some examples of laws can be motor vehicle act, private universities act, national security act, food adulteration act, etc.

Laws are expected to be an expression of the general will of the people and they ensure that governance is done in a uniform manner for all citizens and there is a sense of discipline in the society. St. Thomas Aquinas defined law as "An ordinance of reason for the common good promulgated by him who has care of the community."

It induces a certain action from the people or restrains them from taking a certain action. St. Thomas recognized two kinds of laws—

1. Natural Law
2. Positive Law

Natural law is based on human nature and has evolved over time. They provide ethical guidance on right or wrong action for a human being. Natural laws have two qualities, first, universality which means that it extends to all human beings and second, immutability which implies that it does not change as it is a product of human nature. On the other hand, positive laws like the civil law clarify the natural laws which can often be vague and they often also take up issues which do not fall under the ambit of natural law. There is an obligation for following the principles of natural law and since positive laws also emerge from natural law they should also be followed. Positive laws get their sanction from the existence of a lawful government which has enacted the laws with full authority.

John Austin propounded the command theory of law where the law is a command from a sovereign and is reinforced by sanction or punishment and people are expected to obey them. The above theory excludes the concept of morality from the conception of various laws. Theories of positive law do not accept any connection between positive law and morality though most of the laws emerged from the moral foundations of the society.

We often talk about public servants acting according to the rule of law. This means that they implement the laws of the nation with uniformity and without any discrimination according to the letter and spirit of the law. One of the most important ethical duties of a public servant is to uphold the rule of law. These days political interference sometimes goes to such an extent that civil servants selectively implement the law which is against the integrity expected of them.

Rules and Regulations

Rules and regulations have often the same meaning. In order to implement the laws properly rules are framed by the competent authority giving detailed guidelines on how a particular law is to be implemented, for example, rules relating to the air pollution act would specify what level of pollution is not acceptable, the possible sources of such pollution and the actions that need to be taken to control pollution from all these sources. The executive branch of the government exercises the rule-making powers but the rules cannot go beyond the law and are like subordinate legislation as they have to be ratified by the legislature. Regulations are also issued by a competent authority to regulate a particular activity. For example, the Security and Exchange Board of India regulates the working of the financial markets and the Reserve Bank of India regulates the working of all the banks in the country. Regulations can be said to be directives or statutes enforced by law while rules can be described as guidelines or instructions or doing something correctly and govern the behaviour of a person in an organization or a country. Rules and regulations apply to the working of most institutions like schools, colleges, banks, clubs, offices or corporations. Rules are generally flexible while regulations are rigid. Rules flow from particular conditions and circumstances while regulations flow from an act. Rules can be set by an individual or an organization while regulations are made by government. In general, we can say that rules are a set of instructions issued for the public while rules which are legally accepted by the governing authority are regulations. Both have to be inconsonance with the constitution and are to be followed by the people and are for their good and any violation can lead to penalty.

A public servant in his working has to ensure that the laws, rules and regulations which have been framed by the government are followed. It is his ethical duty to do so and if any public servant does not do so he can be called unethical. A public servant has to see that laws, rules and regulations are implemented properly and there is no negligence in this respect on his part. However, if due to the change in circumstances a public servant finds a particular rule or regulation not corresponding to ethics he should move to get that rule amended. The laws also can undergo a change in different circumstances but they have always to be passed by the legislature. For example, before 1991 as per the Industrial Licensing Act no industry could be set up without obtaining a license from the competent authority. However, this had created an atmosphere where industrial and economic growth in India had been slowed down. In 1991, the act was amended giving freedom of entry and exit to industries and these major reforms transformed the economy of the country.

A public servant has to at all times be guided ethically by rules, regulations and laws in force at that time. If he does not do so his act could be irregular or even criminal and he has to face action or penalty for the same.

Conscience

Conscience is the inner sense of a human being speaking to him and it is the biggest source of moral and ethical guidance. It is said that conscience is the voice of God which enables them to choose good over evil and the just over unjust. It is the moral basis of any human action. That is no external punishment or reward that is the guiding force of conscience. It is the inner sense of morality and that of right and wrong which motivates a person to act as per his conscience. Conscience is much wider than law and its application as it applies to all aspects of human activity. It is an aspect of human intelligence and consciousness and a special faculty innate in man. However, recent theories say that it is the individual and social experience of a human being which guides his conscience and thus it can be considered as a product of social development and individual development. Conscience and law generally should not be opposed to each other and in fact should complement one and the other. For example, there are laws like prevention of corruption act which prohibit corruption in public service and prescribe punishment for indulgeing in corrupt acts. At the same time, the conscience of a public servant would always tell him that committing a corrupt act is wrong and any public servant would listen to his conscience would never be corrupt. It is a different matter that individuals, as well as public servants, often suppress the voice of conscience by giving justifications for their immoral behaviour like a corrupt officer justifying himself by saying that everyone is corrupt or that he requires money for his family needs etc. Repeated snubbing of the voice of conscience makes a human being immoral and unethical.

Government rules are aggregated into systems like budget systems, accounting systems or personnel systems. Government employees tend to focus more on rules and laws and procedures rather than on achieving an outcome. In fact, there are an excess of rules and obsolete regulations and even laws which are coming in the way of the rapid development of the country. Some of these rules are from the colonial era and not suitable for the current economic and political situations. The Government of India and some state Governments have carried out an exercise over the last few years to review all old rules and regulations and weed out those which are no longer necessary. This process must continue on a regular basis if good governance is to be achieved. Recently the plethora of laws relating to labor have been codified into four code by the Government of India and this has made the labor laws easy to understand, comprehensive and suited to modern times. This process engineering has to be a priority otherwise people will continue to criticize the functioning of the Government as being more concerned with red tape than actual delivery of the services. Delivering results is an essential part of the ethics for a public servant. There is an urgent need of eliminating old and dysfunctional legislations and harmonization and unification of statutes. There is also need for sun set provision in the laws so that a statute becomes invalid after a particular period of time.

A public servant has to look towards his conscience as well as rules, regulations and laws for ethical guidance.

Accountability and Ethical Governance

A government system to be ethical has to be accountable. A public servant holds his office in trust and spends public money to bring about development of the country and provide security of life and property to the people. A public servant, therefore, has to be accountable for all his actions and delivering results to the people of this country. His job is to serve them and so he is accountable to resolve all their problems and grievances. Since he deals with public money he is accountable to the tax payer of the country and must perform maintaining the highest standards of ethics and integrity.

It is true that the delivery of public service at the moment leaves a lot to be desired. The quality and efficiency of public service delivery is by and large of a poor quality. One of the main reasons for this is the lack of accountability. Accountability can be brought about by the following measures—

1. Evolving a rigorous performance evaluation system for civil servants which will link their career advancement and promotion to actual performance and delivery on the job. The current system of promotion on seniority subject to merit has to be changed to give more importance to merit. The system of writing annual confidential reports where almost every officer is given a good report encourages mediocrity in the system. The Government of India has now started 360 degree feedback system in promotion. Similar innovations are required so that the system rewards only those who perform.
2. Increasing domain specialization and competence. In most civil services there are now regular in service training

programmes which enhance their leadership qualities and professional competence besides making them aware of the modern challenges and changes in the social, economic and technological environment. Regarding domain specialization, the civil servants have to be protected from the scourge of frequent transfers. A civil servant must have tenure of two to three years in a posting to be able to deliver. Also, after a certain number of years in the service like the IAS the officers should be made to specialize in different domains. There are some who argue about the merits of lateral entry into the service to encourage competition and professionalization but how useful this would be is a matter of debate.

3. It is important to enforce an effective disciplinary regime. It should be possible to take action against a delinquent employee or a corrupt one. This will promote a culture where honesty and good performance is rewarded and the opposite is punished.

Government has to change its work culture to deliver governance that is accountable. There is need to improve the work environment and the rules and procedures need to be streamlined. Decentralization of authority also leads to improvement in accountability. Some countries have created performance based autonomous agencies to improve the accountability. These agencies will have civil servants and executives selected from the open markets working together to achieve a performance contract with the government. They themselves will be on contract. The agency will be given freedom in personnel, financial and operational matters.

The basic reason why public servants fail the accountability test is their not having an ethical compass to guide them. It must be clear that public administration is an activity which has its rules in values and morals and the larger good of the people should always be the goal instead of personal interest.

Public servants have to be accountable to the views and needs of the people and should always respond to the people in public service delivery to ensure accountability. In a democracy, it is the people who elect their representatives who comprise the legislative wing of the government and follow the parliamentary systems to hold the executives responsible. There are committees of parliament which hold a detailed scrutiny of the performance of the executive. The public account committee is an extremely important committee which holds the executive accountable on the basis of the audit report of the comptroller and accountant general. The judiciary also performs the function of ensuring that the executive is accountable to the constitution and the rule of law. Ethical governance implies that there are ethical standards for public service which are reflected in a legal framework and provide ethical guidance to public servants. Ethics in governance is enforced through the code of ethical conduct prescribed for the civil servants. A public servant has to work according to certain values which have been spelt out in the earlier part of this chapter. To ensure ethics we need control systems like having clear policies and procedures and system of oversight accompanied by rigorous monitoring. There is a need for the highly functional audit systems and also a reward and punishment mechanism. Ethical governance means corruption free governance and value based governance. In the chapter on corruption I have discussed this in detail.

In brief, ethical governance is one where a public servant is sensitive to the needs and expectations of people and responds to it in his working. A public servant must comply with all laws and rules and ethical guidelines that apply to their work. They should comply with the orders of the superiors but not carry out illegal orders. They should never waste public money and use public resources as they would use their own. They have to be open, transparent and impartial in their actions. Ethical governance is essential for good governance. Ethical governance also means that you should not remain quiet if you see injustice, illegality or corruption anywhere in the system. Ethical governance is governance dedicated to the welfare of the people which is the highest ethic for a public servant.

Strengthening of Ethical and Moral Values

We have already discussed what constitutes ethical and moral values in public service. The governance system will display these qualities if the public servants think, behave and act in accordance with them. Sadly, today there is a perception in the eyes of the common man that there is a gradual erosion in the moral and ethical values of a public servant leading to a trust deficit between the people and government and is often the cause of social unrest, political agitations or law and order problems. It is clear that all efforts have to be made to develop and sustain these ethical and moral values in our public servants. A question must be asked whether ethical values can be taught. A child imbibes his moral and ethical frame-work from his parents who are the first to set an example for him. Then there is the role played by the school, teachers, friends and society in moulding the character of a person. Today, the society has become more materialistic and public servants and their families aspire for a higher standard of living which includes things like eating out at five star hotels, frequently going abroad or children going abroad for studies or building a palatial house. In essence the public servant has started putting his personal gain ahead of public service which is the very opposite of the ethical and moral conduct expected of a civil servant.

Training is essential to continuously orient the public servants towards an ethical and moral conduct. Despite all the negative factors training can still help in changing the outlook of a public servant and training programs focused on developing a value system should be a regular feature. However, this by itself will not help. It is important to have a fair and impartial reward and punishment system. The public servant sees that the honest and ethical performers do well in their career and rise to the top whereas the unethical or the corrupt suffer. Corruption and lack of integrity should be at high cost and low reward activity and not the opposite as it has become today. I have discussed the institutions that have been created to deal with corrupt practices in the chapter on corruption.

Ethical governance will be strengthened if the bonafide actions of public servants are not used to hold them accountable if they do not get the results. Intention is more important than anything else. Virtues like humility, accessibility and sensitivity are essential for a civil servant. It is important to protect civil servants from arbitrary transfers and other political interferences. The public servant, of course has to be motivated and incentivized to be open, transparent, impartial, objective and result-oriented. When a new entrant to the civil service observes that ethical officers are reaching the top of their career and also being appreciated then they will certainly follow in the footsteps of these officers.

Ethical Issues in International Relations

Ethical issues in international relations are the subject matter of international morality which is a part of international relations. Nations have to relate to each other for their political, economic and security interests and are just like various interest groups in domestic politics. International politics is a process of interaction amongst nations. Every country has its foreign policy which determines how it will conduct its interaction with other nations. The subject of international law defines the legal rights that are available to each nation and form the basis for relationship between them. Customary international morality has been codified in the form of international law. Though states have been in existence since time immemorial the nation states have dominated the modern period in history as it represents the shared heritage, values and culture of the people of a country.

There is no doubt that a nation's international relations policy reflects its own economic and security interests. However, the question is whether nations can be allowed to pursue their own interest even if it is not acceptable or in the interest of other nations. International morality or ethics imposes some limitation on national power so that nations follow those policies which enable them all to live together. We can say that international law is the legal court and international morality the moral court which nations must follow. There are different views regarding the existence or necessity of an ethical dimension to international relations. There are three different thoughts in existence—

1. Denial of existence of international morality—since there is no universally accepted standard of right and wrong in international relations it is felt that international morality does not exist.
2. Personal codes as international moral standards—the advocates of this view are of the opinion that moral standards that guide human beings in their personal behaviour should guide nations in their behavior with one another.
3. A double standard of morals—advocates of this view accept the concept of international morality but are of the view that is not the same as the moral code of any group of individuals or state.

On balance it cannot be denied that there is such a thing known as international morality which consists of moral principles endorsed by a number of nations. The charter of United Nations reflects international morality in many of its provisions, for example, in those related to human rights or maintenance of piece.

International relations theory talks about three dimensions of the role of international morality—

1. Protection of human life in the time of peace between nations. Each nation has to treat human life as sacred and not allow

any immoral means to have an impact on the security of life of the people living in the nations.

2. Protection of human life in war—there is a whole body of law regulating how wars have to be fought, how prisoners of war have to be treated and how war is to be fought between the armies of two belligerent nations and not between the entire populations of two countries. It is a moral and legal duty not to attack, wound or kill non-combatant civilians purposely during of war.
3. Moral condemnation of war—ever since 1945 nations have made all efforts to avoid war as an instrument of foreign policy. Not only is a war a costly affair it has to be shunned on moral grounds and this has become a very strong foundation for international morality. The growing demand for disarmament, arms control and nuclear non-proliferation are examples of this. The United Nations was created with the specific purposes of developing peaceful and harmonious relationships between nations avoiding war.

Theories of International Relations

There are essentially two theories of international relations—realism and idealism.

Realism

This theory believes that power is most important and that no other morality matters. This approach does not believe in any role for a shared ethical system between nations and simply means that a nation should act an its own personal interest even if it is at the cost of others and even if it means going to war against weaker nations or making them a part of your sphere of influence. The famous political philosopher Hegel was of the opinion that there is no higher duty for a state than that of maintaining itself meaning that a state should promote its own interest and advantage against other states. This may not sound very moral but the reality is that most nations follow this realistic policy though they avoid going to war but otherwise try to secure their own interest with little thought of interests of the other nations. The nations feel that they have to work for their own survival than for any other higher ideal of mutual cooperation and well-being. However, though prudence is important, amoral behaviour by nations is not ultimately in their own interest also. Nations have to live together as with globalization the economies of the nations are closely linked to one another.

Realists are of the opinion that morality has no place in international relation and that the nation state is basically anarchic and concerned with its own security and self interest. Even within realism there are those who think that states value, power, security and national interests and do not behave morally and this approach is called descriptive realism. On the other hand, prescriptive realism advocates that state should be prudent in their international conduct.

Idealism

This theory focuses on the existence of common interest which should guide the behaviour of nations and that international relations is not only about the pursuit of power but in having an international order which promotes ethics and morality and where the chances of an armed conflict are avoided. Nations sign treaties and international agreements with each other and it is moral duty to honor them. Immanuel-Kant the political philosopher has observed that no state should interfere by force in the internal affairs of another state and during war not allow such acts of hostility that will make subsequent peace impossible. He also advocates reduction in government spending on military.

The idealists believe that instead of settling disputes by going to war nation should cooperate with each other and create an environment of peace where common interests will unite humanity. The League of Nations and United Nations is the product of this approach.

If we observe the real world we find that all countries pursue self interests but going for a war is the least favoured option. Diplomacy is used to settle most disputes in a manner that is beneficial to both the concerned parties. It is true that most countries are spending huge sums on building up their armed forces but this is only for the purpose of self defence and security. Many countries have got nuclear weapons but this is only to be used as a deterrent. Most countries have an agreement of no first use of nuclear weapons. Nations now cooperate with each other to control international terrorism. They also have trade relations with each other leading to using their import and export related policies to bring about their own development and also be internationally competitive. Bilateral and multilateral treaties are entered into for this purpose. A lot of regional cooperation blocs have emerged. It is now widely believed that countries can work together in mutual self interest. Yet there are countries which are trying to dominate the others and this is a perceived threat for future.

United Nations

The UN came into exist after the second World War for the specific purpose of ensuring peace in the world. It has succeeded to a large extent in achieving this. The UN Security Council has five permanent members—USA, UK, Russia, France and China. They have the power of Veto through which any one member can block a resolution. The current arrangement appears unfair as just five countries enjoy this disproportionate power but this was a reflection of actual political realitics of that time (1945). Things have changed now and there is a demand from many countries to change this unequal distribution of power as it does not reflect the current political reality. The general assembly is a forum for debate and sharing of views amongst countries whereas the International Court of Justice resolves the conflict between nations. There is, thus, an institutional framework for peaceful relations and resolution of conflicts between nations.

The preamble to the charter of the United Nations has listed out the main goals of the organization which are to save the world from the horrors of a war, to reaffirm faith in fundamental human rights, to establish respect to international laws and to promote social progress and better standard of life. The organization was based on the principle of sovereign equality of its members. The UN also emphasizes the need for international cooperation to solve social, economic and environmental problems of the world. Several organizations like UNESCO, FAO, UNICEF, WHO, WTO have been setup for this purpose. The UN has also set the millennium development goals for 2030 which includes issues like eradication of extreme poverty, achieving universal primary education and reducing child mortality. These goals are now called the sustainable development goals and most countries are aspiring to achieve them by 2030.

Climate change is another important area of international cooperation. Many countries like USA which are leading as far as carbon dioxide emissions are concerned have given limited support to measures whereby they would control their emissions overtime. They are following their own economic self interests and showing little concern for international morality which would expect them to be concerned about the future generations and the problems being faced by the developing countries.

Ethical Issues and International Funding

After the Second World War many countries have been giving foreign aid to the poorer countries and international funding organizations like International Monetary Fund and the World Bank have been supporting development programmes through grants or very low interest fund being made available. However, most of these donor countries and organizations are not doing this without any conditions. They are linking this aid to conditions being fulfilled by the recipient country which may not often be in the interest of that country. Sometimes the donors go to the extent of trying to influence the policies of the aid receiving countries which is in the domain of the legislature of that country. Often the local issues and problems are ignored at the time of prescribing conditions. It is also being argued that conditionality infringes on a country's sovereignty.

There is often an ulterior motive for foreign aid and the donor country uses this aid to economically and often politically dominate the recipient country. The recent belt and road initiative of China where it is giving aid to build infrastructure in developing countries is an example of this. Countries like USA have used foreign aid as a tool of diplomacy. In the initial years after the Second World War till the end of the cold war USA and other democratic developed countries used foreign aid to support democracy in other countries and to see that communism does not spread.

Foreign aid, which is primarily focused on serving the strategic and economic interest of the donor countries, cannot be termed as ethical but they do correspond to the reality of the international politics where serving self interests is often viewed as essential.

India and International Morality

Indian foreign policy has been based on morals and can be called enlightened. It was Mahatma Gandhi who set the tone for a moral policy for India with the following tenets—

1. Non-alignment.
2. Non-violence and quest for nuclear disarmament.
3. India should behave as international peace-maker.
4. Moral, diplomatic and economic support for the struggle against colonialism, racialism and apartheid.

After independence India did not only concentrate on its narrow self interests but gave a moral shape to their foreign policy by the five principles of Panchsheel which are—

1. Mutual respect for each other's territorial integrity and sovereignty.
2. Mutual non-aggression.
3. Mutual non-interference in each other's internal affairs.
4. Equality and mutual benefit.
5. Peace and co-existence.

Jawaharlal Nehru said that if all countries follow the Panchsheel model then there would hardly be any conflict or war. Some people criticize the moral approach in Indian foreign policy as it had an adverse impact on the self interest of the country.

India continued the policy of Non-Alignment during the Cold-War years and there is a debate on whether this was the right approach. India even today is taking the lead in developing international peace and cooperation which is the essence of international morality.

Today the whole world is linked to each other and this is the era of globalization. The latter led to mutual cooperation and free movement of human beings and resources between countries. Recently there has been an attack on globalization and most countries have once again started focusing on their national interests. An ethical basis for international politics would be to have a judicious blend of self-interest and overall interest of humanity. Ultimately all countries have to be peaceful and develop economically by economic and technological cooperation with each other.

Corporate Governance

Introduction and Importance

Corporate governance relates to the private and public sector corporations. It represents the value framework, the ethical framework and the moral framework under which business decisions are taken. It is important for a business to make profit but it has to be concerned about legal and moral issues. Increasingly over the years after some poor governance practices were noticed that led to scams; corporate governance has acquired a lot of importance. Corporate governance lays down the framework for creating long term trust between the companies and external provider of capital. It brings in independent directors to the board who ensures that all legal compliances are done and provides valuable strategic thinking to the board using their wealth of experience. It also ensures the integrity of financial reports and carefully articulates the decision-making process to limit the liability of the top management and the directors.

Need for Corporate Governance

There is good corporate governance if public governance is strong. We are aware of the collapse of some Multinational Corporations like Enron due to fraud and dishonesty on the part of the company as well as on the part of the accounting firm Anderson. There have been other scams like those relating to Satyam Computers, Harshad Mehta, Ketan Parikh and others. This called for induction of global governance standards to improve corporate governance in the country. The principles of corporate governance have been brought out in the amended companies acts and securities and exchange board of India guidelines (SEBI). These have emerged from the recommendations of committees such as Kumar Mangalam Birla Committee and Rahul Bajaj Committee. The main Trust is to ensure transparency and full and correct disclosure.

Ethics and Values in Corporate Governance

A business enterprise is not expected to be an economic unit only but also has to be a good corporate citizen and for this there has to be genuine respect for business ethics and values. Unfortunately the perception is that business environment in India is full of unethical acts like bribery, corruption and insider trading. The funds of the share holders used to be siphoned off with impunity before the new guidelines regarding corporate governance. The quality of corporate governance is determined by the manner in which top management particularly the Board of Directors, allocate the financial resources of the company between themselves and other interested groups such as employees, customers, government etc. The basic ethical qualities required in this regard are trust, honesty, integrity, transparency and compliance with the laws of the land. The ethical climate in any business or capital market depends on three factors—

1. The individual's sense of value.
2. Social value accepted by business and industry. Social value depends upon the standards set by professional bodies like the Institute of Chartered Accountants of India.
3. The kind of system that exists and whether it encourages good corporate governance. A proper climate of effective public

governance is required to monitor and guide the working of business enterprise.

Companies Acts and Corporate Governance

The companies act is perhaps the most important instrument of corporate governance in India. The companies act came into being in 1956 and has been amended several times to usher in good governance practices. As a reaction to the scams the amended version of companies act prescribed heavy penalties. This has been questioned in recent times as it is not creating a proper climate for enterprise. The government of India has recently come up with amendments to do away with the stringent penal measures. The provision in the companies act dealing with corporate governance relate to issues like the composition of the board, prescribing essential presence of independent directors and appointment and structure of audit committees to go into the appointments of the auditors and scrutinizing the financial reports to ensure that there is full of honest disclosure of all financial transactions of the company. It also mandates how the remuneration of directors will be determined, the procedure of the board meetings, analysis of the annual reports, disclosure of a director's interests, share holder rights and the compliance level of corporate governance in the annual reports.

The Naresh Chandra committee report of 2002 recommended a professional interface between the company and statutory auditor and the procedure for appointment of auditors and deciding on their fees. It also suggested rotation of statutory audit firm and prescribed certification of accounts by management and the directors and laid down the role of the independent directors amongst other measures. The Narayan Murthy report of 2003 went further to evolve a dynamic system of corporate governance and they felt that if the right standards of corporate governance are followed Indian firms will become attractive for domestic and global capital. The government of India went ahead with the legal and regulatory framework to achieve the required level of corporate governance to inspire confidence in both domestic and foreign investors.

SEBI and Corporate Governance

The SEBI has been continuously trying to reform the capital markets and bring about good governance corporate practices. SEBI setup the Kumar Mangalam committee on this issue and adopted its report in 2000. This committee has given important recommendations for good corporate governance. SEBI through clause 49.2 of the listing agreement regulates the corporate governance of listed companies. This clause has specified the following:

1. Composition of the Board—Board should have a chairman and fifty percent of each of executive and non-executive directors.
2. Constitution of the audit committee—The audit committee should have three independent directors with the chairman having a financial background. A minimum three meetings should be convened every year. The director finance and head of internal audit should be special invitees.
3. The audit committee—This committee is responsible for review of the financial performance and appointment/removal/remuneration of auditors and also reviews the adequacy of the internal control system of the companies.
4. Remuneration of the directors—To be decided by the board and disclosed to the share holders.
5. Board procedures—Board should have at least four meetings in a year.
6. Share holder information—The company should provide a brief resume of new or reappointed directors. Quarterly results should be submitted to the stock exchange and put on company website. Share holders grievance committee should be constituted with an independent director as the chairman. Further a report on corporate governance and a certificate from auditors on complaints of provisions of corporate governance should be provided.

In addition, the clause 49 provides that the board will lay down a code of conduct for all board members and senior members of the management. The CEO's and CFO's have been made directly responsible for risk management and internal control system.

As a result of the above measures the climate of corporate governance has improved a lot in India and a survey on corporate excellence carried out by Credit Lyonnais, three Indian companies—Infosys, Hindustan Lever, Wipro are amongst Asia's top 10 corporations in terms of good governance practices. ICICI, HDFC and Tata group of companies also are known for their good corporate governance. Banks as corporates are also required to have good governance norms and the Reserve Bank of India has taken steps to strengthen corporate governance mechanisms in banks.

We have discussed the need for transparency for public service but it is important to note that a private company also has to be totally transparent in its dealings as it deals with the money of the share holders and it is accountable to them.

In order to encourage good governance practices government of India has instituted an award for excellence in corporate governance in 1999 and Infosys was the first company to get this award. This award evaluated the company on good governance practices like fairness, honesty, transparency and courtesy to all share holders and for deep concern for environment, pioneering social audit, taking good care of its employees and for driving change within the company in terms of knowledge management systems.

The department of company affairs has set up a Serious Fraud Office (SFIO) with the intention of acting on company fraud and improving corporate governance. The SFIO will investigate economic crimes such as bribery by companies trying to win lucrative contracts. The SFIO will also investigate company finances and prosecute them in cases where there has been violation of corporate laws.

Accounting Standards

A very important aspect of corporate governance is to have internationally accepted accounting standard which would let the investors know how their money has been used to further the interests of the company they have invested in, companies have been known to be using wrong practices to hide relevant information. The Institute of Charter Accountants of India has come out with new accounting standards with effect from 1st April 2001. The Indian accounting standards are now of an international level.

Over the last twenty years due to the efforts mentioned in the earlier part of this chapter the standard of corporate governance has improved in India but only a few corporates have concentrated on excellence in governance whereas others have made only cosmetic changes. The challenges of good corporate governance are a soft state, slow moving judicial system, ambivalent value system and poor enforcement of rules and regulations. More work has to be done in these areas to bring about the desired improvement in corporate governance. The good thing is that Indian corporations are slowly realizing the benefits of the good corporate governance practices and making effort to follow them. The exercise of improving corporate governance has to keep going on if the Indian corporate world has to survive in a challenging international business environment and achieve competitive excellence.

Chapter 8

Probity in Civil Services

8.1 Right to Information: Key to Good Governance

Significance

The essence of good governance is transparency, accountability, participation and delivery of public service to the citizens. Right to Information is an extremely significant administrative innovation which relates to transparency in governance. The idea behind this is to open up the government working to the public. This aims to make the government more accountable and also lead to the participation of citizens in the process of delivery of public service. We can say that Right to Information is an essential attribute of good governance.

India is a democracy which implies that government is of the people and by the people. If this ideal is to be attained then people must participate in the process of governance. Right to Information seeks to usher in people centered governance. We are all aware that information is power and sharing of information with the citizens is a tool of their empowerment. India is a welfare state and the objectives of such a state can be best fulfilled if we empower the poor and weaker sections of the society. Aristotle, the great Greek philosopher, has put it beautifully by stating "if liberty and equality, as is thought by some, are chiefly to be found in democracy, they will be best attained when all persons alike share in the Government to the utmost."

Historical Background

The Right to Information act began as a protest movement in Rajasthan where social activists and a group of daily wage workers found anomalies in the wages paid to them and realized this was due to fake muster rolls and siphoning off public funds through this mechanism. This is a common phenomenon in many government schemes. Even the much acclaimed MGNREGA is not immune to this as there are instances of fake job cards being prepared and money drawn against them by corrupt village pradhans and officers. Rajasthan's protest spread to other states and Tamil Nadu and Goa enacted the Right to Information act in their states and Rajasthan followed in 2000. At the national level the Right to Information act was passed in 2005. It applies to all branches of Government but currently focuses only on the executive.

Similar legislations have been promulgated in other countries. Sweden was the first country to do this in 1766 but this was in a different context. USA passed its Freedom of Information law in 1966, Denmark and Norway in 1976 and UK in 2000. Since then most countries have passed such laws.

Official Secrets Act 1923

Prior to the promulgation of the RTI Act the concept of governance was to maintain secrecy about all aspects of government functioning. The major legal provisions regarding this are in the colonial area Official Secret Act 1923 (OSA). This law deals with maintenance of secrecy and confidentiality in matter relating to security, espionage, sedition and other matters affecting the unity and integrity of the Nation. The colonial regime did not trust the citizens of India and so secrecy became the norm rather than being an exception. Though section 5 of OSA was meant to deal with potential breaches of national security it began to cover every issue related to governance. The tendency was to hold back rather than give information. The OSA 1923 is still in existence but will not come in the way of disclosure of information under RTI Act. Section 22 of RTI Act states "The provision of this Act shall have effect notwithstanding anything with inconsistence therewith contained in the Official Secret Act 1923 and any other Law for the time being in force or any instrument having effect by virtue of any Law other than this Act". However the retention of OSA in its current form is an anachronism.

Section 5 of OSA penalizes not only communication of information useful to the enemy but also communicating in an unauthorized manner any kind of secret information which a government servant has obtained by virtue of his office. This implies that even noting in the files can be kept secret. The Government can use this provision of OSA to deny information to the citizens and reduce the efficacy of the RTI Act. The Second Administrative

Reforms Commission 2006 has recommended that OSA 1923 should be repealed and substituted via a chapter in a National Security Act relating to official secrets. The commission further agrees with the Shourie Commission which recommended amendment of Section 5(1) of OSA making the provision applicable only to violations effecting national security.

Indian Evidence Act 1972

The Government enjoys a certain privilege relating to evidence. The Indian Evidence Act 1872 in its section 123 prohibits the giving of evidence derived from unpublished official records relating to affairs of State except with the permission of head of the department. It further adds in section 124 that no public officer shall be compelled to disclose communication made to him in official confidence when he considers that this would adversely affect public interest. The Second Administrative Reform Commission has strongly recommended amendment to these sections.

Oath of Secrecy

It is clear that the Government over the years has been valuing secrecy much more than making information available to the citizens. The Government in this way maintains distance which is against the basic tenet of democracy. All of us must have seen the oath taking ceremonies of the Union and State Ministers on Television. While assuming office the ministers are administered an oath of secrecy which is as follows "I will not directly or indirectly communicate or reveal to any person or persons any matter which shall be brought under my consideration or shall become known to me as Minister for the Union/State except as may be required for the due discharge of my duties as such Minister". It is strange that a Minister who owes his basic allegiance to the people who elect him takes an oath of secrecy which is a legacy of the Colonial era. It would be appropriate in the spirit of democracy that Ministers take an oath of transparency rather than secrecy.

Central Civil Service Conduct Rules

Once again section 11 of the Conduct Rules prohibit any government Servant to communicate any official document or information to any person he is not authorized to do so. Once again the accent is on withholding information. The Second Administrative Reform Commission has recommended that this should also be amended in the spirit of transparency.

Similarly the manual of office procedures also talks of no unauthorized communication in official administration.

From the above discussion it is clear that the Colonial approach to Government was to cloak its actions in a shroud of secrecy. The RTI Act is a revolutionary governance reform which seeks to lift the veil of secrecy and make governance open, transparent and accountable. The OSA continues to be in existence but there are provisions of RTI Act which override the OSA. We have already mentioned section 22 of RTI Act in this connection. There is also the section 8 (2) of the RTI Act that allows any information to be disclosed if public interest in disclosure outweighs the harm to the protected interests. Thus RTI Act can fulfill its purpose even with the OSA continuing in existence. However, in future, the Government can consider repealing of OSA and keeping the relevant sections of this Act as a separate chapter in the National Security Act.

Information Exempted from Disclosure Under RTI

In any case the RTI act also exempts certain information from disclosure and should serve the purpose of the OSA act except for the penalties to be imposed. Some of the items exempted are as follows:

1. Information impacting the sovereignty and integrity of India. Matters relating to security or economic interests of State.
2. Disclosure regarding negotiations with foreign states.
3. Any information whose disclosure has been forbidden by any court or may cause a breach of privilege of parliament or State legislature.
4. Information that would adversely affect the investigation any criminal offence.
5. Cabinet papers.

Process of RTI

This act provides universal access on the payment of a very low fee. Nothing is charged from people below the poverty line. People can ask for information in writing specifying the reason for doing so. Normally information is asked for about notes and extracts of Government file and documents, details about Government projects and works. A person has a right to inspect documents and records and the information can be made available in written or electronic form.

For the purpose of supplying this information every department has designated a senior officer as PIO (public information officer). As soon as he receives the requests for information with a prescribed fee the PIO collects the information and makes it available to the applicant. The Act specifies time limit for furnishing this information. Normally 30 days are allowed but urgent information may have to be supplied within 48 hours.

Implementation Structure

The RTI act has created the Central Information Commission at the national level and the State Information Commissions in the States. These information commissions are statutory bodies. They are independent and look into complaints and appeals regarding information not provided to the public by the Government departments. The Central Information Commission has its headquarter in Delhi and consists of one Chief Information Commissioner and not more than ten information commissioners appointed by President of India. Similarly in the State also there is the post of a Chief Information Commissioner assisted by information commissioners. All these information commissioners enjoy autonomy as they have the power to penalize PIO's who do not supply the correct information to the public.

In order to ensure the independence and status of the information commissioners they are selected by a high level committee. At the national level the committee consists of the Prime Minister as the Chairperson and Leader of Opposition in the Lok Sabha and a Union Cabinet Minister nominated by the Prime Minister as members. Similarly in the state it is the Chief Minister who is the chairperson. Commissioners are expected to be persons of eminence in public life with wide knowledge and experience in law, science, social service, management, journalism and administration. The RTI act also provides that the CIC or IC shall not be a member of parliament or that of any State legislature or hold any other office of profit or be connected with any political party or carrying out any business or pursuing any profession. The Government bodies and even privatized public utility companies and NGOs that receive 95% of its infrastructure funds from the Government are under the ambit of the RTI Act.

The term of office of the Chief Information Commissioner was originally prescribed as five years and that of the information commissioners was also the same. This has been amended in 2018. Instead of five years now the term of the commissioners is as may be prescribed by Central Government. In the original section 13 of the RTI Act the salary, allowances and other terms of service of the CIC was to be the same as chief election commissioner and that of IC to be analogous to the election commissioner. This has been amended to read "shall be such as may be prescribed by the Central Government". Similar amendments have been made in section 16 relating to tenure and status of state CIC and IC. There is a debate on whether these amendments have radically altered the structure of the commission by impacting their independence and putting them under the control of the Government. The Government has justified its decision by saying that the commission is a statutory body and the Government has the power to make rules concerned with it. However, there is also a view that the working of the information act has been considerably weakened by making the information commissioners subservient to the Government.

The duty of the CIC or the SIC is to receive and inquire into a complaint by any person who has not been given the information required by him by the Government. The commissioners while inquiring will have the same powers as vested in a civil court while trying a suit under the code of the civil procedure 1908. Any person who does not receive a decision within the specified time or is aggrieved by a decision of the PIO may file appeal before the CIC or SIC. The CIC and SIC has the power to impose the penalty if he finds information has been knowingly withheld or incorrectly supplied. They can recommend departmental action against officers. However, there is no criminal liability under RTI Act.

In addition to building the institutions of CIC and SIC the implementation involves that record keeping be done in a systemic and modern manner by the Government departments. The spirit of the Act also says that the department should *suo motu* declare information and make public interest disclosure. This is very important. For a proper functioning of democracy the Government should voluntarily make information available to the citizens. These days every department is expected to have a website and updated information about all aspects of the working of the department should be made available on the website. Having a citizen charter also falls under this category of voluntary disclosure.

To implement the act properly regular capacity building and awareness generation programmes for Government officers and also make the citizens aware of their rights under this act. Street plays, radio jingles, printed publications can be used for this purpose. The working of the act should be constantly monitored by the CIC and at the senior most level of the Government. The 10th Finance Commission has given grants for record-keeping and digitization of records.

Evaluation of the Act

The Act has certainly caught the imagination of the people and has definitely empowered the ordinary citizens. It has had a positive impact on reduction of corruption and also increased the accountability of Government officials. In the state of UP itself 30 thousand cases are filed in a year showing the impact of the RTI Act.

However there are some issues which hinder the proper working of the Act. There is a huge pendency of cases in the commission which sometimes creates a situation where information is provided after years making the whole exercise futile. One of the reasons for this is that the vacancies of the posts of CIC and IC are not filled up for several months. Also, there is a tendency of Government departments to delay providing information on some pretext or the other. The commissioners do impose fines in such matters but the Government needs to take a more serious view of such propensity to delay giving of information. Also most of the commissioners appointed are either retired bureaucrats or journalists. People of eminence from other walks of life should be appointed to enrich the commission. The appointment being in the hands of the Government leads to a situation where those who are close to the Government are appointed. Naturally they are soft on the Government and rarely resort to the powers of penalty that are vested in them.

The experience has been that more than the ordinary citizens it is the Government employees and lawyers who seek information. This information is then often used to put up before the Courts or Service Tribunals in matters relating to individual cases. In fact a pernicious tendency has emerged where certain so called RTI activists use this as a tool to blackmail Government officers. Of course the CIC and IC should be able to separate the wheat from the chaff and intervene to eliminate such malpractices.

The RTI Act can truly democratize governance. Civil servants should have a positive attitude towards this Act and ensure that information is made available to the citizen. Actually the basic attitude of a civil servant needs to change. He should not feel that by sharing information he is becoming less powerful. In fact, the attitude should be to voluntarily disclose as much information as possible to the citizens. Also the ordinary citizens has to be made much more aware of the functioning of this Act so that they may utilize its provisions.

8.2 Citizen's Charter

Significance and Concept

The basic function of good governance is efficient and effective delivery of public services to the citizen. The citizen now has to be treated in the same way as a private sector company would treat its customers. You must have heard of the adage that the customer is king. A model public service delivery system has to treat the citizens in a similar manner. This implies that there has to be transparency and accountability in governance and the concerns and the grievances of the citizens should be the prime focus of every Government department or agencies. The Government has to be accountable to the citizens. Each Government officer must know what he is responsible and accountable for and the citizens should also know whom he should approach for which problem. The Citizen Charter is another path-breaking innovation in governance and if properly implemented can make a big difference to the quality of life of the ordinary citizen.

Basically the Citizen Charter of any department will give you the name, mobile number of different officers and what they are looking after. It will give details of the services that are being delivered by the department. The important thing is that quality of standards for each service are determined and put on the charter and also time limit in which a service would be delivered. All possible information about the department will be made available in that charter. In this way it is carrying forward the spirit of the Right to Information Act. The charter will also tell you whom to approach for redressal of your grievances. It will also engage with you in matters of policy formulation and also invite your suggestions about the working of the department as well as your complaints. The Citizen Charter could be made available on the website of departments and should be constantly updated to give a true picture of the current situation. In short, we can say that Citizen Charter is a document that brings out the commitment of an organization towards various services that it provides to the citizens and their quality. It is a means of regular interaction between the citizens and the departments.

Origin of Concept

The concept of a Citizen Charter was initiated by the British Prime Minister John Major in the year 1991 with the intention of improving public services. In 1998, in the UK, the concept was renamed as "services first", there after several countries adopted this concept. In India the concept was first adopted at a conference of Chief Ministers in May 1997. In this conference it was decided that all central and state governments and public sector undertakings shall have a Citizen Charter. It was mandated that these charters will specify service standards, time limit of providing these services and mechanism for redressing grievances of the citizens. The department of administrative reforms and public grievances was given the responsibility of coordinating this activity. Those wanting to know further details may access the website of the departments. More than 700 charters were adopted by various agencies across India. Going one step further the Government of India introduced a bill in this connection called "Bill on the Right of Citizens for time bound delivery of goods and services and redressal of their grievances." This bill required all authorities to publish a Citizens Charter within six months of the enactment of the bill and also recommended setting up of a Public Grievance Redressal Commission. The bill however lapsed due to dissolution of the Lok Sabha in 2014.

In 2007 the Second Administrative Reform Commission had also recommended formulation of Citizen Charter and had even suggested penalties for non–compliance. In 2008 a Parliamentary Committee had recommended giving statutory status to the Citizen Charter.

Components and Features of a Citizen Charter

For a Citizen Charter to be affective should have the following components:

1. Organisation's Vision and Mission statements. The vision statements reflect the ultimate goal and ideal of a department while the mission statement lists out the specific objectives. For instance, the vision of the energy department would be to provide uninterrupted 24×7 power supply to all citizens. The mission would list out objectives like reduction of transmission losses, reducing power theft, building new transmission and distribution substations and operationalising new power generation plants.
2. It should bring out the nature of services rendered by the department as also the quality standards and time frame. It should give full information about the services a department offers and should be written in simple and clear language. The charter should lay down clear standards for delivery services and make them time bound. For example, the power department will mention the services it provides to industries, agriculture and domestic consumer. It would also clearly bring out the standards for quality and regularity of power supply, the system of installing meters, the date by which bills would be sent to the consumer and the mode of online payment of bills and getting a power connection within a time frame.
3. It should spell out the citizens who would be the customers of the services offered.
4. It should clearly give a grievance redressal mechanism. The charter of the power department will clearly show whom the customer should contact in case of power failure, voltage issues, wrong reading of the meter, incorrect billing and corruption. The names, mobiles and e-mails of the concerned officers should be mentioned. It would also point out who should be contacted if grievance is not redressed.

Indian Experiences of Citizen Charter

Though many departments at the Union Government and State Government level have come out with Citizen Charters the objectives and the vision of the innovation have not been fully realized. The primary reasons for this are:

1. The Citizen Charter have been prepared by the departments without proper consultation with employees and citizens. It has become something enforced from the top and the other officers of the departments are not involved with it. Ideally a Citizen Charter should not be prepared in a hurry and the process of preparing this should be participative. It is important for all officers and employees to own Citizen Charter to make it a success otherwise it will remain a mere formality.
2. The officers and the employees of the department have not been fully trained to understand the value of the Citizen Charter.
3. At the senior level there is no proper monitoring of the working of the Citizen Charter. If services of the standard mentioned in the charter are not being provided and grievances not being attended to then the charter becomes only a piece of paper. Rigorous monitoring with fixing of accountability is a must to make the Citizen Charter a success. The unfortunate reality is that the Government officers and employees are reluctant to be held accountable to deliver a certain standard of public service
4. The citizens for whom the charter has been created are often not even aware of its existence. The Government should launch a major awareness drive for this and should continuously keep informing the citizens about their rights.
5. In the current system if a citizen does not get the service promised to him he cannot do much about it. The Second Administrate Reform Commission has talked about penalty for non performance, however, at the moment no action is taken against anybody. The proposed bill on Citizen Charter which has lapsed also provided for penalties to be imposed by public grievance redressal commissioners. To ensure accountability some system of reward and punishment needs to be introduced. Without effective remedy the system loses its credibility.

Suggested Model Citizen Charter

Almost all of us are aware of the working of a municipal corporation and have complaints related to water supply, sanitation, roads or drains. A model citizen charter of Municipal Corporation should have the following:

1. The vision would be to provide complete satisfaction to the citizens in municipal services and make the city the cleanest and most livable.
2. The mission would be provide high quality of all municipal services to the citizen.
3. All the services should be listed out along with the service delivery standard and time limit. For example, sanitation services are to be provided. It would be mentioned that garbage would be collected from the household and no garbage would litter on the roads. Similarly the number of hours of water supply and its quality would be mentioned and any complaints regarding it would be resolved in a given time frame which would be indicated. It would also mention how to apply for a birth or death certificate and in how much time would the Municipal Corporation make it available. Similarly details about online payment of property taxes would be provided and standards and time frame for other services like cleaning of sewers, drains, repairing roads and lanes, street lights and traffic would be provided.
4. The names, designations, telephone numbers and e-mails of officers responsible for each service would be mentioned. The process of contacting them would be specified.
5. Details about how the citizens can access forms relating to making applications for certificates or other matters would be given.
6. Clear system of online complaint redressal system would be specified. For example, if you are not getting proper water supply then you would know whom to approach and in how many days the problem would be solved. Nowadays, most municipal corporations have an IT based system of grievance redressal system where you can use your mobile to make a complaint and you will get a response and the problem would be solved.
7. The charter would also specify the cooperation required from the citizens.

Conclusion

Citizen centered governance is the foundation of a welfare state. It makes government departments responsive, accountable and sensitive to the need to the citizens. It is a major reform to bring about transparency and accountability in Government. The citizen charter seeks to improve the performance of Government and ensure proper public service delivery. All it requires is a political will to make it successful.

8.3 Public Delivery-Concept and Quality Service

The outcome of good governance is high quality of delivery of public services. The very purpose of a welfare state is to provide basic public services like education, health, law and order and security to the people. In fact the government has to play a major role in development of the state and the wellbeing of its citizens. In a welfare state the focus is on the poor and marginalized sections of society and to provide them equality before the law and a basic minimum standard of living. The concept of public service means the provision of public goods and basic minimum services to the citizen by the Government. Not only has a certain quantum of public service to be provided but it has to be of a good quality. For example, it is the responsibility of the Government to provide education to its citizens. However, the Right to Education act, as interpreted by the Supreme Court, clearly says that Right to Education implies right to good quality of education. India is a democracy and its Government consists of the legislature, judiciary and the executive and is based on the principle of separation of powers.

Public representatives to the parliament and state legislature are elected by the people. The political party with the majority forms the Government. The Prime Minister/Chief Minister and other Cabinet Ministers are appointed to govern the state on behalf of the people and bring about their all round development. The political executive decides on policies for the welfare of the people and it has civil servants to assist it in policy formulation and carry out the implementation of the policies. This entire governance is for the people and to look after their interests. The people then are the masters and job of the Government is to serve them. This is the concept of public service and the political representatives and government officers are public servants. During the Colonial regime the civil servants were not accountable to the people and behaved as Kings. This is no longer true. The political representatives and the civil servants are accountable to the people of this nation and have to carry out their responsibilities as public servants.

People pay taxes from which the public servants draw their salaries and implement policies and programs for the benefit of the people. The legislature has the responsibility of making the executive aware of the problems and issues confronting the citizens. They use the parliament and sittings of the legislature for this purpose. The legislature asks questions which the executive has to answer and also raises issues which are debated upon to reflect the concerns of the people. Further, all laws are formulated by the legislature after debate and discussion. There are committees of the legislature which do in-depth study of the draft legislations and also summon the executive for oral evidence in matters of public importance. The third wing, judiciary ensures that all action of the executives is according to the constitution and rule of law and protects the fundamental rights of the citizens. The working of all three leads to delivery of public services though, of course, the primary responsibility is that of the executive.

There are three levels of Governments, the Union Government, State Government and Local Government. The constitution clearly defines the subjects which are in the domain of the Union Government, State Government and in the concurrent list where both State and Central Government can operate. In addition the constitution by the 73rd and the 74th Constitutional amendments has clearly defined the role of the Local Governments – both Urban and Rural. For example, defence and external affairs is purely the responsibility of the Union Government while the law and order and agriculture are state subjects, whereas education and forest come under the concurrent list.

Despite numerous schemes and policies and budget allocations over the years it is a matter of fact that there is a governance deficit. For example, the quality of education in Government schools is extremely poor. There is a problem of teacher absenteeism and teachers not being trained or motivated to teach properly. As a result surveys have found that students of class 5 can not read or do arithmetic which is of the standard of class 2 or 3. Similarly the standard of health care provided in the Government hospitals is of a very low quality. Doctors are not present or do not give attention to the patient and even basic medical equipment is not functional. Similarly, the municipal services of sanitation and dirking water are not up to the required standards. Clearly there is a major problem of quality of public service delivery for which the public servants are accountable.

The Second Administrative Reform Commission has observed that "inefficiency, corruption and delays have become, in public perception the hall mark of public administration in India". Various planned documents have found that corruption is a serious factor in the wastefulness, inefficiencies and inequities in the current public administration system. One of the ex-Prime Ministers was candid enough to mention that the fence had started eating the crop and that Government servants were oppressing the poor and have no work ethics. Yet asnother Prime Minister made a statement that public servants were perceived as agents of exploitation rather than as providers of service.

Reasons of Poor Public Service Delivery

1. The continuance of the Colonial legacy of administration which was not meant to serve the people or be people friendly
2. Lack of accountability in the system. Today no public servant feels that he is accountable to deliver high quality public service to the citizens. They spend money from the budget, show physical progress but are not concerned with the results or outcomes. For instance, the quality of government health care has not improved to the required extent despite so many years of independent India. Most Government servants get promoted on the basis of seniority. Even when merit is a criteria for promotion the standard for judging merit is the annual performance reports of the officers which never depict the true picture as performance appraisals are done in a non-serious manner and except in cases of major corruption officers generally tend to get a good performance appraisal. There is no system of identifying the poor performers. The reason is that performance is not linked to actual delivery of results. Some effort has now been made by government of India by introducing a 360 degree evaluation system for the higher civil services. Thus even if an officer does not deliver outcomes he can be promoted to the top. Any organization which does not have a system of reward and punishment is not likely to give results.
3. The functioning of Government is dominated by a process oriented work culture. There are a huge number of rules and regulations. Most civil servants spend all their time ensuring that the rules, regulations and processes have been correctly followed. They have very little concern for actual outcomes. The reality is that if results or outcomes are not achieved then an officer is not punished. However, if there is any deviation

from rules or processes then the officer is held liable and departmental and even criminal action can be taken against him. The civil servants work under the oversight of the four C's – CAG, CVC, Courts and CBI. None of these hold a civil servant accountable for not delivering results, however, they will hang the civil servant if any violation of rule or law or process comes to light. This is irrespective of the bonafide intention of a civil servant. It is only natural that in such an environment the officers suffer from paralysis of decision-making and the civil servants adopt the "safety first" approach. It is true that Article 311 of the constitution provides job security to the civil servant but facing a departmental or a criminal proceeding can be extremely stressful for an officer and has the potential of ruining his career.

4. There is a lot of political interference in the system which hampers efficient decision-making and professional working of civil servants. In our democratic system the political representative of the people is the master and public servants have to work under the elected public representatives. However, there is a clear demarcation of responsibilities which is not followed in actual practice. It is a job of the civil servant to implement policies but we find that the political executive interferes in the system rendering it inefficient. The classic example of this is the transfers and postings of the officers being done by the political executives when this is in the domain of the officer. An officer does not get the team he wants and is often saddled with non-performers with political connections.
5. Politicisation of services – This is connected to the earlier point. We find that officers have got aligned with political parties and rather than work according to the rule of law you find that they work on the directions of the ruling party. This tendency is more prominent in backward states like UP and Bihar where, unfortunately, the bureaucracy often functions along caste lines.
6. High level of corruption in Government departments – This leads to siphoning off of funds and poor quality of service delivery.
7. Lack of professionalism and domain specialization in government departments. Very little attention is given to training and capacity building. The level of motivation amongst

Governments officers is also low as there is no incentive for high performance.

Measures to Improve Public Service Delivery

1. A system needs to evolved to link performance with promotions and other rewards and punishments.
2. Civil service should be protected from political interference. Transfer and postings should be on an objective criteria and done by service boards rather than politicians.
3. A minimum tenure of two to three years should be given to an officer on a particular post.
4. Domain specialization needs to be encouraged.
5. Too much centralisation should be avoided and public services delivered in a decentralised mode. For example, education, health care can be best taken care of by the the panchayats and local bodies.
6. The community should be involved in delivery of social sector programs. For instance, National Health Mission seeks to achieve its objectives by empowering the community.
7. There should be a much greater use of technology. This would lead to better monitoring and enforcement. For instance using a smart phone, photo graphs and videos of developments programs can Le sent directly to the superior officer to assist in monitoring. Also through use of mobiles direct contact can be made with the beneficiaries of schemes to find out their level of satisfaction. Mobile and internet based grievance redressed systems can help in giving better quality of service to the people. In UP the moment we implemented 108 emergency number for ambulance service the critically ill could reach hospitals in less than one hour vastly improving the quality of health care. Similarly, the implementation of Dial-100 led to a situation where the police reach the spot within 20 minutes thereby greatly improving the law and order situation. Technology can significantly reduce corruption.
8. There should be a zero tolerance policy regarding corruption. Government systems and procedures need to be simplified and made transparent. Technology should be used wherever there is a Citizen-Government interface. Red tape needs to be eliminated.
9. Public private models of public service delivery should be encouraged. For instance in the 108 ambulance mentioned

earlier, the ambulances were operated by private concerns and the payment was made to them from the Government budget.

10. Involvement of the stake holders is necessary in policy formulation to ensure that policies are responsive to the aspirations of the citizens.
11. Strong administrative leadership needs to be developed and encouraged.
12. No effective public service delivery is possible without the existence of a strong political will.

Right to Public Services

The Government of India proposed a bill on the rights of citizens for time bound delivery of goods and services and redressal of their grievances. This bill sought to ensure time bound delivery of public services and give the citizens a mechanism for getting their complaints resolved. This bill aimed to make publishing a citizen charter by all departments compulsory and specify the quality of public services to be provided. Public servants were to be made accountable for this. The bill envisaged establishment of a central and state grievance and redressal commission. A citizen could file a complaint regarding failure in providing goods and services listed in the Citizen Charter or about the functioning of a public authority or violation of any law, policy or programme. There were provisions for imposition of penalties. However, due to various reasons this bill could not see the light of the day. There is no doubt that there is a definite need for some institutional mechanism to ensure efficient public service delivery to the citizen.

Public Services Gurantee Act

Many state Governments have made and attempt to come out with an Act to address this problem of lack of accountability and quality in public service delivery. The pioneer in this was the state of Madhya Pradesh. They came out with the Public Services Guarantee Act in 2010. This Act gave citizens the legal rights to public services and provided for sanctions against officials who did not comply with the deadlines. As many as 428 services are covered under this Act in Madhya Pradesh. Today more than 20 States have promulgated a similar Act. This has definitely led to improvement in public service delivery. For example, in this Act it would be mentioned that you would get a power connection within 30 days of applying and also mention the officer who would be responsible for this. Similarly, the time limits for the services like getting a caste certificate or income certificate or vehicle registration are mentioned. Different States have identified lists of services to be covered under the Public Services Guarantee Act. However, the success of this depends upon the awareness level of the citizens and monitoring and actual fixing of responsibility on the officers concerned. In reality, the monitoring has not been of the required standards. Still it is a very valuable administrative reform.

Yet another major governance innovation to ensure quality public service delivery is outcome budget which means that the actual outcomes achieved by Government departments is the goal to be realized and the effectiveness of Government expenditure has to be evaluated in these terms. For instance, the agriculture department will have to show to what extent the income levels of the farmers has increased due to government policies and schemes. I will deal with this in greater detail in the section on utilization of funds

8.4 Utilisation of Public Funds

Every year the center and the state Governments prepare an annual budget which shows the resources that would be generated that year and the expenditure on various departments and schemes. It is with this budget that the Government seeks to solve the problems of the people and provide public services to them. The quality of governance depends and how these public funds are utilized. Good governance means that these funds are utilized in a manner that the desired results and outcomes are achieved. It is also very important to see that there is complete probity in the use of this money. The entire amount should be spent in public interest and are not siphoned off by officers and others through corruption. In short the canons of financial propriety have to be observed.

Budget

The preparation of the annual budget is a major exercise and attracts a lot of public attention. People expect tax reliefs and new schemes to be announced. The union Government budget is always a topic of discussion and debate. The similar is the experience in the states regarding the state Budget. The entire process takes several months and involves detailed stakeholder consultations at the level of the Government. The budget gives a direction to the economy and is a determinant of economic growth. Each department sends its demand or funds to the finance department. This demand is for recurring items like salary or for various schemes. The finance department reviews the position of resource availability and also looks at the previous year budget provision and expenditure and then finalises the budget for each department divided in various heads and sub heads and each one of them has a separate code. The budget proposals are consolidated in the form of demand for grants. This is then discussed in the legislature. All of you are aware of the budget speech of the finance minister which is very keenly followed by all citizens. The budget speech spells out the priorities of the Government and also any tax relief that is being given to the corporates or citizens. The budget is then debated and passed in parliament. An appropriation Act is passed which gives a legislative authorisation for incurring expenditure. This is an annual exercise. However, if required, the Government comes up with a supplementary budget during the course of the year.

Previously the expenditure used to be categorized into plan and non- plan. Non-plan expenditure used to have what the government spends on so called non-productive areas such as salaries, subsidies and maintenance while plan expenditure pertains to expenditure on productive activities like projects of various departments. This categorization led to a situation where money was not given for maintenance as non-plan expenditure was considered to be having a lesser utility. This led to poor maintenance of assets. This distinction has now been done away with. The budget of every department is divided into revenue and capital items. No appropriation of funds from capital to revenue can be done. For instance budget for construction of a hospital cannot be diverted for payment of salaries. This is a basic canon of financial management. The Government finances its expenditure through capital borrowing and if this money is spent on revenue items then the government falls into a debt trap.

Throughout the year the departments prepare detailed proposals as per the budget and take the clearance of finance department to release this money to field officers to carry out the required activities. This process often takes a long time as departments spend a lot of effort in preparing the proposal and the finance department also has a tendency of putting a lot of objections. It is true that it is the duty of the finance department to ensure financial propriety but sometimes the departments complain of a negative attitude on the part of finance department. This often leads to a situation where funds are not utilized during the course of the year. The funds are lapsable except in certain special conditions. And the funds which are not released lapse at the end of the financial year leading to targets of physical output and results not being achieved.

Issues in Utilization of Funds

1. As already indicated above the process of fund release can be cumbersome and often large amount of funds are not utilized impacting the public service delivery.
2. Very often a situation arises where there is a sudden rush to release funds towards the end of the financial year (March). This phenomenon is often called the March loot. There is no scrutiny of this expenditure and utilization certificates are given by departments even though the actual work may not have been done to the required standards. This leads to corruption. It is true that funds cannot be released by the finance departments in one go as they have to manage the cash flow of the Government also. The resources also come to the government over the year and not in one month. To handle this problem the Government divides the annual target into quarterly ones. For instance the Government may say that 30 percent of the budget should be spent in the first quarter, 20 percent in second because of monsoon, 30 percent in third and 20 percent in last quarter. This way the cash flow issue is also taken care of and departments get sufficient time to carry out their activities. In facts many times the Government has issued orders that no sanctions will be issued in March so that the problem of corruption at the end of the financial year can be tackled.
3. To utilize the budget the schemes requires procurement of material or carrying out the physical works. This involves the process of tendering. There are a lot of complaints of corruption in this process. There are allegations of the tendering process not being transparent and fair and certain contractors and suppliers getting undue advantages. Further, this corruption leads to poor delivery of public services. One way of handling this has been through the use of technology by adopting the system of e-tendering which has helped to make the system open and relatively free from corruption.
4. Technology can be used in a big way to control corruption in utilization of funds. Currently in both Union and State

Governments all the transaction are computerized which enables close and regular monitoring of public funds.

5. One of the mechanisms used to handle this problem has been the increasing use of direct cash benefit transfer. This means that cash is directly transferred to the bank account of the beneficiary rather than being routed through government agencies or departments. For example, the government gives pension to old people who are poor and widows. There used to be a lot of corruption in these schemes. Now the government transfers this money directly to the account of the beneficiary leading to elimination of corruption. The Government of India has come up with an excellent tool called PFMS (Public Financial Management System) which handles this direct cash transfer in a transparent manner.
6. A larger share of taxes goes to the Union Government because the major source of tax revenue like income tax is with them. Now even the goods and services tax (GST) goes to Government of India from where the share of each state is transferred to it. As per the recommendations of the Central Finance Commission a certain percentage (currently 42%) of the revenues of Government of India are transferred to the states. Government of India uses central sector schemes and centrally sponsored schemes (CSS) to give money to state governments against specific schemes or projects. The expenditure on CSS schemes is shared in a certain prescribed percentage between the centre and the states. States often complain that many of these schemes are not relevant for the state because local conditions of each states are different. This often leads to the objective of the scheme not being fully realized. It has now been decided to have greater flexibility in the design of these schemes. This would certainly lead to better utilization of funds.
7. The real issue is that funds are allotted and utilized but the required results are not achieved. In fact the focus should be on physical performance and the output. Most governments are now monitoring both financial and physical achievements. It is important to carry out field inspections to assess the quality of work being done. It could be that despite utilizing the budget and constructing a road the quality could be very poor. Detailed systems can be formulated to check quality.

Also technology helps a great deal. Nowadays photographs and videos of developments projects are regularly transmitted through smart phones to senior officers for better monitoring. The performance of officers should be linked to the actual achievement of results and there should be zero tolerance for corruption.

8. Even focusing on output is not sufficient. It is important that the outcomes are monitored to ensure proper utilization of public money. For example, the education department may utilize its budget and construct the required number of school buildings and pay the salary of teachers. This would mean that the output has been achieved however the outcome would be upto what extent the quality of education has improved. Realizing the importance of this the Government of India and many state Governments have started preparing an outcome budget which would help to fix the accountability of the departments and its officers against the achievements of outcomes which is the real objectives of Government expenditure.
9. Increasingly more and more funds are getting transferred to village Panchayats and urban local bodies for meeting the local needs of the citizens. This decentralization of utilization of funds has led to better results.
10. It is also true that utilization of funds is better in advanced states rather than the backward states. This is because of shortage of staff, lack of training, poor monitoring practices, remoteness of areas and corruption. This poor ability of backward states to absorb funds leads to perpetuation of poverty in these states. Best practices from better managed states should be adopted by these states to improve their utilization of funds.

Audit

The accounts of the central and state Governments are audited by the Comptroller and Auditor General (CAG) of India to ensure that public funds are utilized properly and accounted for as per government financial rules. Those civil service officers who get selected for the Indian audits and accounts services are part of the team of the CAG. The CAG derives his duties and powers from articles 149 to 151 of the Constitution of India and Comptroller and Auditor Generals (duties, powers and condition of service) Act. The CAG is the sole auditor of the accounts of the central Government, state Governments and local bodies. The reports of the CAG are presented to the President of India for union Government accounts and to the Governor for State Government accounts. The CAG mandate covers all receipts and expenditure of the Governments and all financial transactions. It ensures a uniform policy of accounting in the Government.

The CAG carries out this audit of the account to make sure that the expenditure incurred by the Governments has been done in an authorized manner and for the purpose for which the funds were allocated. It also sees whether all financial rules, regulations and processes prescribed for use of public money have been followed. These audits bring to light any cases of financial impropriety or wasteful expenditure. The money that the government spends comes from the people and so civil servants have to be extremely conscious of spending this money wisely, as per rule and for the benefit of the people. If these canons of financial propriety are not followed then the officer concerned is held accountable and faces disciplinary action.

There was a criticism of the CAG audit that it focuses only on voucher audit and does not take into account the fact that Government departments have to deliver results. This criticism has been taken care of to a large extent by the system of performance audit started by the CAG. Every year it takes up some departments or organizations to analyse whether funds have been utilized with efficiency and effectiveness and has achieved the desired objectives.

The audit team of the CAG visits a particular department and scrutinizes its accounts and raises audit objections where it is not satisfied. The concerned department then gives a reply to these objections. If the audit team is satisfied then it drops the objections. If it is not satisfied then it finalises its report carrying the audit paras which according to it points towards irregularities. In both the union and state Government level there is the institution of public accounts committee (PAC) which consists of members of the legislature and is the institutional mechanism of parliamentary control on expenditure. The PAC then convenes a meeting where the secretary of the concerned department appears in person and gives his evidence on these audit paras. The PAC is assisted by a senior officer of the CAG. Some of these meetings can be really very gruelling and I have seen secretaries spending sleepless nights to prepare for this. The secretary has to stand and give evidence and is subjected to a thorough cross examination by the members of the committee. If a satisfactory reply is given by the secretary then the audit para is dropped. If not, then accountability on the concerned officers has to be fixed and action taken. The PAC also suggests systems to be designed to see that there is no recurrence of this impropriety in future.

The above procedure of audit definitely makes sure that public money is spent properly and in public interest. However, it is a fact that executive officers have to take decisions on the spot and sometimes in public interest they may by-pass some procedure. Even though they may have acted in public interest they are liable to be held accountable and face disciplinary action. This is the reason why the civil servants are often accused of not taking decisions or policy paralysis. The officers are more concerned with avoiding audit paras rather than deliver quality public goods to the people in the required time. Some civil servants carry this to such an extent that they forget their dynamism and only focus on upholding the status quo. It is important to come up with a mechanism to balance financial propriety with achievement of results.

In recent times all of you must have read about the 2G scam and the Coal scam. In the former the CAG calculated a notional loss of 1.76 lac crores to the state exchequer. In the latter it questioned the arbitrary allotment of coal mines to private developers. Both these issues captured the attention of the entire nation. CBI enquiries were ordered and the Supreme Court also intervened. Senior officers and ministers were arrested. The cases are still going on. There are different views on the CAG report in these matters. For instance it is felt that the report on 2G scam adversely affected the telecom revolution in India. In any case these issues became so large that it led to the downfall of the Government in power at that time.

Apart from the PAC there is an Estimates committee which looks into the accuracy of budget estimates and also examines the surrender of funds by departments. Then there is a committee on public undertakings which exercises financial control on public sector enterprises.

Conclusion

We have seen that there is an elaborate system of ensuring that public money is spent properly and for the welfare of the people. It is important that the funds are spent in a manner to give maximum benefit to the people. Ultimately the objective of any Government exercise is to develop the country and deliver effective public services with maximum transparency and probity.

8.5 Work Culture

Every individual and organization has a work ethic and work culture. The work culture of an organization relates to its values, attitudes, beliefs and the general norms of conduct and ethics that it follows. It is the work culture which determines the effectiveness of an organization and the means it deploys to achieve its ends. It lays out rules of interpersonal behaviour between employees and their commitment to their duty and towards fulfilling the goals of the organization. The work culture of an organization is reflected in the attitude towards work of its individual employees.

Work Culture in Government

There is a general low perception in the minds of the people regarding the work culture in Government. The common belief is that Government employees have very little commitment to their work. They are considered to be lazy, slothful, immersed in red tape, avoiding decisions and being corrupt. They are perceived as being arrogant, apathetic to the needs of the people, negative in their outlook, not helpful, not having a problem solving approach, not being sensitive to the grievances of the people and inaccessible. In contrast to this negative perception people feel that the private sector has a positive, result-oriented culture and is customer centric. This assessment maybe a little unfair and it is important for the civil service and Government employees to change their approach to their work if they want a better feedback from the people. Actually in the private sector the job is not secure and you can be dismissed for poor performance which is generally measured in terms of profits. Also in private sector your promotion depends upon your merit. In contrast in Government there is total job security. It is next to impossible to dismiss a government servant. The promotions in Government are generally based on seniority. The good, bad and the average performers often reach the top on the basis of the number of years of service put in. There is no incentive for capacity development or learning new things. Thus this system of reward and punishment is the main reason for the difference in the government work culture and private sector. I may add that this is a perception problem also as many government officers are very hard working, intelligent and dedicated to their jobs.

Required Work Culture for Civil Servants

1. To maintain punctuality. In most government offices you can see employees coming late to office and also arriving late for meetings and functions. Bio-metric attendance system and supervision from the top can easily bring in a culture of punctuality.
2. During the office hours the seniors officers must ensure that employees do not waste their time in idle conversation with each other and do not spend long hours in lunch or tea breaks. The office time should be for office work. Meetings must start on time. If an appointment is given to a citizen then it should be maintained and the citizen should not be made to wait long.
3. The citizen should be treated in the same way as a private sector company treats its customers. The work culture should be citizen friendly. The civil servant should not be arrogant and inaccessible. They should have a proactive approach towards solving the problems of the people.
4. There should be total efficiency in the working. Work should not be allowed to pile up and decisions taken promptly.
5. The attitude of the civil servant should be positive and helpful. They should not cultivate the habit of saying "NO" to everything.
6. There should be complete transparency and openness in the working of the government. Participation of citizens should be welcome in all policy formulation and implementation.
7. Government servants should be held accountable for their actions. There should be a system of reward and punishment which incentivizes good work and penalizes poor performance.
8. The civil servants should be fully impartial in their working.
9. The civil servants should maintain complete political neutrality.
10. There should be a work culture which increases working in teams and together achieving goals of the Government.
11. Finally the most important aspect of work culture is to have total integrity—both financial and professional.

Conclusion

Work culture determines the way an organization performs and is perceived by the people. The senior civil servants have a major role to play in bringing about a transformation in the work culture of the government and making it a dynamic outcome oriented organization.

8.6 Code of Ethics and Code of Conduct

Introduction

Most professions including the civil services have their professional code of conduct. These basically prohibit certain set of activities. They are different from a code of ethics. Sometimes people use these terms in an interchangeable manner. The scope of a code of conduct is much narrower than a code of ethics. The former brings out the values, principles and behaviour required of the members of a profession or organization. Code of ethics is a system of morals which covers all aspects of life. It spells out what one should do in life and what one should not do. Violations of the code of conduct can be punished as per the conduct rules but they are not criminal offences.

For civil servants an ethical code could comprise of values which are accepted principles or standards of behaviour affecting their attitudes, preferences, goals and aspirations. It sketches out the moral standards to be followed by the civil servants. Ethics should not be confused with religion or following the law. It covers all aspects of life.

Principles of Public Service Ethics

One should be clear that public service is a public trust. Citizens expect the public servant to work in public interest and utilize the public funds to deliver quality public service. Public service ethics is an essential part of good governance. A public servant does not work for personal gain but for public welfare. He is expected to make decisions on the merits and in a neutral, objective and impartial manner. He should be open and transparent in his behaviour and respect the constitution and rule of law. There should be total integrity in his working. A public servant should be responsive to the problems of the people and be efficient and effective in resolving the grievances of the people and be concerned about delivering outputs and outcomes.

The Nolan Committee in UK laid down seven principle of public life which comprehensively outlines the standards of ethics expected of a public servant. They are as follows:

1. Selflessness – Working purely in public interest and not personal gain
2. Objectivity – Taking every decision on merit in a fair manner.

3. Accountability – Holders of public office should be accountable for their decisions.
4. Openness – Having as much transparency in working as possible.
5. Honesty – Their working should be free of corruption.
6. Leadership – Public servant should promote principles by their own examples.
7. Integrity – Both financial and administrative integrity should be maintained.

Draft Public Service Bill

A draft public service bill is under the consideration of the ministry of personnel. This bill seeks to lay down the generic values expected of civil servant. These include commitment to the ideals of the constitutions, apolitical functioning, good governance, objectivity, impartiality, accountability, transparency, maintaining high ethical standards, avoiding wasteful expenditure, participative functioning and merit based working. This bill envisages penalties for violation of a public service code which it stipulates. The Second Administrative Reform Commission also recommended that there should be a set of public service values stipulated by law.

Ethics Infrastructure

It is felt that to manage ethics in public services simply having a code of conduct or code of ethics will not give the desired result. An ethics infrastructure is required which should contain the following:

1. Political commitment to ethics in governance.
2. An effective legal framework to enforce required standard of behaviour.
3. Efficient accountability mechanisms like audit procedures and systems of performance evaluation.
4. Workable code of conduct—statement of values, roles and responsibility
5. Professional socialization mechanism—education and training.
6. Supportive public service conditions—regarding pay and job security.
7. An ethics coordinating body.
8. Active civic society including media.

In the environment created by the above conditions a system of ethical governance will be able to take shape.

Code of Conduct

Every profession has a code of conduct to maintain uniformity and desired quality of service. Doctors, engineers, lawyers have their own professional code of conducts. The medical profession follows the Hippocratic Oath which says that a doctor will always work for the benefit of the sick and will not indulge in any mischief or corruption. It further says that a doctor will maintain total confidentiality about the patient. In the great epic *Ramayana*, Lord Hanuman brings the *vaid* (doctor) Sushen to treat Lakshman after the latter was struck by an arrow fired by Meghnad. Ram was fighting a war with Lanka and Sushen was the royal *vaid* of Lanka. He was faced with an ethical dilemma because he had been brought to treat an enemy. He however treated Lakshman as he realised that as per the code of conduct of medical profession he had to treat a patient irrespective of his belonging to the enemy camp.

The civil service conduct rules and the All India service conduct rules specify that:

1. Every member of the service shall at all times maintain absolute integrity and devotion to duty.
2. He will maintain political neutrality.
3. He will maintain high ethical standards, integrity and honesty.
4. He will promote the principles of merit, fairness and impartiality
5. He will maintain total accountability and transparency.
6. He will be responsive to the public specially the weaker sections.
7. He will maintain courtesy and good behaviour.
8. He will commit himself to uphold the supremacy of the constitution and the democratic values.
9. He will defend the sovereignty and integrity of India.
10. He will take decisions solely in public interest.
11. He will not misuse the position of a civil servant.
12. He will work according to rule of law.

Apart from the above which were inserted in the conduct rule by amendment in 2014 the original conduct rule of 1968 talk about a civil servant not using his position to get employment to near relatives in companies or private firms, he will not take part in politics or elections. He will take permission before publishing any book or material or participating in media, he will not criticise the Government, he will not in an unauthorized manner communicate any information, he will not take dowry or gifts, he will disclose assets, he will be restrained in consumption of intoxicating drinks or substances and maintain proper decorum and behaviour at all times

Conclusion

It can be seen that there are lot of common points between a code of ethics and a code of conduct. However, a code of ethics goes beyond the conduct required as a member of a profession. It comprises of values and morals of life. Ethics are influenced by the political and social environment in which a person lives. A person inculcates his ethics and morals from his family, school, teachers and friends. The society sets standards which reflect the general moral conscience or principals of social ethics and incorporates them into laws for the state to implement. The public servant by his own example has to set a high standard of ethics to gain the respect and confidence of the people.

Chapter 9

Corruption

Causes and Remedies

Corruption is endemic in the Indian society today and public service is no exception being a microcosm of the society. Elimination of corruption is not only a moral imperative but an economic necessity. The common perception of the ordinary citizen is that the politicians as well as civil servants are notoriously corrupt and nothing moves in government if proper greasing of palms is not done. This is generally true but there are still a number of honest politicians and civil servants who have not fallen prey to the lure of illegal gains and benefits. It is also true that corruption is not restricted to the government or public sector and the private sector is not immune to it. The only thing is that the government deals with large volumes of money over which the government servants have discretionary control leading to widespread corruption. However, it is a fact that for each public servant willing to take bribes there are private individuals or companies who are willing to pay bribes to get their work done. The worst situation is when money is taken or given not for doing illegal things but even for doing genuine and legal things. Financial honesty is an essential part of integrity which is the basic quality that is expected of a civil servant but integrity is much more than that. Integrity stands for basic moral values and the commitment to do the right thing at all points of time and not allow anything wrong or irregular to be done. It implies implementing the rule of law in all situations which means that there is an overall governance structure which gives justice to the people and punishment to the wrong doers. In this chapter the focus will be on financial honesty as the overall aspect of integrity has been discussed in the other chapter. As far as civil servants are concerned corruption can be defined as using public office for private gain. The essence of good governance is to have a corruption free delivery of public services.

Causes

It is difficult to identify one single cause for the prevalence of corruption. In the materialistic society today people want to acquire more and more wealth and enjoy a high standard of living even though they may not be able to legally afford it. This is a matter of values and character and the reason for rampant corruption is the general degradation in the value systems of the individual and in particular government officers. Without values there is no pole star to guide people on the issues of right and wrong.

According to the Second Administrative Reform Commission (SARC) corruption is related to abuse of office which is aggravated by three factors. Firstly, the existence of a colonial legacy of unchallenged authority and tendency to exercise power in an arbitrary manner; Secondly, there is an enormous asymmetry of power in our society with power being concentrated only in a few hands which reduces societal pressure to conform to ethical behaviour and makes it easy to indulge in corruption and thirdly, consciously the Indian government after independence chose a policy framework where there was state control in all sectors of economies and gave a lot of discretionary powers to government officers who used the over regulations and severe restrictions in economic activity to creating an atmosphere of unbridled corruption. Further, the system of state subsidies and plethora of beneficiary oriented development programs led to increased corruption as there was a lot of power in the hands of the officers to distribute patronage.

It cannot be denied that competition and transparency reduce corruption whereas the state having monopoly power is a recipe for enhanced corruption. Also the fact that government functioning has kept its working as a closely guarded secret not sharing anything with the citizens has created a situation of total lack of information which gives birth to corruption. Over centralization has been the mantra in India leading to concentration of authority in a few hands and consequently more corruption. Decentralization always leads to reduction in corruption.

It is also true that officers view corruption as a low risk high gain activity which increases the tendency for them to resort to corrupt practices. If the matters of corruption are taken up seriously and the offenders given exemplary punishment without delay then it would certainly lead to an environment where corruption becomes a high risk activity and people would desist from indulging it.

The most surprising thing today is the acceptance of corruption in the society. A few decades ago there were only a handful of officers who were corrupt and they generally had a very bad reputation and the society looked down on them. Today corruption is becoming the norm rather than an exception and officers are not ashamed to flaunt their ill gotten wealth. It has become the fashion today amongst officers today to own numerous properties, send their children abroad for studies, eat at five star hotels and enjoy luxurious vacations. Somehow the society also does not condemn this behaviour and in fact there is an acceptance of this phenomenon. I have found that many people opt for the civil services with the intention of making money. I recall a case where a person was doing very well in the private sector and earning a good salary but was aspiring for the civil services. I asked him that this would amount to him working at a salary which is one fourth of his current salary. I was aghast when he replied that salary was immaterial and that he would earn much more on the side the moment he becomes a civil servant! If people join the civil service with this kind of motivation then you can well appreciate the kind of corruption that they are mentally prepared for. This is the reason why officers are acquiring a bad reputation from the very beginning of their career.

Corruption is one of the major factors leading to slow economic growth. The deliberate delays in decision-making and harassment have led to the slowing down of the economy. There is, thus, an urgent need to tackle the problem of corruption.

Nature of Corruption

There are different definitions of corruption but we can go by acts of corruption as specified by the central vigilance commission which include the following:

1. Demanding or accepting illegal remuneration or gratification by a public servant for an official act or using his influence with another official for such an act.
2. Obtaining any valuable thing from a person with whom he is likely to have official dealings with and where he can exert influence. This may be with or without consideration.
3. Obtaining any pecuniary advantage by illegal means or abusing position as a public servant.

4. Possessing assets disproportionate to known sources of income.
5. Misappropriation, forgery or cheating or similar criminal offences.

The SARC has widened the definition of corruption and recommended amending the offences under the prevention of corruption act to include.

1. Gross perversion of the constitution and democratic institutions amounting to wilful violation of oath of office.
2. Abuse of authority by unduly favoring or harming someone.
3. Obstruction of justice.
4. Squandering public money.

The above definition given by SARC encompasses all aspects of integrity which is a comprehensive way of looking at the issue of corruption.

The civil servants and other government officers are exposed to three types of corruption in their service. The first one can be termed as extortion where employees are forcibly taking money or bribes in any other form to do illegitimate work. More often than not this extends to legitimate work also. This means that if a person wants an officer to favor him in an illegal manner he pays a bribe to get this work done but very often even to get the right things done people have to forcibly pay bribes. This is the worst kind of corruption. The public servants indulging in this resort to delaying decisions or raising unnecessary objections on files till the citizen is forced to pay a bribe. The second type of corruption is the regular commission that some officers get as part of regular practice of the department. In this category comes the commission taken by engineers from contractors for any kind of construction work done. In many departments a fixed amount of payment made or budget released is shared amongst the officers. The worst example of this that I have observed is monthly money taken from each police station by the district police officers. This type of corruption is unfortunately becoming more and more prevalent with the officers justifying it by saying that there is no consideration involved and this is a regular practice and does not affect their performance as an officer. Nothing can be further from the truth than this kind of reasoning. Such corruption weakens the moral authority of the officer and he will not be able to take action against corrupt subordinates and also it definitely has an adverse impact on the efficiency and performance of an officer. The justification attempted by officers is merely an exercise in self delusion. The third kind appears to be innocent but has negative long term effects. This type of corruption is when an officer does not demand anything and does the work on merit but the opposite party gives him a gift in money terms or kind as a token of thanks. For example, an officer gives the contract of constructing a road to a party on merit but the party later on gives an expensive gift or money to the officer as a token of thanks. The negative impact of this is that the officer gets compromised and then cannot act against the party even if it does not perform as per the standards laid down. Thus corruption in any form is not acceptable and there should be a zero tolerance of corruption at all levels. An officer may be honest himself but if he does not take steps to check corruption in his department then the responsibility for the same comes to him also.

SARC has talked about two kinds of corruption. The first is Coercive corruption in which the bribe giver is a victim of extortion. The second is collusive corruption in which the bribe giver and bribe taker acts as partners and siphon off public money.

Some of the areas in government where rampant corruption is visible are the tenders of various projects and construction activities. More often than not the entire tender process is conducted in a manner to favor a particular party in exchange for a handsome consideration. The other area is recruitment of employees where the competition is tough and people are willing to pay money to get selected and the officers handle the selection process in a manner that only those who pay get selected. This is so rampant that people refuse to believe that any selection process can be fair. Entrepreneurs who want to set up an industry are subjected to illegal demands at each stage from allotment of land, giving of power connection, obtaining no objection from pollution control department and getting clearances from a whole lot of departments including labour and tax. The ordinary citizen faces a lot of harassment at the hands of the tax collection authorities and normally there is a collusion between the two leading to lower realization of revenue by the government. Many citizens would be aware of the corruption at the police stations sometimes just for lodging an FIR. Even worse are cases of corruption in judiciary.

Political Corruption

Political corruption is the very fountainhead of corruption. If corruption has to be eliminated then we have to start from the top and it is political corruption which has to be tackled on priority. In our elected democracy it is the political executive who is at the apex of the governance structure. Unfortunately over the years there has been a situation where more and more money is being spent by the candidates contesting elections and much of this money is raised in an illegal manner. Some part of the expenditure is borne by the political parties but even here there is no transparency in how the funds have been raised by them. The parties are allowed to take donations from individuals and corporations but there is no transparent disclosure of this. The representation of peoples act provides for ceilings on election expenditure and Supreme Court has made it necessary for political parties to file Income Tax Returns and Wealth Tax details as per the acts. The election commission also deputes senior officers as observers to keep a check on the election expenditure of the election candidates. However, despite all these measures and often even strict actions it is a fact that a large amount of money is spent in the elections which are not accounted for. This is the very basis of political corruption. A candidate who spends a huge amount of money to get elected tries to earn this money or even more if he becomes a minister or holds any other important position of power. This leads to unwanted interference in the process of governance and the transfer posting industry in many states is a result of this. The instances of corruption in government tenders, contracts and projects are also a consequence of this malady. Political parties in power are known to accept illegal money in the name of building a party fund to contest elections. When this corruption starts from the top it travels down the line to government officers and employees completely vitiating the governance atmosphere.

The parliament has passed the law on political funding which makes it mandatory for a political party to disclose finances and contributions over ₹ 20,000 and gives full tax exemption to individuals and corporates giving donations to political parties. Even then we cannot say that there has been any improvement in the level of corruption related to political funding. The SARC has recommended partial state funding of political parties to reduce the use of illegal money in elections but one is not sure that even this would help. Candidates are known to go to the extent of distributing cash and liquor to get votes. In some countries there is total state funding of elections but so far this model has not been found feasible for India. It would not be an exaggeration to say that this political funding of elections through illegal means is at the root of all corruption in the society. Things have become so bad that one hears of candidates paying huge amounts of money to get an election ticket from some political parties. Any politician who gets elected in this manner would certainly like to recover his expenditure through illegal means.

Apart from money power the elections are influenced by muscle power and it is a shocking thing to find that a large number of legislatures have a criminal record and many are facing charges of a very serious nature. The current law allows them to contest till they are finally sentenced. The legal process takes a long time and these legislators have the power to delay and influence the proceedings and as a result of which they continue to be elected representatives despite having serious charges against them. The Supreme Court and the Election Commission have intervened by making it mandatory for a candidate to declare any conviction by a court or pendency of any criminal case against him. The candidate is also expected to declare his assets and liabilities. The Supreme Court has ruled that persons convicted of a criminal offence are disqualified from being legislators. This does help to minimize the criminalization of politics in some way.

The Election Commission has prescribed a court of conduct for all political parties insisting on daily expenditure statements and appointing large number of observers. Also policing arrangement have been ensured for free and fearless polling and the introduction of electronic voting machine has also made a difference. Also photo identity cards have been made available for all voters to prevent impersonation and electoral rolls have been computerized.

There has been a reduction in the size of council of ministers to 15% of total members of the parliament or state legislature as another political reform. Another form of corruption that is visible these days is elected legislatures shifting loyalty to another party and bringing down the government in power after accepting huge amounts of money. It is a shameful spectacle to see elected representatives being herded in five star hotels and resorts to protect them from being lured away by promises of money or posts. The anti-defection law states that at least one-third of the members of a political party should shift to another party to avoid being disqualified as members of parliament or legislature. This has helped to some extent but still these kinds of cases keep coming up and even if they are disqualified they get money and contest the elections again.

It must be admitted that the election commission of India has done a wonderful job in conducting free and fair elections. We must ensure that nothing is done which would adversely impact the independence and the autonomy of the election commission.

To handle matters of political corruption by ministers there is the institution of "Lokayukt' in most states and after prolonged agitations the office of the Lokpal has been set up at the government of India level with full powers of investigation, enquiry and action. The ministers according to a codes of conduct prescribed for them have to furnish every year a declaration of their assets and liability and they have to refrain from starting or joining any business. They are not expected to use their office for private gain or to demean their office in any manner and have to maintain transparent integrity.

Anti-corruption Laws and Agencies in India

At the time of independence the Indian penal code was used to combat corruption. Thereafter efforts were made to come up with a legal framework to tackle this menace and the prevention of corruption act 1988 (PC) came into being. This act does not define corruption but lists offences of bribery and its penalties. These offences cover illegal gratification as a motive or reward for doing or not doing any official act or favoring or disfavoring any person, or obtaining anything valuable without consideration, misappropriation or having assets disproportionate to income. The PC act also lays down the penalties. According to SARC the PC Act should be amended to provide for a special offence of collusive bribery. An offence could be classified as collusive bribery if the outcome or intended outcome of the transaction leads to a loss to the state and is against public interest. In such matters the public servant and the beneficiary of the decision would be committing an offence of collusive bribery.

Sanction for Prosecution

In order to protect an honest civil servant from being harassed for decisions taken in a bonafide manner the section 19 of the PC act provides for previous sanction of the competent authority before a court takes cognizance of the offence. Some people are of the view that this provision should be done away with as it is used as a shield by corrupt public servants. This may be true in some cases but in the larger context this provision is to help an honest officer and if this provision would be removed then officers will avoid taking decisions. The SARC has suggested some measures to deal with this situation. The first recommendation is that if a public servant is caught red-handed taking bribe or in cases of there being clear evidence of his having assets much beyond his known sources of income then there should be no need of taking sanctions before prosecution. The SARC also feel that there should be no need for a sanctioning authority to be summoned in a trial court as witness as often the cases take a long time and it is possible that the concerned authority may not recollect all aspects of the case. There are also complaints of delay in giving sanction by the authority which gives protection to the corrupt. This can be solved by prescribing a time limit for giving sanctions. The SARC has argued for the power of sanction to be given to the central and state vigilance commissions to ensure fairness.

Earlier on the PC act provide for a public servant to be liable for action even if he had not derived any pecuniary advantage and had taken a decision which had benefitted a private party. This section was causing a lot of hardship to honest public servants who despite being honest were facing trials in cases of corruption. This also created an atmosphere of policy paralysis in the government as officers began to avoid taking decisions, for in economic matters any decision of a public servant would benefit some private party. Fortunately this provision has now been removed from the Act.

Very often the cases under PC act go on for years considerably reducing their impact. Speedy trial of these cases has to be ensured if they have to act as a deterrent to corruption. SARC has recommended that:

1. Time limit should be fixed for various stages of trial.
2. The special judges handling PC act cases should not be loaded with other work or responsibility.
3. Proceedings in such courts should be on a day to day basis.
4. The Supreme Court or high courts should lay down guidelines to see that there are no unnecessary adjournments and avoidable delays.

SARC has also recommended that if a public servant causes loss to the state or its citizens by their corrupt acts they should be liable to make good the loss and pay damages. It is true that prosecution of dishonest civil servant takes place in a very limited number of cases and this encourages corruption as it is perceived by the dishonest as a low risk high gain activity.

Corruption Involving the Private Sector

Corruption is not the exclusive preserve of the public servant or the public sector. The private sector or private people are very much involved in this process. Cases of corruption have been seen in NGO's handling government projects. However, SARC is of the view that bringing the activities of the entire private sector within the fold of PC act is neither desirable nor practical and should be handled by the existing laws and regulations. However, SARC has recommended that PC act should be suitably amended to include in its purview private sector provider of public services and also NGOs who receive substantial funding from the government.

Confiscation of Illegally Acquired Properties

It is necessary that strict action should be taken against corrupt public servants and for this purpose the PC act provides for confiscation of the properties of public servants in excess of their known source of income but this has proved inadequate because such forfeiture is possible only on conviction and the procedure of attachment of property can start only after the court has taken cognizance of the offence which may allow the corrupt person to hide or adjust his ill-gotten wealth. In fact, the Law Commission in its 166th report (1999) went to the extent of observing that PC act has failed to check corruption. It further noted that even though India is one of the most corrupt nations the number of prosecutions for corruption and moreover the number of convictions are extremely low. In the same report Law Commission has suggested enactment of a law for forfeiture of property of corrupt public servants. The SARC was of the view that in matters of assets in disproportion to income the burden of proof in cases of confiscation of property should be on the corrupt public servant.

Benami Transactions

These are transactions where a corrupt public servant acquires property in the name of another person. To control this, benami transactions prohibition act has been promulgated (1988). The government, even after the passage of so many years, has not prescribed rules under this act affecting its efficacy. The SARC has recommended strict implementation of this act.

Protection to Whistleblowers

Whistleblowers play an important role in exposing acts of corruption. Public servants working in departments know about illegal activities going on but are afraid to act. However, if adequate protection is provided to them it is likely that they will give the required information. Such people in the organization are known as whistleblowers and it is important to keep their identity secret so that they may not face action in revenge. Whistleblowers are people who are part of the organization about which they give information. SARC has recommended that there is need to enact legislation for protection of whistleblower to prevent their victimization and harassment. The government of India moved a bill known as "The Whistleblower Protection Bill 2011" but though it has been passed by the Lok Sabha it has not yet been considered by the Rajya Sabha.

Serious Economic Offences

There is a rise of economic offences which has become a matter of concern and is an offshoot of the pace at which the economy is diversifying and growing. These economic offences include tax evasion, counterfeiting, distorting share markets, falsification of accounts, frauds in the banking systems, smuggling, money laundering, insider trading and others of a similar nature. There are a large number of acts governing such offences which include the Indian penal code, the banking regulation act, the company act, the income tax act, the customs act, prevention smuggling act and foreign exchange management act etc. Most states have established economic offences wings to handle such cases. The Central Bureau of Investigation (CBI) also takes up such cases if they are referred to them. A Serious Frauds Investigation Office (SFIO) was setup in 2003 as a specialized multi–disciplinary organization to deal with cases of serious corporate frauds. SFIO carries out investigation under the provision of companies act. The SARC has recommended for more stringent laws to curb serious economic offences.

Article 311 Constitutional Protection to Civil Servants

Part XIV of the constitution regulates the conditions of the service of the civil servants. Article 309 stipulates about recruitments and conditions of service of people appointed to public services and article 310 says that they would hold office during the pleasure of the president or Governor of the State. The exercise of this pleasure is circumscribed by provisions of article 311. The article says that no civil servant shall be dismissed or removed or reduced in rank by any authority subordinate to that by which he was appointed and that no such action shall be taken except after an inquiry has been held and he has been given a reasonable opportunity of being heard in respect of charges framed against him. However, these provisions do not apply if the actions mentioned are taken against civil servants if he has been convicted on a criminal charge or if the empowered authority records in writing that it is not practical to hold such inquiry or if the President or the Governor is satisfied that such inquiry cannot be conducted in the interest of the security of the State.

The purpose of this provision and procedure laid down in article 311 is intended to provide a security of tenure to government servants and provide safeguards against arbitrary dismissal of government servants or reduction to a lower rank.

There has been much debate about this article and those in favor are of the view that giving an opportunity of being heard is a fundamental principle of natural justice which would be applicable even if article 311 was to be repealed. Also, it is only logical that the appointing authority be vested with powers to decide on major punishment. This is in line with the principle of hierarchy in government. Moreover, it is only fair to allow to the civil servant to respond to charges and actions against him to be taken after due process of inquiry. The judicial pronouncements of the honorable Supreme Court also indicate that this article is not an obstacle in dealing with delinquent public servants. The courts do not sit in appeal against the findings of the departmental proceedings and they only ascertain whether enquiry was fairly or properly conducted.

Those who are in favor of repealing article 311 are of the view that this provision has the potential to protect corrupt public servants as these provisions are used by some public servants to tie down inquiries against them on mere technicalities. Some point out that reasonable opportunity of being heard should be provided to a government official but this should not be excessive and the delayed action should not become a reason to embolden errant officials to keep committing acts against public interests. They feel the constitution provided this safeguard to protect the civil servant in the aftermath of partition and post-Colonial administrative upheavals when the bureaucracy had to face a lot of difficult challenges these safeguards are not necessary now. Permanency in the civil services is also being questioned and people are talking of contractual appointments to senior positions. The SARC is in favor of repealing article 311 and also article 310 and they recommend suitable legislation should be provided with all necessary terms and conditions provided under article 309 to protect bonafide action taken in public interest and this should provide necessary protection to a public servant against arbitrary action.

This author is of the view that in the emerging political scenario it is necessary to retain article 311 as more and more governments are becoming vindictive and begin to take action against public servants on flimsy grounds for political reasons. Recently we have seen a trend of IAS officers being suspended if they do not carry out the irregular orders of the political executive. The Union Public Service Commission is the appointing authority for the civil servants and the powers of major punishment should vest with them otherwise this will lead to all civil servants becoming committed to political parties in power rather than to the constitution and the rule of law. Article 311 is essential to protect the independence of the civil servant.

Disciplinary Proceedings

Disciplinary proceedings are initiated against civil servants to deal with any misconduct on their part which could be an irregularity or even an act with criminal intent. The procedure of holding such proceedings has been prescribed and conforms to the principles of natural justice. The government as the competent authority after a preliminary or fact finding inquiry takes a decision to start departmental proceedings against an employee or officer. The officer is then given a statement of charges and an inquiry officer is appointed who issues these charges to him. The officer has to respond within a certain time period which may be extended at the discretion of the inquiry officer. The concerned officer can ask for the documents to be made available to him to file a satisfactory reply and he may also seek to be heard in person. The inquiry officer after providing reasonable opportunity shall give his findings on the basis of which the officer being inquired against can be exonerated or awarded minor or major punishments or it may also be recommended to start criminal proceedings against him. Minor penalties include censure, withholding of promotion to employees for a specified period or withholding of increments while major penalty implies dismissal, reduction in rank or removal or compulsory retirement. Departmental proceedings are in the nature quasi judicial proceedings and the Chief Vigilance Commissioner (CVC) has fixed time lines for disposal of inquiry. However, in most departmental inquiries there are a lot of delays often owing to technical reasons. Strict monitoring of pending departmental inquiries at an appropriate level can speed up the matters. During the pendency of a departmental inquiry the officer cannot be promoted.

Institutional Framework to Deal with Corruption

The administrative vigilance division in the department of personnel and training is the nodal agency dealing with vigilance and anti-corruption in government of India. The main institution created for this purpose is that of the CVC.

Central Vigilance Commission (CVC)

The Santhanam Committee on prevention of corruption recommended the setting up the CVC which was created by Government of India in 1964. It was accorded statutory status consequent to the judgment of the Honorable Supreme Court in Vineet Narayan vs Union of India through the CVC act 2003. The CVC advises the union government on all matter pertaining to maintaining of integrity in administration. It exercises superintendence over the working of the central bureau of investigation (CBI) and also over the vigilance administration of various ministries and other organizations of the government of India. The CVC consists of a chairperson and not more than two Vigilance Commissioners as members who are appointed by the President for four years or till they attain the age of 65 years whichever is earlier. The CVC supervises cases involving all India services officers working with the central government and all other group-A officers of central government and officers of central public sector and autonomous organizations. The commission can order investigation into complaints it receives about the involvement in offences under the Prevention of Corruption Act (PC). It can review the progress of investigation but cannot interfere with the process of investigation. The commission tenders advice to central government on matters of vigilance.

Every ministry in Government of India and every central public sector undertaking have a vigilance department under a CVO whose appointment is approved by the CVC. In matters where CBI requests for sanction for prosecution against officers the CVC examines the matter and tenders advice to the department. The CVC has also identified areas of corruption in government working and issued guidelines to prevent the same like the CVC guidelines on tender and procurement procedure. Similarly the CVO in each department also developed systems to eradicate corruption in the department and he also creates awareness about vigilance matters. As per the directions of the CVC a vigilance week is observed every year to make officers and employees aware about issues related to corruption and integrity and creating an environment of probity.

Central Bureau of Investigation (CBI)

The CBI is the main investigative agency of the government of India in anti-corruption matters and derives its power from Delhi special police establishment act 1946. The CBI has three units.

1. anti corruption division,
2. economic offences wing and
3. Special crime division.

The CBI also investigates cases against public servants of state government if the cases are entrusted to them. The CBI director is selected by a committee consisting of the Prime Minister, Chief Justice of India and the leader of the largest opposition party and holds office for two years. This high level committee has been set up to ensure complete fairness in the selection process and the director and the CBI under him is expected to work with complete impartiality. However, there is a general criticism that this powerful agency is often used by the government in power to meet its political ends. Matters came to such a pass that the honorable Supreme Court referred to the agency as a "Caged parrot". Recently many state governments which are under the control of political parties different from the party in power at the centre have refused to allow CBI to automatically investigate matters lying within the jurisdiction of the state governments. To act as the principle agency against corruption the CBI needs to work with total autonomy, independence and be perceived as an impartial agency.

Vigilance Systems in State Governments

All the states have vigilance mechanisms to deal with matters of corruption. The institutional structure varies from state to state but there are common elements, for example, in UP there is a Principal Secretary rank officer looking after all cases related to corruption. In some states the Home Secretary has this as an additional responsibility while in some others the Chief Secretary is holding this post. There is a vigilance wing in the police under a Director General of Police (vigilance) who is of the same seniority as the Director General of Police and supervises all vigilance investigations and reports to the government. In addition there is also a state vigilance commission headed by a state vigilance commissioner. However, the state vigilance commission is nowhere as powerful as the CVC is at the centre and often inconvenient IAS officers are parked there without any substantive powers. In addition there are the anti-corruption and economic offences wings in the police department to look after cases relating to these offences.

Lokpal

The Indian Lokpal is based on the idea of the institution of ombudsman existing in Scandinavian countries. There was a lot of agitation by civil society for a Lokpal act to take action against corruption at the highest level. The Anna Hazare movement is best remembered in this connection. After much debate and discussion the Lokpal and Lokayukta act was passed in 2013 and came into force from 1st January 2014. According to the act the Lokpal will have a chairperson and up to eight members, four of whom will be judicial members. The chairperson can be a serving or retired Chief Justice of India, Supreme Court judge or an eminent person. Similarly the judicial member could be a serving or retired judge of the Supreme Court or retired Chief Justice of the High Court. The non-judicial members have to be persons of impeccable integrity and domain knowledge. 50 percent of the members should belong to schedule castes, scheduled tribes, other backward classes, minorities and women. The selection committee for the chairperson and members will consist of the Prime Minister as the chairperson and the Speaker of the house, leader of the opposition, Chief Justice of India and one eminent jurist recommended by committee members to be nominated by the President. The chairperson and members can hold office for five years or till the age of seventy.

The Lokpal deals with complaints against public functionaries which includes the Prime Minister, Ministers, members of parliament and group A and group B officers or equivalent. The Lokpal will have an enquiry wing and a prosecution wing. There will be a procedure for handling complaints and the Lokpal can order CBI investigation also. The Lokpal can attach the proceeds of corruption in the possession of public servants. As per the Lokpal act there is no provision for seeking prior sanction before taking action against public servants for corruption.

The setting up of the institution of the Lokpal had to confront several challenges. The first one was regarding the inclusion of the Prime Minister in the bill. There were different views and finally the act provide that the Lokpal can inquire into allegations of corruption against the Prime Minister if it refers to subjects other than international relations, external and internal security, public order, atomic energy and space but the full bench of the Lokpal would have to consider the matter and at least two-third of the members should approve the enquiry which should be held in camera.

The second issue was regarding the conduct of members of parliament inside the parliament. The tradition is that all activities inside the parliament are regulated by the Speaker or by the house itself. Lokpal act excludes the conduct of members of parliament inside the house from Lokpal's scrutiny. The members of the army, navy and air force are excluded from the purview of Lokpal. There was some dispute about the inclusion of group C and D category of government employees. These are in large numbers and including them would lead to creation of a huge parallel bureaucracy and also harassment and illegal action. Finally the act passed by Lok Sabha covers these employees. Then there was an issue of including or excluding the judiciary from the ambit of the Lokpal. However, after much deliberation the judiciary has been excluded.

Every state government is expected to establish a body known as Lokayukta for the state by a law made by the state legislature to deal with complaints relating to corruption against certain public functionaries. Most states have established the Lokayukta and the performance of the institution have been mixed. There is a general reluctance of the state governments to appoint a Lokayukta and often the appointment to this crucial post is greatly delayed. Even though the selection committee has the Chief Justice of the High Court and leader of opposition as the members along with the Chief Minister the ruling party tries its level best to select a member of the judiciary with whom they have good relations. For the institution to succeed it is important that the selection should be absolutely fair and on the merit with total integrity and impartiality being the main criteria. In state governments it has also been observed that several reports of the Lokayukta are kept pending if they have recommended something which is not acceptable to the party in power. However, there is a provision that in case of any disagreement the entire issue has to be put up before the legislature. I have seen instances where the Lokayukta has taken up with the Governor about non action on its reports and the Governor has asked for a report from the state government. There have also been cases where the Lokayukta has resigned due to non compliance by the state governments. There have also been cases where the Lokayukta has severely indicted a minister and the latter has had to resign.

The Lokpal and Lokayukta are valuable governance reforms in the direction of curbing corruption at the highest levels of governments and if the chairperson and members perform their duties with complete integrity then they can certainly make a big difference to the climate of probity in government.

Social Infrastructure

• Citizen's Initiatives

The civil society which led to the creation of Lokpal has been increasingly active over the years and raising issues of corruption and demanding accountability from the government. The civil society groups like NGOs, media, professional associations and informal groups of people have given voice to the demand of the citizen to control and take action against corruption. They play a very important role in creation of awareness. Traditionally the governments are responsible to parliament elected by people but the civil society groups have been demanding accountability to the citizen. The institution of Citizens Charters have also been created to deal with this concept of accountability to citizens and transparency in government. The SARC in its report has quoted the example of independent commission against corruption of Hong Kong which has produced exemplary results in the fight of civil society against corruption. In India the civil society has been active since the early 1990s and some examples of these are public interest litigations, Jansunwai by Mazdor Kissan Shakti Sanghatan Rajasthan and campaign for electoral reforms by Loksatta Hyderabad. Civil society groups have exerted pressure on governments to reform and have also made people aware about corruption in government. They have thus been a major initiative in the hands of the common man to fight corruption. The government, if it is keen to combat corruption, must engage regularly with these civil society groups by disseminating all possible information to them and inviting them to oversee government programs. The government should establish credible complaints mechanisms, enforce access to information, educate society on the events of corruption, use public hearings to audit government activity and periodically carry out surveys to assess the quality of public service delivery. The Citizen's Charter and Right to Information act are steps in this direction.

- **Social Audit**

We are aware of the audit conducted about financial transactions of the government by the CAG and also performance audit of departments and some important schemes. However, there are various beneficiary oriented development initiatives of the government where social audit has evolved as an accountability tool that measures, evaluates and identifies gaps in service delivery and then proposes to rectify these gaps. This entire process is done by the direct participation of the intended beneficiaries. There are usually complaints that there are a lot of leakages in these development schemes and that often the benefit is not going to the intended beneficiary implying that the funds have not been utilized effectively and the objective of the scheme not fully realized. Sometimes this is as a result of inadequate understanding of the provisions of the schemes but more often it is because of corruption at the level of the bureaucracy and the Pradhans or Sarpanches at the village level. One of the major schemes where social audit has been used is MGNREGA. The social audit of this scheme collects all records like muster rolls and studies them. Surveys are then prepared and conducted and on the spot inspections are done. The participants of the survey are called for a public hearing which is attended by Gram Sabha members, local administrative officer, the point person for the scheme and sometime even local politicians. The citizens are empowered in this manner by being made aware of the provisions of the scheme and fund utilization and work done. Follow up action is promised and taken. This has been extremely useful as the society through participation finds out where the scheme is going wrong and takes corrective measures.

Most states have set up a directorate of social audit as an autonomous body which studies one village after another to assess the real impact of various development schemes. In UP, we had a system where the working of the social audit directorate and its findings was done at the level of the Chief Secretary to give it due importance. The findings of the audit were uploaded on a portal which was visible to all making the entire exercise transparent. The Gaon Sabhas has been mandated to conduct social audit of all the schemes in their jurisdiction. The mid-day-meal scheme has also been subjected to successful social audit. The officers have a tendency to avoid cooperating with social audit as they feel that it would expose them. The socio-economic power structure of a village is such that the stronger castes and the better offs tend to appropriate most of the benefits of the government schemes which are supposed to reach the needy and the poor. For this reason the social audit exercise faces a lot of resistance in the beginning and can succeed only if it has the support of the District Magistrate and the senior most level at the Secretariat level. The government in power stands to gain a lot from successful social audits and should provide all support to them.

The number of social audits and the schemes being taken up for social audit has been going up regularly but still it has not got the desired success. The main reason has been that action to rectify the gaps and defects has not been taken. This makes the whole exercise wasteful. It is thus important to rigorously monitor action taken on the reports of the social audits. Moreover, in many states the selections of the officers for the directorate is subjected to political influences and often it is used as a parking ground for favoured retired bureaucrats who are not committed to social audit and are afraid to point out defects in the implementation of the schemes as they do not want to embarrass the government in power or disrupt the existing power structure. There is no doubt that this is a very powerful tool of curbing corruption in social and rural development schemes and effective utilization of government funds. However, to succeed these audits need the complete support from the senior levels of government.

Systemic Reforms

There is no denying that corruption exists in a big way in government and various surveys done by transparency international have rated India high on the corruption index. This makes it necessary to take steps to control if not eradicate corruption completely. The SARC has analyzed corruption beautifully by giving the following equation:

Monopoly + Discretion – Accountability = Corruption.

It follows that systemic reforms are required to increase competition, reduce discretion and enforce accountability to reduce or eliminate corruption. There has to be an optimum mixture of preventive and punitive measures to reduce corruption. The preventive measures come under the ambit of systemic reforms. E-governance has been another major initiative in tackling corruption and the railway ticket booking has been the biggest example of this. There have been numerous best practices followed where the government systems and processes have been made simpler and more transparent thereby reducing corruption.

Promoting Competition

There is always a scope for corruption in government schemes because government often provides public services in a monopolistic setting. If competition is introduced in the delivery of public services then it can control corruption significantly. The major examples of this have been the opening up of the telecom and aviation sector to competition which has reduced corruption and also provided better services to the citizen. We have to guard against private sector corruption also and to ensure that the interests of the citizens are looked after and for this purpose a regulatory mechanism has to be created. Today such regulatory mechanisms exist in a large number of areas including telecom and electricity supply. The recent agriculture reforms allowing a farmer to sell his produce to any consumer anywhere in the country has been done with the objective of breaking the monopoly of the agriculture Mandis where rampant corruption had started prevailing. However, the farmers are opposing it and the matter is being deliberated.

Simplifying Transactions

A major problem with the working of the government is the existence of a complex network of procedures, rules and regulations about which the citizen has no knowledge and the government employees use these systems to hold back clearances, licenses, permits and other approvals and force the public to pay bribes to get their work done. Since only the government employee has knowledge of these systems he uses them selectively leading to harassment of the people and consequent corruption. It is thus important that the processes of all government transactions should be simplified so that the citizens are not exploited. A single window system for all clearances certainly helps. For example, industrialization was not taking place due to numerous clearances required to set up an industry and the time and harassment involved in the process. This was reflected by a low rank in the ease of doing business in India amongst all countries. Now with the focused attention of government of India and state governments things have improved considerably and the rank of India in ease of doing business has become much better leading to an improvement in the investment climate. This was done by introducing single window system for industries and reforming the procedures involved. For many clearances self certification has been allowed and the time period for which approvals are given has been increased in most cases from one year to three or five years. This has led to reducing the interface between the industrialist and government departments and consequent reduction in corruption. For example, pollution control board used to give no objection (NOC) every year which meant that the industrialists will have to apply every year and grease the palms of the concerned officer. Now in most cases this NOC is being given for five years and has to be given within a fixed time period. Most state governments have passed a public service delivery act whereby specific officers have been made accountable to give approvals regarding their departments in a stipulated time period or else they will be penalized. Simple things like approval of map for construction of a house or obtaining an income or caste certificate used to be a herculean task and it was not possible to get these documents without payment of bribes. All these activities have now been simplified and they come under the public service act so that the citizen is not made to run endlessly from one officer to another.

In government of India as well as state governments a business engineering process has been undertaken to weed out archaic laws and irrelevant processes. Much work needs to be done to streamline these procedures. We have to trust the citizen and not bind him down by rules which are taken advantage of by unscrupulous officers and employees.

Use of Information Technology

Information technology (IT) have been a game changer as for as reduction in corruption is concerned. In the earlier example given about ease of doing business the single window has been made possible only because of the system of online filing of applications and online clearances which means that a prospective entrepreneur does not have to physically approach government departments as information technology ensures that his work is done virtually.

There used to be a lot of corruption in delivery of subsidies and also scholarships and pensions which have been reduced considerably by IT which enables the transfer of the money directly into the account of the beneficiary so that there are no leakages of the type that can take place in a manual process. These direct cash benefit transfer schemes have greatly reduced the incidence of corruption. Another major area where technology has reduced corruption has been the computerization of land records in most states following the example of the Bhoomi Project in Karnataka and making an extract of land record available to the individual online. This has greatly reduced the corruption that used to take place in the maintenance, updating and availability of land records. However, information technology becomes useful only after the government processes and procedures have been thoroughly re-engineered. Nowadays more and more apps are being developed to make it easy for the citizens to avail public services online and also lodge grievances and complaints on the apps. It is important that complaints are monitored in a manner that the citizen gets the ends results and there should be fixation of responsibility if there is any lapse. Mobiles are also being used to identify and verify the beneficiaries of various schemes and redress the grievances of the people where they can lodge a complaint using their mobile and get a response also. Smart phones are being used to take photographs and videos to monitor the physical progress and quality of construction projects greatly reducing the chances of corruption.

Reforming the Civil Services

The SARC is of the view that systemic reforms have no meaning without reforming the civil services. It is important to ensure accountability of civil servants to reduce corruption and mis-governance. The duties and responsibilities at each level of the civil service should be clearly delineated. There should also be an in-built system of rewards and punishments. Regular performance audit would also help.

Risk Management for Preventive Vigilance

An office which has higher level of discretion and public interface is more prone to corruption and can be called a high corruption office risk. For example, the Tax Assessing officers post can be categorized as high risk. Individual government servants vary in their level of integrity. A risk management system to control corruption can minimize risks by posting upright officers to high risk jobs and vice-versa. The risk profiling of officers should be done by a committee of eminent persons, at least once in every five years. Some organizations assess the integrity of the person through an integrity test. The practice is followed in some developed countries to identify suspected corrupt persons.

Audit

CAG carries out audit of government departments and corporations and submits his report before the state legislature or Parliament. The recent 2G scam and Coal scam came to light as a result of the report of the CAG. CAG in its audit points out the irregularities done and the possible loss to the state exchequer. Many audit observations lead to enquiries and often expose cases of corruption. SARC has recommended that the audit team should be imparted training in forensic audit.

Proactive Vigilance on Corruption

The Santhanam Committee in 1964 gave emphasis to proactive vigilance by identifying suspected corrupt elements and then devising mechanisms to see that they do not occupy sensitive positions. The SARC commission has listed the following measures for proactive vigilance:

1. List of officers of doubtful integrity should be maintained.
2. An agreed list of suspect officers should be prepared and these officers kept under watch.
3. A list of undesirable middlemen, touts dealing with sensitive departments should be prepared.
4. Every office should ensure timely submission of his annual property returns and these should be in the public domain.
5. For every major appointment vigilance clearance from the CVC should be taken.
6. There should be mandatory review of officers at the age of 50 or 55 to screen out those with doubtful integrity.

Vigilance Network

A large number of corruption cases remain pending with various authorities and need to be reviewed by senior officers. SARC recommends creation of a national database for this.

Integrity Pacts

Integrity pacts are added to public contracts to reduce corruption. This pact is an agreement between a public agency procuring goods and services and the bidder for a public contract where the bidders give assurance that they have not paid and shall not pay any bribes to get the contracts. These pacts are supervised by independent observers. *The Defence Procurement Procedure manual* 2006 provides for adoptions of these pacts in Defence contracts.

In general we can say that systemic reforms to reduce discretion, improve accountability and a working environment of accessibility and responsiveness goes a long way in reducing corruption.

Protecting the Honest Civil Servant

Just as it is necessary to take action against corrupt officers it is also important to protect the honest civil servant otherwise they will not take decisions which will hamper the development of the nation. Systems are necessary to ensure that no honest civil servant suffers for bonafide mistakes made by him in the course of taking decisions. The current system has the shield of taking sanction from the concerned government before investigating a civil servant on charges of corruption or charge-sheeting him. The CVC is the body authorised for this purpose in government of India and the state vigilance department does this in the states. It is important that every allegation of corruption against a public servant must be examined in depth before any enquiry is conducted against him and this should take into account the circumstances under which a particular decision has been taken.

Chapter 10

Case Studies in Ethics

Introduction to Case Studies

The fourth general studies paper for the main examination for civil service is on ethics, integrity and aptitude. In the previous chapters we have seen the importance of ethics in life and of public service ethics in civil service. This paper is divided into two sections. Section A deals with the theory of ethics while section B, which carries equal marks, relates to application of these theories to real life situations. Accordingly case studies or scenarios are given with various alternatives and the candidate is expected to choose the right course of action. There is, of course, a word limit and the candidate is expected to logically analyse the case study and come to a decision within this word limit.

Approach to Handling Case Studies

The objective of the case studies is to assess the ethical and moral foundation of a candidate's values system, his attitude, aptitude and also sense of commitment to integrity in public service. The case study method has been used extensively in management education. I had done my MBA from IIM Ahmedabad before entering the IAS and there the entire method of teaching the principles of management was through case studies. There are a large number of case studies available in management but very few related to public administration. The problem has been very little documentation of real life situations in administration. Public administration is an applied subject and administrator has to deal with people and countless pulls and pressures. Administration is a science as well as an art. The case studies bring out these aspects of the job of a civil servant and as such are very relevant to bring out the value system, principles and character of a candidate.

The first thing to do when answering a case study question is to read the case study properly with great attention to minute details and fully comprehend the problem situation. There are many aspects mentioned in a case study and one should understand all the nuances. For this each word of the case study is important as it denotes what the examiner is trying to say and also indicates what your answer should address. Often after a problem various alternatives are given. You have to choose the alternatives which according to you best address the problem. Sometimes you are expected to go beyond the alternatives given and come out with the solution of your own. Though there is a word limit you should start your answer by mentioning the problem and then take each alternative, analyse it and then select the best alternative to handle the situation and give justification for the same. This is a paper on ethics and so your answer should be according to the right ethical approach that a public servant should have. For example, a public servant should have total financial integrity and never indulge in any kind of corruption. Accordingly the candidate must choose a solution where no corruption is involved or is against desired ethical value system of a civil servant. You are expected to use the ethical framework given to you by the earlier chapters of this book which deal with the theory of ethics. The examiner would like to see how you apply ethical values of life and of public service to a real life problem situation. It is true that in real life situations one has to often use diplomacy and tact to get the desired results but one should never deviate from his ethical code.

In this book I have taken up case studies that appear in the main examination from the years 2013 to 2019 and given the solutions to the same. Thereafter, on the basis of my experiences in the civil service I have prepared case studies which cover all aspects of the syllabus and give solutions to the same. Sometimes I have not adhered to the word limit but this is deliberate as I have tried to give examples and also discuss in detail. The candidate, of course, has to stick to the word limit and therefore must be very brief and concise.

CASE STUDY: UPSC GENERAL STUDIES-4 PAPERS – 2013

Case 1 (Question 10)

A Public Information Officer has received an application under RTI Act. Having gathered the information, the PIO discovers that the information pertains to some of the decisions taken by him, which were found to be not altogether right. There were other employees also who were party to these decisions. Disclosure of the information is likely to lead to disciplinary action with possibility of punishment against him as well as some of his colleagues. Non-disclosure or part-disclosure or camouflaged-disclosure of information will result into lesser punishment or no punishment.

The PIO is otherwise an honest and conscientious person but this particular decision, on which the RTI application has been filed, turned out to be wrong. He comes to you for advice.

The following are some suggested options. Please evaluate the merits and demerits of each of the options:

1. The PIO could refer the matter to his superior officer and seek his advice and act strictly in accordance with the advice, even though he is not completely in agreement with the advice of the superior.
2. The PIO could proceed on leave and leave the matter to be dealt by his successor in office or request for transfer of the application to another PIO.
3. The PIO could weigh the consequences of disclosing the information truthfully, including the effect on his career, and reply in a manner that would not place him or his career in jeopardy, but at the same time a little compromise can be made on the contents of the information.
4. The PIO could consult his other colleagues who are party to the decision and take action as per their advice.

Also please indicate (without necessarily restricting to the above options) what you would like to advise, giving proper reasons.

Answer

The Public Information Officer under RTI Act has to decide whether to disclose information asked for even though disclosure would make him liable for punishment as the information pertains to some wrong decisions taken by him. The key words are that the PIO is an honest and conscientious person but has made a mistake. Also the case study says that non-disclosure or partial-disclosure would lead to lesser or no punishment. The examiner wants you to examin the merits and demerits of the option. The examiner wants you to indicate the action that you would take without restricting yourself to the alternatives given. The hint is clear that none of the four alternatives is the right one. You have to suggest a better alternative of your own.

The subject relates to RTI Act. This Act has been promulgated to bring transparency and accountability in Government and also ensure citizen participation. Since this is an Act the PIO has to give information as desired.

The first alternative is not feasible as under the Act it is a PIO who is responsible to give information and he has to take a decision on it. There is no provision of officially taking advise from seniors in this matter. Of course, informal consultation can be held.

The second alternative has no meaning. A public servant cannot run away from his duty by proceeding on leave or requesting for transfer. He has to take a decision at his level as per law.

The third alternative would mean that he is giving incorrect information to safeguard his career. This means he is putting personal gain above public interest which is against public service ethics. This alternative is not acceptable.

The fourth alternative is not available. The PIO may consult his other colleagues who are also likely to be held liable for this decision informally. However, ultimately he has to act as per his conscience and the law.

The right course of action for the PIO would be to do his duty as a PIO under the RTI Act. The PIO is an honest and conscientious person. He has taken a wrong decision but it has been done in a bonafide manner. There is no malafide intent. The PIO must disclose the complete information as desired under the RTI Act. as he would have done even if the information related to a wrong decision by some other officer. Honesty and integrity are essential attributes of a public servant.

For discussion's sake I must point out that it is possible that the disclosure of this information could lead to departmental proceedings against him. However, he would be asked to give an explanation where he can spell out the circumstances under which the decision was taken. As he has a reputation of honesty, in all probability no action would ultimately be taken against him. I must point out that if a public servant takes a decision with the right intention then he eventually does not get punished for his actions.

Case 2 (Question 11)

You are working as an Executive Engineer in the construction cell of a Municipal Corporation and are presently in-charge of the construction of a flyover. There are two Junior Engineers under you who have the responsibility of day-to-day inspection of the site and are reporting to you, while you are finally reporting to the Chief Engineer who heads the cell. While the construction is heading towards completion, the Junior Engineers have been regularly reporting that all construction is taking place as per design specifications. However, in one of your surprise inspections, you noticed some serious deviations and lacunae which, in your opinion, are likely to affect the safety of the flyover. Rectification of these lacunae at this stage would require a substantial amount of demolition and rework which will cause a tangible loss to the contractor and will also delay completion. There is a lot of public pressure on the Corporation to get this construction completed because of heavy traffic congestion in the area. When you brought this matter to the notice of the Chief Engineer, he advised you that in his opinion it is not a very serious lapse and may be ignored. He advised for further expediting the project for completion in time. However, you are convinced that this was a serious matter which might affect public safety and should not be left unaddressed.

What will you do in such a situation?

Answer

The main issue in this case study relates to an executive engineer of a Municipal Corporation who is responsible for day to day reporting to the Chief Engineer about quality of construction and progress of a flyover. The Executive Engineer is getting report from two junior engineers working under him. They have reported that work is going on as per specification but when the Executive Engineer carries out a surprise inspection he finds serious lapses the rectification of which would delay the project. There is lot of public pressure for early completion of project. The chief engineer also advises the executive engineer not to raise the issue as it would delay the project. The examiner wants to know if you were the Executive Engineer how you would handle the situation.

The first option of following the advice of the Chief Engineer and not reporting the matter is an ethically incorrect response. The Executive Engineer is in charge of construction of the flyover and it is duty to see that flyover is constructed as per the desired specifications. Public money is involved and this has to be utilized properly. A poor quality construction means that public money is being wasted and also points towards corruption. In fact the two Junior Engineers working under the Executive Engineer have given a clear report about the quality of construction and they seem to be either very negligent or corrupt. The Chief Engineer could also be involved in the corruption or he simply wants to complete the project on time to get appreciation from his superiors. The Executive Engineer should not follow the advice of the Chief Engineer to ignore the issue.

The second option is a sound one. The Executive Engineer must give a detailed report in writing and with his analysis put up the report to the Chief Engineer. It would be very difficult for the Chief Engineer to overrule in writing. Any enquiry later on would hold the Chief Engineer directly responsible. The Executive Engineer in his report should mention that if the flyover collapses after construction it could lead to lot of people losing their lives.

Before writing to the Chief Engineer the Executive Engineer should call for an explanation from the Junior Engineers and issue orders to the contractor for necessary corrections within the project period. This is the responsibility of the Executive Engineer. He does not need the advice of anybody to do this. It is a question of his ethical system. Also, this is what is officially expected of him.

The fourth alternative has to be avoided. In government it is not correct to go over your boss and report to his superior. In fact the latter will ask you as to why you have not reported the matter through official channel.

The fifth alternative is totally unacceptable as a public servant cannot and should not run away from his responsibility.

Thus, he has to first act as per the third alternative and go for the second alternative. This is a case of an ethical dilemma. On one side is the issue of completing a public project on time and on the other side is the issue of the quality of the construction which could lead to a major tragedy in the future where the Executive Engineer would be held squarely responsible and even face criminal action. So he must perform his duty even if this leads to a delay in the project.

Case 3 (Question 12)

Sivakasi in Tamil Nadu is known for its manufacturing clusters on firecrackers and matches. The local economy of the area is largely dependent on firecrackers industry. It has led to a tangible economic development and improved standard of living in the area.

So far as child labour norms for hazardous industries like firecrackers industry are concerned, International Labour Organization (ILO) has set the minimum age as 18 years. In India, however, this age is 14 years.

The units in industrial clusters of firecrackers can be classified into registered and non-registered entities. One typical unit is household-based work. Though the law is clear on the use of child labour employment norms in registered/non-registered units, it does not include household-based works. Household-based work means children working under the supervision of their parents/relatives. To evade child labour norms, several units project themselves as household-based works but employ children from outside. Needless to say that employing children saves the costs for these units leading to higher profits to the owners.

On your visit to one of the units at Sivakasi, the owner takes you around the unit which has about 10-15 children below 14 years of age. The owner tells you that in his household-based unit, the children are all his relatives. You notice that several children smirk, when the owner tells you this. On deeper enquiry, you figure out that neither the owner nor the children are able to satisfactorily establish their relationship with each other.

Answer

The issue in this case relates to implementation of the law regarding child labor. Sivakasi is known from manufacturing firecrackers and matches and provides large scale employment to the people bringing about an improvement in the standard of living and leading to economic development. The use of child labor which is below the age of 14 years in India is not allowed in registered and non registered entities but units which are household based can legally take work from children of their own family under the supervision of the parents. On your inspection as an officer you find that a unit which is household based is employing a lot of children below 14 years. The owner tells you that they are all his relatives but a deeper inquiry shows that it is not true.

The basic ethical issue involved is taking work from children against the law. In fact it is a duty of the state to provide education to these children under the Right to Education Act. Making firecrackers and matches is a hazardous industry and thus children are exposed to great danger of injury and other serious consequences if work is taken from them. It is important to ensure that the industry functions properly as it leads to employment and all round development. However, this cannot be done at the expense of the life and safety of children. The officer has found that a particular unit is violating the law. The ethical response from him would be to take action against the unit as per law.

A public administrator has to look beyond a specific case. This incident clearly shows that there are many units which would be violating the law in a similar manner and the Junior Level Officers are in collusion with them. The officer should order a detailed inspection of all the units and wherever there is a wrong classification as a household unit action as per law should be taken against those units and they should be taken out of the category of household units. Also the concerned officer who had not reported these violations earlier on should face disciplinary action.

However, detailed inspections cannot be carried out frequently. As an officer you must devise a system to see this kind of a situation does not occur in the future. Random inspections by different groups of officers should be carried out regularly. Further, an awareness drive should be launched to educate the people about the provisions of the law.

The officer could go one step further in the interest of children. He should send a detailed recommendation to his superiors in the government requesting that law be amended to disallow children working even in household units or at least to have very strict norms for this and provision for heavy penalty in case of violation.

Case 4 (Question 13)

You are heading a leading technical institute of the country. The institute is planning to convene an interview panel shortly under your chairmanship for selection of the post of professors. A few days before the interview, you get a call from the Personal Secretary (PS) of a senior government functionary seeking your intervention in favour of the selection of a close relative of the functionary for this post. The PS also informs you that he is aware of the long pending and urgent proposals of your institute for grant of funds for modernization, which are awaiting the functionary's approval. He assures you that he would get these proposals cleared.

1. What are the options available to you?
2. Evaluate each of these options and choose the option which you would adopt, giving reasons.

Answer

The issue involved in this case study is selecting a candidate for the post of professor because the PS of the senior officer has recommended him and not carry out selection on merit.

The first option is to comply with the direction of the PS so that the senior functionary is happy and sanctions the proposal of your institute for funds for modernization. This is ethically not correct. A civil servant must be impartial and objective. Also this means selection of the wrong candidate which will affect the quality of teaching of your institute and also be unfair to the students.

The second option is to bluntly tell the PS that this is not possible and selection will be done on merit. Ethically this would be the right approach as it would ensure the fairness in the selection process. However, this will antagonize the senior government functionary who would then not approve funds for your institute and also not cooperate in any other matter affecting the overall performance of the institute.

The third option is to politely explain that there is a selection committee and there are other members and selection is done on the basis of the views of all the members. You can say that you will try your best provided the candidate does well in the interview. It may even be better to meet the senior functionary and explain this to him in person. Sometimes the PS may be acting of his own volition. The senior functionaries are normally more amenable to reason. You can explain how it is important to select a person on merit and that a committee would never agree on a candidate who does not perform well. Thereafter, the selection should be done on merit. In real life such situations are quite common. If in the interview two candidates including the candidate of the functionary perform equally then you can exercise your discretion in favor of the latter. You can make it clear to the functionary that no injustice will be done to his candidate. In administration you have to learn the art of politely saying no and not being blunt or aggressive.

Case 5 (Question 14)

As a senior officer in the Finance Ministry, you have access to some confidential and crucial information about policy decisions that the Government is about to announce. These decisions are likely to have far-reaching impact on the housing and construction industry. If the builders have access to this information beforehand, they can make huge profits. One of the builders has done a lot of quality work for the Government and is known to be close to your immediate superior, who asks you to disclose this information to the said builder.

1. What are the options available to you?

2. Evaluate each of these options and choose the option which you would adopt, giving reasons.

Answer

This case relates to you as a senior finance ministry officer being privy to confidential and crucial decision that a government is about to announce. If the builders get this information beforehand then they will make huge profits. Your immediate superior asks you to disclose this information to one builder who has done quality work for the government and is close to your immediate superior.

The first option is to comply with the directions of your superior. However, this would be a totally unethical thing to do. This falls under the category of corruption and is against the code of ethics and conduct of an officer. Oral orders of your superiors which are illegal and unethical should not be complied with.

Therefore, the second option is not to follow the orders of your superior. You can politely tell him that this would not be possible and if this act comes to the knowledge of others later on then you will face criminal action for this. Moreover, this act would be violation of the ethics and values of government functioning. The superior may not like it but you have to be firm in this matter. The builder doing quality work should have no effect on your decision. If you disclose the information beforehand then you would be allowing builders and corrupt officers to make illegal money. This would be a straight case of corruption. Hence the officer should not listen to his superior and disclose information to the concerned builder.

Case 6 (Question 15)

You are the Executive Director of an upcoming Infotech company which is making a name for itself in the market.

Mr. A, who is a star performer, is heading the marketing team. In a short period of one year, he has helped in doubling the revenues as well as creating a high brand equity for the company so much so that you are thinking of promoting him. However, you have been receiving information from many corners about his attitude towards the female colleagues; particularly his habit of making loose comments on women. In addition, he regularly sends indecent SMSs to all the team members including his female colleagues.

One day, late in the evening, Mrs. X, who is one of Mr. A's team members, comes to you visibly disturbed. She complains against the continued misconduct of Mr. A, who has been making undesirable advances towards her and has even tried to touch her inappropriately in his cabin. She tenders her resignation and leaves your office.

1. What are the options available to you?
2. Evaluate each of these options and choose the option you would adopt, giving reasons.

Answer

In this case you are the Executive Director of an upcoming Infotech company and a outstanding marketing manager. Mr. A has doubled the revenue of your company and built a brand in the market. You find him eligible for promotion but there are reports about him showing indecent behaviour towards his female colleagues. In fact one Mrs. X comes to you and makes a specific complaint of inappropriate behaviour by Mr. A and tenders her resignation.

The options available to you are:

1. To keep quite because the manager is a star performer and hush up the issue.
2. To call both Mrs. X and Mr. A and convince them to patch up the matter.
3. You may call Mr. A and admonish him strongly and let him off with an oral warning.
4. You should take strong action and sack Mr. A to ensure that the ethical standards of the company are maintained.

Acting as per the first alternative would be a terrible mistake. Matter of sexual misconduct in an organization should never be tolerated howsoever meritorious the accused person maybe.

Second option is also not advisable. Mr. A has acted like this not only against Mrs. X but other women also. Further this is too serious a misconduct to call for a compromise solution. The dignity of Mrs. X has been violated and cannot go unpunished.

The third option will also not give results. Mr. A is evidently a habitual offender and mere admonishment will not change him. Besides the grievance of Mrs. X remains unresolved. It also gives a bad signal about the working culture of the organization.

The fourth option is the best one. Mr. A should be sacked. Cases of sexual misconduct in an organization should never be tolerated. In fact every organization has to mandatorily have a policy to deal with such incidents. It is important for the culture of the company to protect the honour of its women employees.

Short term benefits of profitability must not cloud the decision-making of the Executive Director. This is a basic principle of good corporate governance also.

CASE STUDY: UPSC GENERAL STUDIES PAPERS-2014

Case 1 (Question 10)

Suppose one of your close friends, who is also aspiring for civil services, comes to you for discussing some of the issues related to ethical conduct in public service. He raises the following points:

1. In the present times, when unethical environment is quite prevalent, individual attempts to stick to ethical principles may cause a lot of problems in one's career. It may also cause hardship to the family members as well as risk to one's life. Why should we not be pragmatic and follow the path of least resistance, and be happy with doing whatever good we can?
2. When so many people are adopting wrong means and are grossly harming the system, what difference would it make if only a small minority tries to be ethical? They are going to be rather ineffective and are bound to get frustrated.
3. If we become fussy about ethical considerations, will it not hamper the economic progress of our country? After all, in the present age of high competition, we cannot afford to be left behind in the race of development.
4. It is understandable that we should not get involved in grossly unethical practices, but giving and accepting small gratifications and doing small favours increases everybody's motivation. It also makes the system more efficient. What is wrong in adopting such practices?

Critically analysis the above view points. On the basis of this analysis, what will be your advice to your friend?

Answer

This case study relates to a close friend of yours aspiring for the civil services seeking your advice relating to issues about ethical conduct in public service.

1. He has to be clearly told that the first argument is not acceptable. It is unethical to follow the path of least resistance and abandon ethical principles just to avoid problems in one's career or hardships to family or risk to one's life. It shows total

lack of integrity if you put personal gains above serving the public interest.

2. This argument is also not valid. A public servant has to maintain his ethics and morals and lead by his example. Just because others are adopting wrong means you should not become like them. Even one individual can make a difference so it does not matter if you are in a minority. Further, an individual is answerable to his conscience and ethical standards and adopting the attitude of following the majority in being unethical shows moral weakness.
3. There is no ground to believe that following ethical considerations will hamper economic progress. In fact, corruption and lack of integrity lead to slower economic growth. Good governance is necessary for economic growth.
4. Accepting small gifts or gratifications compromises the integrity of a public servant in the same way as larger issues of ethical misconduct. It definitely does not lead to making the system more efficient. It affects the objectivity and impartiality of an officer and adversely effects his ability to take decisions in public interest.

Your advice to your friend should be unequivocal. In matters of ethics in public service there can be no compromise or dilution of standards. If the friend wants to work in public interest and according to a code of ethics he should aspire for civil services otherwise he should consider some other career for himself.

Case 2 (Question 11)

You are a no-nonsense, honest officer. You have been transferred to a remote district to head a department that is notorious for its inefficiency and callousness. You find that the main cause of the poor state of affairs is the indiscipline of a section of employees. They do not work and also disrupt the working of others. You first warn the troublemakers to mend their ways or else face disciplinary action. When the warning had little effect, you issue a show cause notice to the ringleaders. As a retaliatory measure, these troublemakers instigate a woman employee amongst them to file a complaint of sexual harassment against you with the Women's Commission. The Commission promptly seeks your explanation. The matter is also publicized in the media to embarrass you further. Some of the options to handle this situation could be as follows:

1. Give your explanation to the Commission and go soft on the disciplinary action.
2. Ignore the Commission and proceed firmly with the disciplinary action.
3. Brief your higher-ups, seek directions from them and act accordingly.

Suggest any other possible option(s). Evaluate all of them and suggest the best course of action, giving your reasons for it.

Answer

In this case an honest and strict officer trying to improve the working of his department by taking action against those indulging in indiscipline and inefficiency has got into trouble as a false complaint has been engineered against him.

A woman employee has been instigated to make a complaint of sexual harassment against you and the Women's Commission has asked for your explanation and the media has also publicized the issue. The officer cannot ignore the Commission which is a legal authority. He must give a detailed explanation to the Commission and also bring out the actions he has taken to control indiscipline and how these complaints are a result of this. He should not go soft on the disciplinary action as this would imply that he was doing something wrong. Also, it shows that he is a weak person and not able to take a stand for his ethical conduct.

In fact, as per the second alternative after giving explanation to the Commission he should proceed firmly with the disciplinary action.

It will not help if he seeks directions from his higher-ups and acts accordingly. He has to be responsible for his actions and should have the moral courage to take a stand for his values in the interest of the efficient working of the organization. However, the media has raised the issue and people tend to believe the media. It would, thus, advisable for him to brief his superiors fully about the matter and seek their support. This would ensure that they do not carry any wrong notions about him. Further, in such matters it will help if the officer talks to the editors of the media who have publicized the false news and give them a complete factual picture. They would be obliged to publish the statement of the officer. Such incidents are quite common especially when you join a new organization and want to take strict action against the trouble-makers. The motive behind the false complaints is to make you stop taking disciplinary action. However, if you persist then they will realise that you are an officer of values and courage and slowly they will fall in line.

Case 3 (Question 12)

Suppose you are the CEO of a company that manufactures specialized electronic equipment used by a government department. You have submitted your bid for the supply of this equipment to the department. Both the quality and cost of your offer are better than those of the competitors. Yet the concerned officer is demanding a hefty bribe for approving the tender. Getting the order is important both for you and for your company. Not getting the order would mean closing a production line. It may also affect your own career. However, as a value conscious person, you do not want to give bribe.

Valid arguments can be advanced both for giving the bribe and getting the order, and for refusing to pay the bribe and risking the loss of the order. What those arguments could be? Could there be any better way to get out of this dilemma? If so outline the main elements of this third way, pointing out its merits.

Answer

In this case study you are the CEO of company manufacturing specialized electronic equipment for a government partner. You have submitted a bid to the department but the concerned officer is demanding a hefty bribe. The order is important for your company but you are also a value conscious person. Arguments can be advanced for both, giving the bribe and refusing to pay the bribe.

The arguments in favor of giving the bribe can be—

1. Your company will get more profits and not have to close a production line which could lead to losses and loss of employment to labor.
2. The company manufactures specialized electronic equipment used by this particular department. By not paying the bribe the officers of the department would be unhappy with the company and will try to harm the company by not placing orders on them in the future also. Since the company manufactures a specialized equipment this may amount to it losing its main customers and force the company to have heavy losses.
3. Losing the current and future orders could possibly adversely affect the career of the CEO.

On the other hand the arguments against giving a bribe are as follows—

1. Giving bribe is an illegal and immoral act. If this comes to light in the future then the company and CEO can face criminal action.
2. It is against the basic principles of good corporate governance and a company which deviates from these principles eventually suffers.
3. The CEO is a value conscious person. He would be sacrificing his values for commercial gains and this would be counter to his standard of ethics and morals. Values are of no use if they can be compromised whenever there are obstacles in its path.
4. Earning profits by unethical means is wrong no matter what the situation may be.

It is clear that the CEO should not pay the bribe to the government officer thereby maintaining a high standard of integrity. He can approach the superiors of the concerned government officer and bring the matter to their knowledge. Generally the superiors would intervene and ensure fairness in the transaction. If, still the company's bid is rejected illegally it can make a written representation. In the days of Right to Information Act it is not easy for the government department to act in an arbitrary manner. In the worst case scenario he can approach the courts.

Case 4 (Question 13)

Rameshwar successfully cleared the prestigious civil services examination and was excited about the opportunity that he would get through the civil services to serve the country. However, soon after joining the services, he realized that things are not as rosy as he had imagined.

He found a number of malpractices prevailing in the department assigned to him. For example, funds under various schemes and grants were being misappropriated. The official facilities were frequently being used for personal needs by the officers and staff. After some time, he noticed that the process of recruiting the staff was also not up to the mark. Prospective candidates were required to write an examination in which a lot of cheating was going on. Some candidates were provided external help in the examination. Rameshwar brought these incidents to the notice of his seniors. However, he was advised to keep his eyes, ears and mouth shut and ignore all these things which were taking place with the connivance of the higher-ups. Rameshwar felt highly disillusioned and uncomfortable. He comes to you seeking your advice.

Indicate various options that you think are available in this situation. How would you help him to evaluate these options and choose the most appropriate path to be adopted?

Answer

This case relates to an honest civil servant who finds unethical practices in the department he is assigned to. He also finds cheating taking place in the recruitment of staff with the connivance of his superior officers. Rameshwar is disillusioned and comes to you for advice.

1. He can listen to the advice of his seniors and close his eyes to all the unethical practices including cheating in recruitment. However, this would mean that he totally compromises his integrity. Not taking an action against wrong or illegal activities makes you a part of them. You are as dishonest as others. Such behaviour is contrary to the ethics of a public servant and ultimately it is the citizen who suffers. This alternative is not acceptable
2. It is the responsibility of Rameshwar to see that working in his department is done in an honest and fair manner and government resources are not misused for personal needs. He is accountable for the working of his department and cannot ignore his responsibility by taking shelter behind the advice of seniors. He should act immediately to rectify things. He can take the following actions.
    a. He should personally implement a system of invigilation and supervision in the recruitment process to ensure that there is no cheating. He should take extremely strict action against those who persist in cheating.
    b. He should issue instructions that official facilities will not be used for personal needs. He should then monitor to see that his instructions are followed.
    c. He should get an immediate audit done of the funds for various schemes and grants and take action against any misappropriation. He should design a system to ensure that there is complete financial propriety and financial rules are followed.

d. His actions could annoy his superiors. He should make a detailed report in writing and send it to his superiors. Once things have been brought on paper no senior officer would be able to disagree with him. They may try to get him transferred but one should not worry about this. Dishonest officers do not have the moral courage to harm an honest civil servant.

Case 5 (Question 14)

In our country, the migration of rural people to towns and cities is increasing drastically. This is causing serious problems both in the rural as well as in the urban areas. In fact, things are becoming really unmanageable. Can you analyse this problem in detail and indicate not only the socio-economic but also the emotional and attitudinal factors responsible for this problem? Also, distinctly bring out why—

1. Educated rural youth are trying to shift to urban areas;
2. Landless poor people are migrating to urban slums;
3. Even some farmers are selling off their land and trying to settle in urban areas taking up petty jobs.
4. What feasible steps can you suggest which will be effective in controlling this serious problem of our country?

Answer

This question relates to the important problem of rural people migrating to towns and cities causing serious problems in both rural and urban areas.

There are limited opportunities for employments in rural areas for educated youth and they want to migrate to urban areas to get better jobs. They do not want to work on their farms as they feel that they will not be able to earn as much as they would in a job in the city. Agriculture has also become unremunerative and very little industrialization is taking place in rural areas.

Landless poor people also migrate to urban slums as they get higher wages working in the construction industry and the factories in urban areas. It is for the same reason that farmers sell off their land and take up small jobs in urban areas. In fact with the growth of population the average size of the land holding in the villages has become very small and agriculture is slowly becoming unviable. The farmers are also not able to get a fair price for their produce.

Migration to urban areas is a natural phenomenon and has happened in every country. However, the problem is that they are not getting very high wages in urban areas and forced to live in an unhealthy environment in slums. The situation needs urgent policy reforms in the following areas.

1. System to see that farmer gets right price for his produce and that his income steadily increases.
2. Make inputs and credit available to the farmer at subsidized rates.
3. Have a comprehensive crop insurance policy to take care of natural calamities.
4. Combine agriculture with income earning activities of animal husbandry or fisheries.
5. Create hubs of agro-industries in the rural areas and in general encourage industrialization in rural areas.
6. The physical infrastructure in rural areas needs to be improved. Better roads, power, schools and hospitals have to be provided to give the people living in the villages a good quality of life.

CASE STUDY: UPSC GENERAL STUDIES PAPER—2015

Case 1 (Question 9)

A private company is known for its efficiency, transparency and employee welfare. The company though owned by a private individual has a cooperative character where employees feel a sense of ownership. The company employs nearly 700 personnel and they have voluntarily decided not to form union.

One day suddenly in the morning, about 40 men belonging to a political party gate-crashed into the factory demanding jobs in the factory. They threatened the management and employees, and also used foul language. The employees feel demoralized. It was clear that those people who gate- crashed wanted to be on the payroll of the company as well as continue as the volunteers/members of the party.

The company maintains high standards in integrity and does not extend favours to civil administration that also includes law enforcement agency. Such incident occur in public sector also.

(a) Assume you are the CEO of the company. What would you do to diffuse the volatile situation on the date of gate-crashing with the violent mob sitting inside the company premises?

(b) What can be the long term solution to the issue discussed in the case?
(c) Every solution/action that you suggest will have a negative and a positive impact on you as (CEO), the employees and the performance of the employees. Analyse the consequences of each of your suggested actions.

Answer

This is a difficult situation for the CEO. 40 men belonging to a political party have gate-crashed in to the factory threatening management and employees. The company has a culture where there is an excellent relationship between management and employees because of which employees are not unionized. The company also maintains high standards of integrity and does not give favors to political parties and government officers. The employees have total faith in the management and this incident has demoralized them. The CEO has to ensure their security. He should use the security force of the company to protect the workers and the property. However, it appears that the security forces are not able to control the intruders. They have illegally entered the factory and are threatening violence. The CEO should immediately lodge a complaint with the police. He should talk to the higher officers like District Magistrate (DM) and Superintendent of police (SP) and request for immediate action to protect life and property.

Along with senior officers the CEO should call leaders of the mob and hold discussion with them. They should reason with them that this kind of behaviour is not acceptable. They should be told that as per company rules one cannot be on the payroll of the company and also be a member of a political party. They should also be told that there is a process of giving a job which will have to be followed. The company cannot employ people just like this. It is possible that they may agree otherwise police will have to evict them.

The long term solution would be to approach senior officers, ministers even the Chief Minister of the State. It should be put forward that the factory will not be able to function in this manner and the management will have no option but to close down the factory and go to another state. This will lead to unemployment in this state. No Government would allow this to happen and action would be taken by them. It is necessary to approach the minister and Chief Minister because people indulging in this kind of behaviour would most likely be from the ruling party and would have to be politically controlled as sometimes the district administration is also reluctant to act against the ruling party workers. This will raise the morale of the employees and they will perform better as they will be confident that the management is taking all steps to protect their life and property and maintaining total integrity in recruitment of employees.

Successful handling of situation will raise the image of the CEO in his company and help his future career. However, the CEO, even though the company does not extend favors to administration, must develop good social relations with DM and SP so that he keeps getting support in the future also.

Case 2 (Question 10)

You are the Sarpanch of a Panchayat. There is a primary school run by the government in your area. Midday meals are provided to children attending the school. The headmaster has now appointed a new cook in the school to prepare the meals. However, when it is found that cook is from Dalit community, almost half of the children belonging to higher castes are not allowed to take meals by their parents. Consequently the attendance in the schools falls sharply. This could result in the possibility of discontinuation of midday meal scheme, thereafter of teaching staff and subsequent closing down the school.

(a) Discuss some feasible strategies to overcome the conflict and to create right ambiance.

(b) What should be the responsibilities of different social segments and agencies to create positive social ambiance for accepting such changes?

Answer

This is a case study related to the evils of the caste system in India. The parents of the students are not allowing them to take mid day meal cooked by a new cook from Dalit community. This state of affairs is totally not acceptable. The Sarpanch should use his authority to call a meeting of the Panchayat and convince all parents that they should not object to the new cook. It would be better if he takes the help of government officers also. Together they should convince the people that this amounts to untouchability which is a crime in India and such action will lower the image of the village in the country and if mid day meal is discontinued or school closes down then the students of this village will suffer. This is a serious issue and it would be advisable to inform the district collector, chief development officer and superintendent of Police about this. High level of intervention will be able to get a positive response from the people.

The Sarpanch along with the members of panchayat and enlightened members of upper caste should continue to educate others that this kind of caste discrimination is not correct. The Government officers also have to play a positive role in this. The local MLA and MP and other opinion leaders can also be involved.

Case 3 (Question 11)

One of the scientists working in the R&D laboratory of a major pharmaceutical company discovers that one of the company's bestselling veterinary drugs has the potential to cure a currently incurable liver disease which is prevalent in tribal areas. However, developing a variant of the drug suitable for human being entailed a lot of research and development having a huge expenditure to the extent of Rs. 50 crores. It was unlikely that company would recover the cost as the disease was rampant only in poverty stricken areas having very little market otherwise.

If you were the CEO, then—

(a) Identify the various actions that you could take; and

(b) Evaluate the pros and cons of each of your actions.

Answer

One alternative action for CEO is to drop the project as it is financially not viable. The aim of companies is to maximize profit and development of this drug would not lead to recovery of costs. However, this is not an ethical way of looking at things.

Companies also have a responsibility towards society. This drug has the potential of curing a liver disease which is rampant in poor people of the area. For the benefit of the society the research and manufacturing of this drug is essential. Profitable companies are expected to spend two percent of their average net profit on corporate social responsibility. The CEO can take this project under corporate social responsibility.

It is possible that the huge expenditure of 50 crore is not possible under the corporate social responsibility. The best course of action would be take up the matter with the government whose primary duty it is to look after the health of the people specially in tribal areas. The government can certainly support the research cost of the company and also come up with a policy of subsidizing the production costs. Many such projects are taken up in public private partnership (PPP) mode. It is the responsibility of the government and the moral duty of the company to produce a drug which can cure an incurable disease.

Case 4 (Question 12)

There is a disaster prone state having frequent landslides, forest fires, cloudbursts, flash floods and earthquakes, etc. Some of these are seasonal and often unpredictable. The magnitude of the disaster is always unanticipated. During one of the seasons a cloudburst caused devastating floods and landslides leading to high casualties. There was major damage to infrastructure like roads, bridges and power generating units. This led to more than 100,000 pilgrims, tourist and other locals trapped across different routes and locations. The people trapped in your area of responsibility includes senior citizens, patients in hospitals, women and children, hikers, tourists, ruling party's, regional president along with his family, additional chief secretary of the neighbouring state and prisoners in jail.

As a civil services officer of the state, what would be the order in which you would rescue these people and why? Give justifications.

Answer

A devastating cloudburst has taken place leading to high casualties. Major infrastructure like roads and bridges have been damaged. One hundred thousand pilgrims are trapped and have to be evacuated. It is not possible to move everybody at the same time. In such matters, the civil servant has to prioritize. He should first shift those people who are most vulnerable and facing the greatest risk.

He should first rescue the patients in hospitals as they require immediate medical attention otherwise many lives could be lost.

Next should be the women and children. They belong to the vulnerable section and any delay in moving them could cause injury or even loss of life.

After this he should evacuate the senior citizens because aged people will not be able to withstand the hardships and could even lose their lives. Senior citizens are normally weak and suffering from other diseases.

Next should be the tourists as they would need food and medicines and most of them would not be equipped to handle the situation.

After this he should evacuate the ruling party's regional president along with his family. The justification for this is that he is accompanied by his family which would need attention.

After this the additional chief secretary of the neighbouring state should be rescued. He is a senior officer of another state and therefore needs to be rescued. Also he would be of an advanced age.

I would then evacuate the prisoners in the jail. They would be of different age groups and may not be physically very strong.

Finally the hikers should be evacuated as they would be young, physically strong, able to adjust to the situation and having the capacity to survive longer in this difficult situation.

It is possible that there are women and children in the family of the ruling party's president. They should be evacuated along with other women and children. In this situation it may even be advisable to rescue the additional chief secretary as he belongs to a neighboring state before the regional party president and adult male member of his family. The party president can help the administration in organizing the rescue also.

Case 5 (Question 13)

You are heading a district administration in a particular department. Your senior officer calls you from the State Headquarters and tells you that a plot in Rampur village is to have a building constructed on it for a school. A visit is scheduled during which he will visit the site along with the chief engineer and the senior architect. He wants you to check out all the papers relating to it and ensure that the visit is properly arranged. You examine the file which relates to the period before you joined the department. The land was acquired for the local panchayat at a nominal cost and the papers showed that clearance certificates are available for the two of the three authorities who have to certify the site's suitability. There is no certification by the architect available on file. You decide to visit Rampur to ensure that all is in the order as stated on file. When you visit Rampur, you find that the plot under reference is a part of Thakurgarh fort and that the walls, ramparts, etc., are running across it. The fort is well away from the main village, therefore, a school here will be a serious inconvenience for the children. However, the area near the village has potential to expand into a larger residential area. The development charges on the existing plot, at the fort, will be very high and question of heritage site has not been addressed. Moreover, the Sarpanch, at the time of acquisition of the land, was a relative of your predecessor. The whole transaction appears to have been done with some vested interest.

(a) List the likely vested interest of the concerned parties.

(b) Some of the options for action available to you are listed below. Discuss the merits and demerits of each of the options:

   (i) You can await the visit of the superior officer and let him take a decision.

   (ii) You can seek his advice in writing or on phone.

   (iii) You can consult your predecessor/colleagues, etc, and then decide what to do.

   (iv) You can find out if any alternate plot can be got in exchange and then send a comprehensive written report.

Can you suggest any other option with proper justifications?

Answer

(A) There are many parties with vested interest in this case.

   1. The Sarpanch at the time of acquisition of land definitely wants the school to be located at the proposed site and he has a monetary interest.
   2. The predecessor of the current officer also has a vested interest. Actually a handsome compensation is likely for the land acquired for the school and the officer and the Sarpanch are likely to gain monetarily from this.
   3. Further locating the school there would enhance the potential value to a builder constructing a residential colony. It is likely that the builder is in collusion with the Sarpanch and the officer.

(B) It is clear that the location of the school is not suitable. It is far away from the main village whereas a school should be near the habitation to enable children to attend without inconvenience. Further, it is part of Thakurgarh Fort which means that it is being located in a heritage area which is not correct as heritage sites have to be protected. Further there are walls, ramparts running across the land making it totally unsuitable for a school. Moreover, there is no certification by an architect available on the file.

   (i) The first alternative is not acceptable. After knowing the facts the officer cannot wait for the decision of his superior officer.

(ii) This alternative is also is not acceptable. He is aware of the facts and there is no need of advice in writing or on phone.
(iii) There is no need to consult the predecessor or any colleague. Particularly as the predecessor clearly has a vested interest in the matter.
(iv) This alternative has got merit. It is his responsibility to see that a school comes up in the area to meet the needs of the children. Also, the current proposed land is totally unsuitable. A public servant has to meet multiple objectives and he has to not only indicate a problem but come up with a solution. Thus he should select an alternate plot for the school and move for necessary clearances and also send comprehensive written reports to his superiors clearly rejecting the current land proposed for the school giving his reasons and give his fresh proposal.

One other option is to send a detailed report rejecting the current land proposal and actually show it to the team which is coming for a visit. Various alternatives can be shown to the team and a new piece of land selected through mutual consultation.

Case 6 (Question 14)

You are recently posted as District Development Officer of a district. Shortly thereafter you found that there is considerable tension in the rural areas of your district on the issue of sending girls to schools.

The elders of the village feel that many problems have come up because girls are being educated and they are stepping out of the safe environment of the household. They are of the view that the girls should be quickly married off with minimum education. The girls are also competing for jobs after education, which have traditionally remained in boys' exclusive domain, adding to unemployment amongst male population.

The younger generation feels that in the present era, girls should have equal opportunities for education and employment, and other means of livelihood. The entire locality is divided between sexes in both generations. You come to know that in Panchayat or in other local bodies or even in busy crosswords, the issue is being acrimoniously debated.

One day you are informed that an unpleasant incident has taken place. Some girls were molested, when they were *en route* to schools. The incident led to clashes between several groups and a law and order problem has arisen. The elders, after heated discussion, have taken a joint decision not to allow girls to go to school and to socially boycott all such families, which do not follow their dictate. (250 words) (25 Marks)

(a) What steps would you take to ensure girls' safety without disrupting their education?

(b) How would you manage and mould patriarchist attitude of the village elders to ensure harmony in the inter-generational relations?

Answer

This is a serious case of differences in attitudes and values system of two generations. The matter relates to education of girls.

A. Law and order problem has to be attended on priority. The District Development Officer must immediately brief the District Magistrate and Superintendent of Police and see that strict action is taken against those involved in molestation of girls and in violent clashes. The action should be strict enough to see that this kind of situation does not recur. The safety of the girls can be ensured by police patrolling on the route to the school. Police should also take preventive action against all anti-social elements. Girls may be advised to move in groups. Sensible people from the village can be used as volunteers to escort the girls to the school.

B. The officer should hold meetings at the village level with all the groups involved. He should take the help of the District Magistrate also. The village people should be convinced about the advantages of sending girls to school. The older generation which is opposing education of girls has some misapprehensions which need to be removed by giving them examples of other villages and the benefit of schooling of girls to their families and village. It should also be made clear that this is part of government policy. Within the older generation also there would be some people in favour of education of girls. They can be used as opinion leaders to convince others. In such situations the local MLA or MP can also be very effective as they have a good rapport with the people.

CASE STUDY: UPSC GENERAL STUDIES PAPER-4 – 2016

Case 1 (Question 9)

A fresh engineering graduate gets a job in a prestigious chemical industry. She likes the work. The salary is also good. However, after a few months she accidentally discovers that a highly toxic waste is being secretly discharged into a river nearby. This is causing health problems to the villagers downstream who depend on the river for their water needs. She is perturbed and mentions her concern to her colleagues who have been with the company for longer periods. They advise her to keep quite as anyone who mentions the topic is summarily dismissed. She cannot risk losing her job as she is the sole bread-winner for her family and has to support her ailing parents and siblings. At first, she thinks that if her seniors are keeping quiet, why she should stick out her neck. But her conscience pricks her to do something to save the river and the people who depend upon it. At heart she feels that the advice of silence given by her friends is not correct though she cannot give reasons for it. She thinks you are a wise person and seeks your advice.

(a) What arguments can you advance to show her that keeping quiet is not morally right?

(b) What course of action would you advise her to adopt and why?

Answer

A. It is clear that whatever the personal situation the engineering graduate should not keep quiet about toxic waste being dumped into the river by the chemical industries. Firstly, it is against the environmental laws relating to water pollution act. No industry is allowed to discharge toxic effluents into rivers and they have to install an effluent treatment plant. Having knowledge of an illegal act and not doing anything about it means that you are also part of the illegality being committed.

Secondly this waste would destroy the fish and the other aquatic animals and plants which is also a criminal act and adversely impacts the bio-diversity of the region.

The people of the village use this water for drinking and other needs. This could lead to serious diseases in the people and even cause shortening of their lives.

It is also morally incorrect to ignore one's conscience and allow an unethical practice to continue. On the basis of all the above reason she should not listen to the advice of her colleagues and raise the issue.

B. It seems the company dismisses anybody who raises the issue. The girl is getting a good salary and is the sole bread-winner of the family and has to support her siblings. She should raise the matter in writing. It is not easy for the organization to ignore issues put up in writing. Further there is now a policy of the government and applicable to corporations to have a whistleblower protection policy. She should raise the issue as a whistleblower and the company cannot summarily dismiss her. A clever way of doing it would be to quietly brief the media. The moment it becomes a media story then the government authorities would immediately take action and the company will also have to take corrective measures or face closure. Sometimes such steps have to be taken for a larger benefit to society. Further she should start looking around for alternative jobs and move as soon as she gets one because this company does not seem to be following ethical standards and it is wise not to continue working for them for a long time.

Case 2 (Question 10)

Land needed for mining, dams and other large-scale projects is acquired mostly from *adivasis,* hill dwellers and rural communities. The displaced persons are paid monetary compensation as per the legal provisions. However, the payment is often tardy. In any case, it cannot sustain the displaced families for long. These people do not possess marketable skills to engage in some other occupation; they end up as low paid migrant labourers. Moreover, their traditional ways of community living are destroyed. Thus, the benefits of development go to industries, industrialists and urban communities whereas the costs are passed on to these poor helpless people. This unjust distribution of costs and benefits is unethical.

Suppose you have been entrusted with the task of drafting a better compensation-cum-rehabilitation policy for such displaced persons, how would you approach the problem and what would be the main elements of your suggested policy?

Answer

This case study relates to a typical ethical dilemma in administration. Constructing a dam or large scale projects leads to development of the state and the people. However, to get land for the project the traditional communities like *adivasis* are displaced causing a low of hardship to them. The compensation provided is often not sufficient and the poor people end up as low paid migrant laborers. The rich gain and the poor lose. This is unethical.

One has to acquire land for a major infrastructure project. The first step to be taken is that a complete rehabilitation cum compensation plan should be prepared for which a policy is required. This plan should have the following provisions—

1. Generous, financial compensation should be awarded. The new land acquisition policy accounts for this.
2. A proper new habitation should be chosen for relocation which meets the social and economic needs of the people.
3. The new settlement should be properly planned providing for broad roads, drains, water supply, power supply and other basic amenities.
4. There should be a provision for schools and hospitals to provide service to the displaced community.
5. At least one member of the family should be given a job in the project.
6. Skill development training should be provided to the youth so that they can get gainful employment.
7. The benefits of various government schemes should be extended to them. For example, the houses may be constructed under the government scheme for housing.
8. Care should be taken that there is no disturbance to the culture and social mores of the people.

Case 3 (Question 11)

Suppose you are an officer in-charge of implementing a social service scheme to provide support to old and destitute women. An old and illiterate woman comes to you to avail the benefits of the scheme. However, she has no documents to show that she fulfils the eligibility criteria. But after meeting her and listening to her you feel that she certainly needs support. Your enquiries also show that she is really destitute and living in a pitiable condition. You are in a dilemma as to what to do. Putting her under the scheme without necessary documents would clearly be violation of rules. But denying her the support would be cruel and inhuman.

(a) Can you think of a rational way to resolve this dilemma?

(b) Give your reasons for it.

Answer

A. The scheme is to provide support to old and destitute women. The woman who comes to you is old and illiterate but has no documents to prove her eligibility for the scheme. Your enquiries have revealed that she is deserving but you cannot violate rules. This is an ethical dilemma. A public servant must work as per rules but also have compassion for the poor and destitute. In this case it would be advisable for you to make a special case for this woman and include her in the list of beneficiaries. You can take a report about her income status from the Tahsildar and also conduct on the spot enquiry and make a record of it. Statements of people living nearby can be taken as evidence. On this basis you can give the benefit to this woman and also inform your superiors about the action taken by you.

B. The justification for the above action is that the human being is more important than a mere mindless application of rules. It is clear that the woman is eligible but only that she does not have the required documents. The officer should take initiative and create the documents so that the outcome of the scheme is achieved. In administration the procedures are important but it is more important that you get the right results and outcomes. This is the essence of ethical public service delivery. In addition you can write to the concerned department to amend the scheme for the future to allow for inclusion of deserving cases that do not have the required documents and ask for a procedure to be prescribed for this.

Case 4 (Question 12)

You are a young, aspiring and sincere employee in a government office working as an assistant to the director of your department. Since you have joined recently, you need to learn and progress. Luckily your superior is very kind and ready to train you for your job. He is a very intelligent and well informed person having knowledge of various departments. In short, you respect your boss and are looking forward to learn a lot from him.

Since you have a good tuning with the boss, he started depending on you. One day due to ill-health he invited you at his place for finishing some urgent work.

You reached his house and before you could ring the bell you heard shouting noises. You waited for a while. After entering the house the boss greeted you and explained the work. But you were constantly disturbed by the crying of a woman. At last, you inquired with the boss but his answer did not satisfy you.

Next day, you were compelled to inquire further in the office and found out that his behaviour is very bad at home with his wife. He also beats up his wife.

His wife is not well-educated and is a simple woman in comparison to her husband. You see that though your boss is a nice person in the office, he is engaged in domestic violence at home.

In such a situation, you are left with the following options. Analyse each option with its consequences.

(a) Just ignore thinking about it because it is their personal matter.
(b) Report the case to the appropriate authority.
(c) Your own innovative approach towards the situation

Answer

This is a peculiar case of an ethical dilemma. The director of the department is very nice to his assistant, he trains him and depends upon him and he is very good at his work also. The assistant also respects him a lot. However, it comes to his knowledge that the director is engaged in domestic violence at home which is a crime as well as an inhuman and immoral act.

A. He could think of ignoring the matter as it is a personal issue and has nothing to do with the professional aspect of the work of the director. His relationship with his boss is purely official and the boss has been treating him very well also. Further he has not seen his boss indulging in domestic violence. He has only heard about it when he went to the house of his boss he heard shouting noises and the sound of a woman crying. He has no definite information about what the real issue is. Thus, he could think about ignoring the matter but here the personal ethics and morals of a person come into play. A woman is evidently being abused by her husband. This could lead to more violence or even suicide if not checked. The assistant has to answer to his conscience also. So he cannot ignore the issue and think of an innovative way to handle the situation.
B. Reporting the case to the police or commission for women or even to the higher-ups in the company would be a direct way

of handling the situation. However, this would lead to enmity with the director and it is also possible that no evidence is found for domestic violence. Even the wife may not like to speak before the authorities about her domestic matter. In such a situation nothing would be done and the assistant would also lose his job.

C. The director likes the assistant and depends upon him also. The assistant should meet his director alone and tell him that there is general talk in the office that the relations between him and his wife are not good and they even say that he indulges in domestic violence. He should say this very politely and say that he wants nothing to effect the reputation of his boss. He should gently suggest that the matter can come to the knowledge of the superiors and also get taken up by media. There is a lot of sensitivity about gender issues in society today and if the matter becomes public it would harm the reputation and career of the director. You may suggest that he takes steps to rectify the issue. It is possible that the director will mend his ways after this. Most probably the director would listen to him and reform himself.

Case 5 (Question 13)

ABC Ltd. is a large transnational company having diversified business activities with a huge shareholder base. The company is continuously expanding and generating employment. The company, in its expansion and diversification programme, decides to establish a new plant at Vikaspuri, an area which is underdeveloped. The new plant is designed to use energy efficient technology that will help the company to save production cost by 20%. The company's decision goes well with the Government policy of attracting investment to develop such underdeveloped regions. The Government has also announced tax holiday for five years for the companies that invest in underdeveloped areas. However, the new plant may bring chaos for the inhabitants of Vikaspuri region, which is otherwise tranquil. The new plant may result in increased cost of living, aliens migrating to the region, disturbing the social and economic order. The company sensing the possible protest tried to educate the people of Vikaspuri region and public in general that how its Corporate Social Responsibility (CSR) policy would help overcome the likely difficulties of the residents of Vikaspuri region. In spite of this the protests begin and some of the residents decided to approach the judiciary as their plea before the Government did not yield any result.

(a) Identify the issues involved in the case.

(b) What can be suggested to satisfy the company's goal and to address the residents' concerns?

Answer

A. This is a classic case of conflict between development and its impact on the inhabitants of that area. The issues involved in this case are—

1. Underdeveloped regions have to be developed and this is the government policy also. The government is giving attractive incentives to the csompanies to invest in backward areas. It is the duty of a welfare state to develop such areas.
2. The company also wants to expand and generate employment and that is why they are planning a set up a new plant at Vikaspuri. They are also using energy efficient technology and their action would lead to the development of the area.
3. The company is also prepared to spend its corporate social responsibility funds to protect the interests of the inhabitants of that area. The intentions of the company are good and they do not want to exploit the people.
4. The inhabitants are unhappy as they feel that this plant would lead to an increase in cost of living, aliens migrating to the region and disturbances to the social and economic order.
5. The inhabitants are not satisfied with the response of the government and want to approach the judiciary.

B. The best method of handling such situation is by holding direct talks with the concerned people. There would be some opinion leaders whom the company can engage in discussion. It would also be advisable if officers of the government also join the talks. First they should try and understand the problems of the people and then think of solutions and satisfy the people with the remedies offered. They should explain to the people how development of the area would lead to more employment and a higher quality of life for them. The government should offer a relief package giving roads, schools, hospitals to the area under various government schemes. The company should also draw a corporate, social responsibility plan in consultation with the people. Specific measures can be suggested to provide basic necessities at an affordable cost. Also it can be discussed how the social and economic order is not disturbed even though there would definitely be a change but overall the people would gain from the project. They can also assure that a regular dialogue will be kept with the people to keep resolving their grievances. Once the people feel that this project would give them a better quality of life they would accept.

Case 6 (Question 14)

Saraswati was a successful IT professional in USA. Moved by the patriotic sense of doing something for the country she returned to India. Together with some other like-minded friends, she formed an NGO to build a school for a poor rural community.

The objective of the school was to provide the best quality modern education at a nominal cost. She soon discovered that she has to seek permission from a number of government agencies. The rules and procedures were quite confusing and cumbersome. What frustrated her most was the delays, callous attitude of officials and constant demand for bribes. Her experience and the experience of many others like her have deterred people from taking up social service projects.

A measure of government control over voluntary social work is necessary. But it should not be exercised in a coercive or corrupt manner. What measures can you suggest to ensure that due control is exercised but well meaning, honest NGO efforts are not thwarted?

Answer

Saraswati is an idealist IT professional who out of patriotism leaves her job in USA, comes to India and starts an NGO to build a school for the poor. She wants to provide best quality education at a nominal cost. However, the government system is such that there are a lot of permissions and approvals to be taken for setting up a private school. The system is cumbersome. Moreover, there is a negative perception about NGOs in government and so they do not easily grant approvals. The worst part is that there is an abnormal delay and demand for bribes at each stage.

The government should encourage individuals, NGOs and others to take up social service projects in the interest of the development of the community. However, it is true that government must exercise control also so that a uniform standard of work is done and there is no siphoning of funds by NGOs and the work is done as per norms.

The government must have rules and procedures for approving social projects like schools by NGOs. However, firstly the rules should be reviewed to ensure that no unnecessary rule or procedure is there. Process engineering is required. Then they should fix time limits for each approval and also indicate the name of the officer responsible for this. Ideally the department should have a Citizen's Charter where all details would be given and accountability indicated. To prevent corruption information technology should be used. There should be no need for Sarswati to go from one office to another for clearances. She should be able to apply for all clearances online and also be able to track status of each clearance online. This should eliminate the problem of bribes being asked at each level. The government should have a system where a social entrepreneur can make a complaint against delays, harassment or corruption. They should be monitored at the top level and strict action should be taken against the delinquent officers. The system should also require total transparency from the NGO who should give all details about itself and its accounts on its website. In this way the honest and genuine NGO's would be encouraged to invest in social projects leading to the development of the poor.

CASE STUDY: UPSC GENERAL STUDIES-4 PAPERS – 2017

Case 1 (Question 9)

You are an honest and responsible civil servant. You often observe the following:

(a) There is a general perception that adhering to ethical conduct one may face difficulties to oneself and cause problems for the family, whereas unfair practices may help to reach the career goals.

(b) When the number of people adopting unfair means is large, a small minority having a penchant towards ethical means makes no difference.

(c) Sticking to ethical means is detrimental to the larger developmental goals.

(d) While one may not involve oneself in large unethical practices, but giving and accepting small gifts makes the system more efficient.

Examine the above statements with their merits and demerits.

Answer

(a) It is true that there is a general perception that ethical conduct does not pay and those who indulge in unfair practices often reach the top. This is sometimes true but not always. Ethical conduct always helps an officer in the long run. You may have to suffer frequent transfers or get insignificant postings and sometimes even face enquiries. If you take action against corruption then often the life and security of your family is in danger. Even then one must realise that those who follow unfair practices can get caught and face criminal action which would ruin their career. In any case those who are unethical have a poor reputation which does not allow them to reach the top of their career. Honest people face difficulties but ultimately succeed in life and career.

(b) Even a small drop makes a difference. Even if honest and responsible civil servants are in a minority they can change the system and make the working of government ethical, transparent and accountable. They earn the respect of people which the unethical officers are never able to do.

(c) This is absolutely incorrect. In fact corruption or unethical practices mean that public money is not utilized properly leading to poor public service delivery and slowing down the process of growth. Studies have shown that just control of corruption can significantly increase the GDP of a country.

(d) There is no such thing as a small or large unethical practice. A theft of a pencil is as much a criminal act as stealing gold jewelry. The moment an officer starts compromising himself by taking small gifts he is on the road to becoming corrupt and very soon will graduate to larger unethical practices. It is a fallacy to think that accepting small gifts can make the system more efficient. In fact any compromise of ethics leads to inefficiency in the system.

Case 2 (Question 10)

You are aspiring to become an IAS officer and you have cleared various stages and now you have been selected for the personal interview. On the day of the interview, on the way to the venue you saw an accident where a mother and child who happen to be your relatives were badly injured. They needed immediate help.

What would you have done in such a situation? Justify your action.

Answer

It is your dream to become an IAS officer and you have been selected for personal interview. However, as you are going for your interview you witness an accident where a mother and child who are your relatives are badly injured and need immediate help. It is possible that if you stop to help then you may be late for your interview which can put an end to your dream of becoming an IAS officer. However, it is important to be a good human being even if it means sacrificing something. A mother and child are hurt badly. You have to act to save their lives and give them urgent medical attention. It does not matter whether they are your relatives or not.

The first thing to do would be to inform the police and call for an ambulance by using the call center numbers. If you are in a car you can use your car to take the injured to the nearest hospital. Alternatively you can stop some vehicle on the road and request him to take the injured to the nearest hospital and you should accompany them. If they are your relatives then you should immediately call up other relatives and ask them to reach the hospital. Even otherwise you can take the numbers of the close relatives of the injured from them and inform them.

You can accompany the injured to the emergency wing of a hospital. After they start getting medical attention and some of their relatives reach the spot you can excuse yourself and rush to the venue of the IAS interview. It may be that you reach on time. You can then have a glass of water, relax and mentally prepare for the interview. In case you have missed your turn you should immediately meet the senior officers available and explain the reasons for the delay. You can give it in writing also. The senior officer shall certainly consider your case and you will be called for interview.

It is always advisable to reach the interview venue well in advance of the appointed time. Thus it is very much possible for you to send the injured to the hospital, inform their relatives and reach the interview venue on time.

Case 3 (Question 11)

You are the head of the Human Resources department of an organisation. One day one of the workers died on duty. His family was demanding compensation. However, the company denied compensation because it was revealed in investigation that he was drunk at the time of the accident. The workers of the company went to strike demanding compensation for the family of the deceased. The Chairman of the management board has asked for your recommendation.

What recommendation would you provide the management?

Discuss the merits and demerits of each of the recommendations.

Answer

The worker has died on duty. However, it has come to knowledge that he was drunk at the time of the accident. The workers are threatening to go on strike demanding compensation which the company has denied due to the worker being drunk on duty.

The chairman has asked for your recommendation as head of human resources department of the organization. One view that can be taken is that since the worker was drunk at the time of the accident and this is against the rules he should be denied compensation. But this is a very narrow and inhuman view of the situation. It is also not proven that the accident took place because of the worker being drunk. He has lost his life and it is the moral duty of the organization to compensate him. In the event that company decides not to pay compensation then this would lead to lowering the morale of the workers and employees of the organization. This would not be in the interest of the company as it would affect the performance and productivity. Also workers will go on strike leading to loss of production and adversely affect industrial relations in the company.

You should recommend that compensation must be given. It is not established that accident took place because of his being drunk. Also being drunk on duty is an act of indiscipline but now that he is dead it does not matter. For future the company should take steps that no drunk person is allowed to enter the factory. The reasons for the accident should be evaluated and preventive measures taken so that there is no recurrence of such an incident in the future. Payment of compensation would also mean that workers do not go on strike and good relations will be maintained between workers and management and there will be no loss of production due to a strike. Moreover, the family of the employee would get relief and not languish in poverty. The morale of the workers would also be boosted leading to better performance in future.

Case 4 (Question 12)

You are the manager of a spare parts company A and you have to negotiate a deal with the manager of a large manufacturing company B. The deal is highly competitive and sealing the deal is critical for your company. The deal is being worked out over a dinner. After dinner the manager of the manufacturing company B offered to drop you to the hotel in his car. On the way to hotel he happens to hit motorcycle injuring the motorcyclist badly. You know the manager was driving fast and thus lost control. The law enforcement officer comes to investigate the issue and you are the sole eyewitness to it. Knowing the strict laws pertaining to road accidents you are aware that your honest account of the incident would lead to the prosecution of the manager and as a consequence the deal is likely to be jeopardized, which is of immense importance to your company.

What are the dilemmas you face? What will be your response to the situation?

Answer

This case brings out the conflict between professional gain and private morality. You as a manager of a spare parts company are very keen to close a deal with a large manufacturing company as this would be crucial for your existence and profitability. After dinner the manager of company B is dropping you to your hotel in his car when because of rash driving he hits and badly injures a motorcyclist. You are the sole eye witness and the law enforcement officer has come to you to investigate.

You are aware that the accident has taken place due to the rash driving of manager of company B. If you tell the truth the police will take action to prosecute the concerned manager. This would certainly put an end to your chances of getting orders from company B. This would affect the profitability of your company adversely and the management of the company could be unhappy with you and even dispense with your services. So, by telling the truth you stand to lose a lot. However, telling lies to a law enforcement officer is itself a criminal act and you yourself may be prosecuted against. It is also ethically and morally wrong to tell a lie considering a motorcyclist has been injured badly. Thus, on balance, you cannot choose the option of telling a lie to the police.

You have to tell the truth which would certainly lead to prosecution of the manager of company B. You have to now handle the situation in a manner that minimum damage is done to your company and career. You should brief your seniors in the company about the incident and your stand which is legally and morally correct. It is very possible that your seniors would understand and not take action against you. Your company's senior managers should have a meeting with the senior management of company B and explain the situation to them. It is possible that company B would go ahead with the deal with your company.

Case 5 (Question 13)

A building permitted for three floors, while being extended illegally for six floors by a builder, collapses. As a consequence, a number of innocent laborers including women and children died. These laborers are migrants of different places. The government immediately announced cash relief to the aggrieved families and arrested the builder.

Give reasons for such incidents taking place across the country. Suggest measures to prevent their occurrence.

Answer

In this case a builder has illegally extended a building he is constructing from three floors to six floors as a result of which it collapses and a number of innocent labourers including women and children have died. These labourers are mostly migrants. The government has announced cash compensation to the aggrieved families and arrested the builder. These are right actions taken by the government but it should also take action against its officers responsible for monitoring construction of buildings as per approved maps.

Such incidents often take place. The main reason is the greed of the builders who want to commit illegal acts to make more money. Thus the government has to take all possible action as per law to make sure that such incidents do not happen.

Secondly the main reason is that government officers who are responsible for ensuring that constructions are taking place as per approved maps and building rules and regulations do not do their duty properly. In fact there is large scale corruption in this. The officers join hands with unethical builders and take bribes and allow such illegal constructions. The government can prevent this by holding officers accountable and in such serious cases as in the case study criminal action should be taken against the officers. This would act as a deterrent to the others.

The map when it is submitted for approval is certified by an architect who is supposed to supervise the construction as per norms and approvals given. He is accountable for the kind of violation that is taken place in this case. The government should pass orders clearly stating that if such a case comes to knowledge the architect would also be prosecuted against and also be black listed for the future. The builder should also be black-listed for the future. If such strong action is taken in some cases then it will create a deterrent environment which will prevent such incidents in the future.

Women and children have died. Children should never have been employed. The builder has violated labor laws. Action needs to be taken against officers of labor department and the builder. The working conditions for women are also unsafe. The concerned authority responsible for safety of workers should be held accountable. It is advisable for the government make strict laws about working conditions to be ensured in such projects.

The government should have a system of registering contractors who would give an undertaking that all possible precautions would be taken. Lastly the government should create a lot of public awareness about such issues so that the people themselves become vigilant.

Case 6 (Question 14)

You are a Public Information Officer (PIO) in a government department. You are aware that the RTI Act, 2005 envisages transparency and accountability in administration. The act has functioned as a check on the supposedly arbitrarily administrative behaviour and actions. However, as a PIO you have observed that there are citizens who filed RTI applications not for themselves but on behalf of such stakeholders who purportedly want to have access to information to further their own interests. At the same time there are those RTI activists who routinely file RTI applications and attempt to extort money from the decision-makers. This type of RTI activism has affected the functioning of the administration adversely and also possibly jeopardizes the genuineness of the applications which are essentially aimed at getting justice.

What measures would you suggest to separate genuine and non-genuine applications? Give merits and demerits of your suggestions.

Answer

The RTI Act is a great administrative innovation to ensure transparency and accountability in governance. However, some citizens have made it a business to act on behalf of others and get information for their own interests. Everywhere you find that RTI activists have mushroomed who are misusing this act to extract money from officers. This has given a bad name to the RTI act and also adversely affects the functioning of the administration. The PIO in this case study is in a similar situation.

It is the duty of the PIO as per RTI Act to give information asked for if it is permissible as per the Act. However, if he feels that the information being asked for is due to ulterior reasons he can reject it recording reasons. However, there are provisions for appeal against the orders of the PIO if he refuses information. Actually it is the duty of the Information Commissioners and Chief Information Commissioner to see that such kind of misuse of information does not take place. They should not allow information to be given in such situations. It is not very difficult for them to assess the genuineness of the applications.

It is also necessary to see whether the person asking for information has any stake in it. Also the departments and Information Commission can make out a list of RTI activists who use the act to extract money and treat their applications as non genuine and reject them. Of course, there are public spirited individuals and even media which ask for information to take up genuine public interest issues. There has to be a balance between giving information for public interest and also preventing its misuse.

It has been noticed that maximum use of RTI is made by government employees in matters relating to their service conditions. You cannot prevent this as the officer needs this information to take up his matter before the service tribunals and the courts. At the same time if any other officer or citizen wants information about the service matter of an employee then it should not be given. A lot of awareness needs to be created about the RTI Act so that citizens can make proper use of it.

There should be some amendments in the act allowing an officer senior to PIO to disallow those applications for information which are not genuine or frivolous.

The RTI Act is new and has a noble objective. There would be teething problems. However, there should be a regular review of the working of the Act at the level of the Chief Secretary or Secretary to department and also at the level of the Chief Information Commissioner.

Such reviews will lead to close cooperation between the government and the commission and this would result in the objective of the act being achieved. Just because some people are indulging in malpractices does not mean that transparency should be reduced. RTI Act should not be unnecessarily diluted.

CASE STUDY: UPSC GENERAL STUDIES-4 PAPERS – 2018

Case 1 (Question 7)

Rakesh is a responsible district level officer, who enjoys the trust of his higher officials. Knowing his honesty, the government entrusted him with the responsibility of identifying the beneficiaries under a health care scheme meant for senior citizens.

The criteria to be a beneficiary are the following:

(a) 60 years of age or above.
(b) Belonging to a reserved community.
(c) Family income of less than 1 Lakh rupees per annum.
(d) Post-treatment prognosis is likely to be high to make a positive difference to the quality of life of the beneficiary.

One day, an old couple visited Rakesh's office with their application. They have been the residents of a village in his district since their birth. The old man is diagnosed with a rare condition that causes obstruction in the large intestine. As a consequence, he has severe abdominal pain frequently that prevents him from doing any physical labour. The couple has no children to support them. The expert surgeon whom they contacted is willing to do the surgery without charging any fee. However, the couple will have to bear the cost of incidental charges, such as medicines, hospitalization, etc., to the tune of rupees one lakh. The couple fulfils all the criteria except criterion 'B'. However, any financial aid would certainly make a significant difference in their quality of life.

How should Rakesh respond to the situation?

Answer

This case presents a typical ethical dilemma between acting as per rules and humanitarian considerations. Rakesh is honest and responsible and trusted by his seniors so he has been entrusted by his seniors to select beneficiaries according to set of four criteria. And old man comes to him diagnosed with a serious ailment and is very poor.

The surgeon is willing to do the surgery free but hospitalization and medication would require rupees one lakh which the old couple cannot afford.

As a sensitive human being and officer one option for him is to include the name of the old man in the list of beneficiaries of the health care scheme for senior citizens so that he is able to meet the hospitalization and medication expenses of the surgery which would greatly improve his quality of life. However, he does not full fill criterion "B" of the scheme. This criterion says that the beneficiary should be belonging to a reserved community which the old man does not. Clearly the old man is not eligible for benefit under the scheme. If Rakesh wrongly gives him the benefit of the scheme even with the right intention it would be violation or rules which is not an option available to officers. He can later on be penalized for not following the rules. It may look inhuman but rules are made to ensure uniformity and to reduce discretion which is often the cause of corruption. So Rakesh should not include the name of the old man in the list of the beneficiaries.

One option for him is to write to his superiors requesting for the criteria to be amended. He can suggest that instead of the beneficiary belonging to a reserved community the income level of the beneficiary should be the criteria and not limited to any community. However, it would take a long time for a decision to come and maybe of no use to the old man whose condition is clearly critical. Besides the government normally comes up with schemes for the benefit of the reserved and other marginalized communities and most probably would not change the criteria.

The best option for the district officer Rakesh is to raise funds from philanthropic organizations or associations of traders or industries or NGOs and provide assistance to the old man. He can then also see under what government scheme further benefits can be given to the old couple to improve their quality of life.

Case 2 (Question 8)

As a senior officer in the Ministry, you have access to important policy decisions and upcoming big announcements such as road constructions projects before they are notified in the public domain. The Ministry is about to announce a mega road project for which the drawings are already in place. Sufficient care was taken by the planners to make use of the government land with the minimum land acquisition from private parties. Compensation rate for private parties was also finalized as per government rules. Care was also taken to minimize deforestation. Once the project is announced, it is expected that there will be a huge spurt in real estate prices in and around that area.

Meanwhile, the Minister concerned insists that you realign the road in such a way that it comes closer to his 20 acres farmhouse. He also suggests that he would facilitate the purchase of a big plot of land in your wife's name at the prevailing rate which is very nominal, in and around the proposed mega road project. He also tries to convince you by saying that there is no harm in it as he is buying the land legally. He even promises to supplement your savings in case you do not have sufficient funds to buy the land. However, by the act of realignment, a lot of agricultural lands has to be acquired, thereby causing a considerable financial burden on the government, and also the displacement of the farmers. As if this is not enough, it will involve cutting down of a large number of trees denuding the area of its green cover.

Faced with this situation, what will you do? Critically examine various conflicts of interest and explain what your responsibilities are as a public servant.

Answer

The course of action for a public servant of integrity is quite clear. He has to refuse to realign the road as insisted by the Minister.

The road project is important for the development of the country and its people and nothing should come in the way of its implementation. However, because of the project real estate prices have gone up in the area and it is a common practice that builders, politicians and bureaucrats take advantage of this and start buying land in the area to make money. All steps should be taken to disallow such practices.

In this case the minister wants to realign the road so that it comes close to his 20 acre farmhouse. Obviously this would raise the value of his farmhouse which would be acquired by the government for the road project. The minister wants to make money out of this project even though it would lead to cutting of more trees, increase the cost of land acquisition and thereby the cost of the project. The minister is looking for his personal gain at the cost of loss of public money. As an officer one should refuse to agree with the minister.

The minister is also trying to make the officer dishonest by saying that he should buy a plot of land in the name of his wife so that he also gains when the price of the land goes up because of the road project. An officer should never agree to such suggestions as this amounts to blatant corruption and unethical conduct.

Further this realignment would lead to acquiring more agricultural land than the earlier option which again is unethical. Government always wants to take least amount of agricultural land for infrastructure projects as agricultural land is required for food production which is necessary for the food security of the country. Also, it would displace a lot of farmers causing issues of rehabilitation and both these factors would lead to greater financial burden on the government and this is not a proper utilization of public money.

Another important point relates to environment. A large number of trees will be cut in this realignment leading to a drastic reduction in green cover which leads to increase in air pollution and other issues and is not advisable. It is important to preserve the forest wealth (trees).

For all the above reasons the officer should send the report in writing supporting the proposed alignment and rejecting the alternative alignment proposed. This is his duty and responsibility as a public servant.

Case 3 (Question 9)

It is a state where prohibition is in force. You are recently appointed as the Superintendent of Police of a district notorious for illicit distillation of liquor. The illicit liquor leads to many deaths, reported and unreported, and causes a major problem for the district authorities.

The approach till now had been to view it as a law and order problem and tackle it accordingly. Raids, arrests, police cases, and criminal trials—all these had only limited impact. The problem remains as serious as ever.

Your inspections show that the parts of the district where the distillation flourishes are economically, industrially and educationally backward. Agriculture is badly affected by poor irrigation facilities. Frequent clashes among communities gave boost to illicit distillation. No major initiatives had taken place in the past either from the government's side or from social organizations to improve the lot of the people.

Which new approach will you adopt to bring the problem under control?

Answer

The Superintendent of Police (SP) is responsible for controlling crime in his area. Despite prohibition being in force the district is notorious for illicit distillation of liquor leading to many deaths. It is his duty to enforce the law and he should gather intelligence about liquor mafias and people involved in this illegal trade, carry out raids, arrest the offenders and lead a major campaign against these criminals.

However, he has studied the situation and he finds that illegal distillation exists in industrially, educationally and economically backward areas. The agricultural productivity in these areas is low due to poor irrigation and the people are very poor leading to clashes amongst communities. It is clear that these problems will have to be attended to if the problem of illicit liquor distillation has to be tackled.

Clearly developmental initiatives have to be taken. However, development is not the direct responsibility of the police department and the development officers do not work under the SP. However, the District Magistrate (DM) is the officer responsible for development and he coordinates and supervises the working of the development departments. The DM is also responsible for law and order and in this case enforcing the government directive on prohibition. The DM and SP have to work closely together to handle the situation. The SP should brief the DM about the situation and give his analysis. Thereafter the DM and SP can jointly convene a meeting of all the development departments and draw an action plan for attending to the backwardness of the district. It would even be a good idea if the DM and SP along with concerned officers visit the villages where maximum illegal distillation takes place and understand the needs of the people and address them along with creating awareness about the government policy of prohibition and ill effects of consuming illicit liquor. Steps should be taken to provide employment to people under schemes like MGNAREGA and National Livelihood Mission. Schemes for improvement of irrigation should be started and concrete measures taken to improve agricultural productivity. Schools should be opened in the area and parents motivated to send their children to the school. They should also make an effort to motivate an entrepreneur to set up an industrial unit in the area. All other development needs like roads, drinking water and health facilities should be attended to. The people should be involved in this process of development. Assistance from state headquarters in terms of projects and funds should be sought.

It would also be advisable to take the help of NGOs and religious leaders and other opinion leaders to bring about an attitudinal change in the people. Continuous dialogue with the people will help in changing their behaviour. A combination of tough action against criminals, spreading of awareness and bringing about development in collaboration with the DM and other officers would help in bringing the problem under control.

Case 4 (Question 10)

A big corporate house is engaged in manufacturing industrial chemicals on a large scale. It proposes to set upon the additional unit. Many states rejected its proposal due to the detrimental effect on the environment. But one state government acceded to the request and permitted the unit close to a city, brushing aside all opposition.

The unit was set up 10 years ago and was in full swing till recently. The pollution caused by the industrial effluents was affecting the land, water and crops in the area. It was also causing serious health problems to human beings and animals. This gave rise to a series of agitation in whichs thousands of people took part, creating a law and order problem necessitating stern police action. Following the public outcry, the state government ordered the closure of the factory.

The closure of the factory resulted in the unemployment of not only those workers who were engaged in the factory but also those who were working in the ancillary units. It also very badly affected those industries which depended on the chemicals manufactured by it.

As a senior officer entrusted with the responsibility of handling this issues, how are you going to address it?

Answer

The main issues involved in this case study are an industrial chemical unit located close to a city has been damaging the environment by causing pollution through its effluents leading to serious health problems to the people. There has been an agitation leading to a serious law and order problem and police action. State government has ordered closure of the factory. This has led to unemployment of the workers engaged in the factory and ancillary units as well as impacting industries who bought the chemical from this factory.

One option before you could be to recommend to the government to allow the opening of the factory so that people do not suffer due to unemployment. However, you cannot ignore the serious issue of pollution. You should have a technical committee to examine the matter and see whether it is possible that the factory can install an effluent treatment plant which can eliminate the release of toxic material in the environment. The factory would have to agree to install this equipment at its own cost and give an undertaking to never release untreated effluent. You can give the responsibility to the pollution department to monitor the use of effluent treatment plant by the factory. This should be technically possible. In fact many polluting industries like distilleries and cement plants are allowed to function after they install effluent treatment or zero discharge technologies.

Since the people have been agitated it would be important to hold meetings with all sections of the affected people and take them into confidence about the measures being taken. They can be assured that the factory would be closed down if it releases untreated effluents any time in the future. You can also deploy medical teams to attend to those whose health has been adversely impacted by the pollution.

Normally such a technological solution is possible but if it is not then the only alternative to shift the plant to another location where there would not be any habitation nearby and so it would not affect life and livelihood of people. In this way the workers would also not get unemployed and the industries dependent on these chemicals would be able to continue their production.

In either of two solutions you have to balance the problem of pollution with that of unemployment. A solution can certainly be found which can resolve both the problem issues.

Case 5 (Question 11)

Dr. X is a leading medical practitioner in a city. He has set up a charitable trust through which he plans to establish a super-specialty hospital in the city to cater to the medical needs of all sections of the society. Incidentally, that part of the State had been neglected over the years. The proposed hospital would be a boon for the region. You are heading the tax investigation agency of that region. During an inspection of the doctor's clinic, your officers have found out some major irregularities. A few of them are substantial which had resulted in considerable withholding of tax that should be paid by him now.

The doctor is cooperative. He undertakes to pay the tax immediately. However, there are certain other deficiencies in his tax compliance which are purely technical in nature. If these technical defaults are pursued by the agency, considerable time and energy of the doctor will be diverted to issues which are not so serious, urgent or even helpful to the tax collection process. Further, in all probability, it will hamper the prospects of the hospital coming up.

There are two options before you:

1. Taking a broader view, ensure substantial tax compliance and ignore defaults that are merely technical in nature.
2. Pursue the matter strictly and proceed on all fronts, whether substantial or merely technical.

As the head of the tax agency, which course of action will you opt and why?

Answer

1. The first option is to take a broader view, ensure substantial tax compliance and ignore technical defaults. This option is in the larger interest of society as Dr. X is opening a super specialty hospital which would be a great boon for the region for the people. As a tax officer it is your duty to collect taxes which is essential to raise resources for the development of the country. You have found some major irregularities but Dr. has cooperated and has undertaken to pay the tax. You must ensure that he immediately makes this payment. As regards the technical compliances it is evident that they would not lead to any further collection of tax and not even be helpful to the tax collection process. It does not appear to be advisable to pursue this. As it is the government wants to create a system of tax administration that does not harass the professionals or businessmen. Unnecessary focus on minor technicalities amounts to harassment and also waste of precious time of the tax department. In fact these are the matters which often lead to corruption. I feel that the tax officer should take a broader view which would mean that tax revenue has been collected and the super specialty hospital also setup in time to serve the people.
2. The second option is one that normally tax collection departments follow. It is their duty to collect taxes and also ensure procedural compliances. It is not very often that the

tax officer looks at the larger interests of society and they can claim that it is not their lookout whether a hospital comes up or not. Besides if he ignores the technical compliances his superiors may hold him accountable for the same at a later date and he may face disciplinary action. Ironically, in government, an officer suffers for minor procedural lapses and the larger objectives that he has achieved are ignored. This leads to a safety first attitude and it is more than likely that in this case the tax officer would insist on all compliances.

On balance as a tax officer I would go by the first alternative as the larger benefit of the society is the goal of all public servants. Besides tax has been collected and there is no loss of revenue to the government. It would also be advisable to prepare a note in writing and inform and take the approval of your superiors for this course of action so that you are not made to face the music later on.

Case 6 (Question 12)

Edward Snowden, a computer expert and former CIA administrator, released confidential Government documents to the press about the existence of Government surveillance programmes. According to many legal experts and the US Government, his action violated the Espionage Act of 1971, which identified the leak of State secret as an act of treason. Yet, despite the fact that he broke the law, Snowden argued that he had a moral obligation to act. He gave a justification for his "whistle blowing" by stating that he had a duty "to inform the public as to that which is done in their name and that which is done against them."

According to Snowden, the Government's violation of privacy had to be exposed regardless of legality since more substantive issues of social action and public morality were involved here. Many agreed with Snowden. Few argued that he broke the law and compromised national security, for which he should be held accountable.

Do you agree that Snowden's actions were ethically justified even if legally prohibited? Why or why not? Make an argument by weighing the competing values in this case.

Answer

Edward Snowden has released confidential government documents to the press about government surveillance programmes. Legal experts find this as a violation of Espionage Act of 1971 which treats his act as one of treason. However, Snowden justifies himself by saying that it is a moral obligation to brings this matter to the knowledge of people as it is a violation of privacy and so an issue of social action and public morality. He sees himself as a whistle-blower.

I do not agree that Snowden's actions are ethically justified. You cannot violate the law and claim that you are acting morally. Treason is a serious crime against the State and cannot be condoned on any grounds. If such Acts are allowed it would lead to anarchy and create a situation where no governance is possible. His act does not fall in the category of whistle-blowing. It is true that there are laws and conventions which protect the whistle-blower. However, the whistle-blower points out illegal acts or matters of corruptions being indulged into by an organization. In this case his action is against the law and, hence, he cannot claim protection as a whistle-blower.

It could be that Snowden genuinely feels that the government is intruding into the privacy of the individuals and the State should not have such powers. In the larger context of the rights of the individual versus the state, Snowden can claim that his action is a matter of public morality and for liberty of the individual. However, the path of releasing confidential documents to the press that he has chosen is definitely illegal. The option before him is to approach the courts and ask for amendment to the Espionage Act and also request the court to give a ruling on the extent to which governments can have surveillance programmes through which they can intrude into the privacy of individuals.

Thus the Act of Snowden is not ethically justified as it is illegal. Nothing that is illegal can be ethical. However, laws can be challenged in the courts and if Snowden feels that it is his moral duty to raise the issue he should approach the courts. This would also start the process of debate in the media on the important issue of the definition of the right to privacy.

CASE STUDY: UPSC GENERAL STUDIES-4 PAPERS – 2019

Case 1 (Question 7)

You are heading the rescue operations in a area affected by severe natural calamity, thousands of people are rendered homeless and deprived of food, drinking water and other basic amenities. Rescue work has been disrupted by heavy rainfall and damaged to supply routes. The local people are seeding with anger against the delayed limited rescue operations. When your team reaches the affected area, the people there heckle and even assault some of the team members. One of your team members is even severely injured. Faced with this crisis some team member plead with you to call off the operations freeing threats to their life.

In such trying circumstances, what will be your response? Examine the qualities of a public servant which will be required to manage the situations.

Answer

This kind of situation often takes place. It is the duty of a public servant to conduct rescue operation in areas affected by severe natural calamity. The rescue operations are often delayed by excessive rainfall or damage to supply routes. In such a situation the local people lose patience and become violent. This does not mean that a public servant should call off the rescue operations. A public servant has to have the qualities of patience, compassion, empathy and a large heart. He has to use his emotional intelligence and handle the situation with a positive attitude, tact and calmness. He should talk to the people; convince them that you have come to give them all possible help and request for their cooperation. The officer will have to explain to the people the steps that they would take to provide relief and ask them to remain patient and not indulge in violence which will further hamper rescue operations.

At the same time as an officer one has to look at the morale of his team members also. One of them has been severely injured by the assault. He should be given immediate medical attention and shifted to a hospital. The other team members are also feeling threatened. The officer must talk to them and assure them of their security and impress upon them the necessity of continuing rescue operations. It is advisable to call the police also so that your team members feel secure. You should also tell the affected people that if they resort to violence then legal action would also be taken against them. In a mob there are always some trouble makers. They should be made to realize that stern action would be taken against them if they indulge in violence.

The office has to show exemplary qualities of leadership and team spirit and ability to motivate and inspire his team and also win the trust of the people with his show of sincerity and sense of public service.

Case 2 (Question 8)

Honesty and uprightness are the hallmarks of civil servants. Civil servants possessing these qualities are considered as a back bone of any strong organizations. In line of duty, they take various decisions, at time some become bonafide mistakes. As long as such decisions are not taken intentionally and do not benefit personally, the officer cannot be said to be guilty. Though such decisions may, at times, lead to unforeseen adverse consequences in the long term.

In the recent past, a few instances have surfaced where civil servants has been implicated for bonafide mistakes. They have often been prosecuted and even imprisoned. These instances have greatly rattled the moral fiber of the civil servants.

How does this trend affect the functioning of civil services? What measures can be taken so that honest civil servants are not implicated for bonafide mistakes on their part? Justify your answer.

Answer

Resent instances have unfortunately implicated honest and upright civil servants for bonafide mistakes and there have been shocking cases of imprisonment and prosecution of some civil servants who have been known to uphold the highest standards of integrity and competence. This has dented the self confidence of the civil servants leading to lowering of their morale and creating a general atmosphere of administrative lethargy and inaction. A civil servant has to take several decisions in a day and he takes them on the basis of the information put up to him and the existing policies and conventions. It is possible that a genuine mistake would be made. It is not possible in any organization for the top person to take hundred percent correct decisions. The important thing is intention. If the intention is malafide then the civil servant should be prosecuted but if the mistake is a bonafide one then the officer should not be made to suffer. We are all aware that the current spate of criminal proceedings against honest officers has led to an environment of policy paralysis. Civil servants are now avoiding taking decisions and the result is that it is having an adverse impact on the development of the country. Sometimes officers are facing prosecution for some procedural errors which do not constitute criminal liability as there is no *mens rea* (criminal intention) involved. These can at best be termed as irregularities and not criminal acts. The CBI, ED and similar agencies are quick to charge a civil servant simply because he has signed the file without looking at the circumstances of the case.

Time and again from the highest level of governance assurance is given that civil servants will not suffer for bonafide decisions even if they turn out to be wrong, however, in reality no protection is given in these matters. The worst situation is when Government changes and they try to implicate the earlier government and it is the civil servant who faces the brunt of this political vendetta.

Recently the government has amended the Prevention of Corruption act. Now an officer is not held liable if his decision has helped somebody if it has been taken in a bonafide manner. It is important that before any matter is referred to an investigative agency it should be enquired into at the administrative level giving full opportunity to the civil servant to explain his case. Then only if malafide is apparent the matter should be referred to an investigating agency. This agency also should enquire whether bribe has been paid or consideration given in kind to charge a civil servant. They should see whether there is a money trail. If there is no evidence of money being taken then criminal action should not be taken and disciplinary action is recommended. Even if criminal action is proposed then th e sanction for prosecution must be taken from the concerned government. Further, the civil servant should not be held liable if a mistake has been made but he has followed the rules and procedures. Also for collective decisions taken or for those where there is an approval of the minister the civil servant should not be made to suffer.

Case 3 (Question 9)

An apparel manufacturing company having large number of women employees was losing sales due to various factors. The company hired a reputed marketing executive, who increased the volume of sales within a short span of time. However, some unconfirmed reports came up regarding his indulgence in sexual harassment at the work place.

After sometime a women employee launched a formal complaint to the management against the marketing executive about sexually harassing her. Faced with the companies' indifference, in not taking cognizance of her grievances, she lodged an FIR with police.

Realizing the sensitivity and gravity of the situation, the company called the women employee to negotiate. In that she was offered a hefty sum of money to withdraw the complaint and the FIR and also give in writing that the marketing executive is not involved in the case.

Identify the ethical issues involved in this case. What options are available to the women employee?

Answer

This case study raises very serious ethical issues. It involves a serious matter of sexual harassment. The company is being indifferent to the complaint of the women employee. This shows that the management is not following ethical practices and ignoring such a serious issue for the sake of protecting an executive who is giving them profits. Just to gain profits allowing unethical and immoral activities in the organization is totally against the ideals of good corporate governance and is also violation of the law. It also shows a high degree of insensitivity towards women employees and their safety.

Even after the employee has lodged the FIR with the police the company is calling the woman employee to negotiate and offering her a hefty sum of money to withdraw the FIR and save the marketing executive. This is further compounding the criminal and unethical act by the management. They are trying to bribe an employee who has suffered sexual harassment. The management is giving a signal that as long as the company makes profits it is willing to condone any unethical and immoral act. Such thinking is detrimental to the work culture of the organization and no woman employee would want to work in such an organization. Thus, the behaviour of the management needs to be strongly condemned.

The woman employee did the right thing by lodging a complaint with the management and after the latter did not take any action she lodged an FIR with the police. She should firmly refuse the sum of money offered by the management and persist with her FIR. If she agrees to the management then she shows her own moral weakness and she is likely to face similar harassment in the future. So she should not even think of negotiating with the management. These are serious matters. The police will take action against the marketing executive. The company would also have to dismiss him. The company cannot dare to take any action against the woman employee because she is morally correct.

Case 4 (Question 10)

In a modern democratic polity there is a concept of political executive and permanent executive elected people's representatives forms the political executive and bureaucracy forms the permanent executive. Ministers frame policy decisions and bureaucrats execute these.

In the initial decades after independence, relationship between the permanent executives and the political executives were characterized by mutual understanding, respect, and cooperation, without encroaching upon each other's domain.

However, in the subsequent decades the situation has changed. There are instances of the political executive insisting upon the permanent executives to follow its agenda. Respect for an appreciation of an upright bureaucrats has declined. There is an increasing tendency among the political executive to get involved in routine administrative matters such as transfers, postings etc. Under this scenario, there is a definitive trend towards 'politicization of bureaucracy'. The rising materialism and acquisitiveness in social life has also adversely impacted upon the ethical values of both the permanent executive and the political executive.

What are the consequences of this 'politicization of bureaucracy? Discuss.

Answer

It is true that the relationship between the political executive and permanent executive have deteriorated over the years. Initially the relationship was based on mutual respect, cooperation and understanding of each other's role. Today the political executive is encroaching on the domain of the officer by getting involved in matters like transfers and postings. Things have come to such a pass that the political executive is giving very little time to policy formulation and concentrating on routine administrative issues like transfers. This has vitiated the working atmosphere as junior officers are paying bribes to the ministers to get postings of their choice even though they are incompetent. This adversely affects the efficiency of governments and also creates a situation where a senior officer cannot take work from or punish a subordinate because the latter has political connections.

It is also true that everywhere in society there is an increasing trend of materialism and acquisitiveness leading to general erosion of values and integrity. The same trend is reflected in the decline in ethical values of the political executive and the civil servant because they come from the same society. This has led to widespread corruption amongst the civil servants and political executives. The worst scenario is when both collude and together siphon off public money. This has an adverse impact on the process of development of the nation and also leads to total unethical and poor governance. In this situation complete politicization of the bureaucracy takes place. One hears about civil servants being attached to political parties on the basis of caste or colluding for corruption. This implies that the civil servant is no longer impartial, objective, transparent and responsive and is merely concerned with personal gain at the cost of giving good governance or efficient public service delivery. Serious governance reforms are required to see that the politician and the civil servant focus on their role and not encroach on each other's domain. Also reforms should see that politicization of bureaucracy does not take place and that dishonesty and lack of integrity is punished and ethics and morality rewarded.

Case 5 (Question 11)

In one of the districts of a frontier state, narcotics menace has been rampant. This has resulted in money laundering, mushrooming of poppy farming, arms smuggling and near stalling of education. The system is on the verge of collapse. The situation has been further worsened by unconfirmed reports that local politicians as well as some senior police officers are providing surreptitious patronage to the drug mafia. At that point of time a woman police officer, known for her skills in handling such situations is appointed as Superintendent of Police to bring the situation to normalcy.

If you are the same police officer, identify the various dimensions of the crisis. Based on your understanding, suggest measures to deal with the crisis.

Answer

In this case study you are a woman police officer posted as Superintendent of Police and known for her competence in a narcotics infested district. The narcotics trade has led to money laundering, extensive poppy farming, arms smuggling and stalling of education. The situation is very bad. Local politicians and seniors police officers are providing patronage to the drug mafia.

It is indeed a tremendous challenge. To begin with she must take strong action against those involved in illegal narcotics trade, money laundering and arms smuggling. FIRs should be lodged against known offenders, raids conducted and firm action taken under various special acts like the National Security Act and Gangster Act along with Provision of Narcotics Act and Money Laundering Act. She should create a team of honest and dedicated police officers to tackle this menace. She should identify those officers who are in league with the mafia and initiate criminal and departmental action against them. This will send a strong message to the entire district. She should also coordinate with the Enforcement Director for money laundering and National Narcotics Bureau for the narcotics related offences.

She should also send a detailed report to the home ministry in the State and Director General of Police. This is necessary so that she gets support from the top which is essential as senior police officer and local politicians are involved in the matter. It would also be advisable if she maintains close coordination with the District Magistrate and together both of them should take an appointment and brief the Chief Minister even telling him the name of the local politicians involved. This will give her all round support without which she will not be able to handle this complex situation.

Then along with the DM and agriculture department she should hold meetings in the villages with farmers to identify the areas of poppy farming and convince the farmers not to grow poppy. Alternative crop giving a better return can be suggested to the farmer who should be motivated to take up this new crop.

It is also important to involve social leaders, opinion leaders and religious leaders to create a district wide awareness about the menace of narcotics and the impact it is having on the health and education of the people. Media should also be regularly briefed so that they do extensive coverage of the campaign being launched by her. Education suffered in the district. Along with the DM and officers of the education department and NGOs a major drive should be taken up to improve the enrolment, attendance and learning in the schools. Children should be specially educated about the evils of taking drugs.

Case 6 (Question 12)

In recent times, there has been an increasing concern in India to develop effective civil service ethics, code of conduct, transparency measures, ethics and integrity systems and anti-corruption agencies. In view of this, there is need being felt to focus on three specific areas, which are directly relevant to the problems of internalizing integrity and ethics in the civil services. These are as follows:

1. Anticipating specific threats to ethical standards and integrity in the civil services;
2. Strengthening the ethical competence of civil servant; and

3. Developing administrative processes and practices which promote ethical values and integrity in civil services.

Suggest institutional measures to address the above three issues.

Answer

It is true that in recent times there is a lot of concern about the fall in ethics and increasing corruption amongst civil servants. Codes of conducts have been amended, Right to Information Act and Citizen Charter introduced to bring about more transparency and accountability and the institution of Lokpal established to check corruption in government, the role of Chief Gigilance Commission (CVC) has been strengthened but still there is a lot of criticism about the continuous falling ethical standards in civil services.

1. There is a general decline in morals in society and a surprising acceptance of corruption because of the increasing allure of materialism and desire for a more ostentatious style of living. The civil servants are products of the same society and their integrity also gets compromised by these changes in societal values.

   The performance evaluation system in civil service does not weed out the corrupt and inefficient. Officers find that there is not much risk in being corrupt as they are not likely to be caught or prosecuted and despite having a bad reputation they can reach the top.

   Further there is an atmosphere of increasing interference in administration by politicians and the politician makes a civil servant, who does not toe his line, suffer. The result is that civil servants, for career advancement, are ready to crawl before the wishes of the political executive without being concerned about right or wrong. Politicization of civil servants is a big threat to their integrity.

   Thus it is important for civil servants to anticipate above threats to their integrity and protect themselves from them. The civil servants must persist with objectivity, transparency, impartiality and integrity in their dealings. They should not bow to illegal demands made of them by the political executives.

2. The ethical competence of civil servants can be greatly strengthened by training them in ethics, values and morals specifically with reference to public service. This would be very

beneficial internalizing integrity and ethics in civil servants. These trainings should be held at a periodic interval and focus on best practices and inspiring examples as well as making them conscious of their code of conduct and code of ethics.

3. It is very important to develop administrative processes which make sure that a civil servant acts in public interests and with absolute integrity. The nexus with the politicians needs to be broken by making the transfers and postings of civil servants independent of political interference and based on merit. Also processes need to be evolved to see that a politician does not encroach upon the domain of the civil servant.

Further the processes should ensure objectivity, transparency and accountability and the performance of a civil servant should be evaluated on the basis of the outcomes he delivers and standards of ethics that he maintains. The system should be such that only the real performers reach the top. Decision-making should be encouraged and the system should be such that an honest officer does not suffer and the dishonest is not able to get away. Use of technology should be encouraged and accountability of civil servants ensured.

CASE STUDIES ON OTHER TOPICS OF THE SYLLABUS

Case 1

Mr. Ram Kumar joined the IAS with a lot of idealism. Very soon he was known in the service as an officer of integrity and competence. He was from a humble background and had seen the problems of shortage of money but he was determined to remain honest. He was appointed as the Municipal Commissioner of a large city and soon realized that there was a lot of corruption in his department. The public used to complain of cases of corruption and especially the engineering wing had the reputation of very poor quality of construction and charging high commission from the contractors. He was wondering how to control this corruption. One day his Chief Engineer who was twice his age and a very religious person but having a negative image about integrity asked him for an appointment at home to discuss some issues. Ram Kumar was surprised when the Chief Engineer handed him a packet and told him that this was his commission from the engineering department and would be made available every month. Ram Kumar protested but the Chief Engineer told him that this was not against any favor to be granted but it was a tradition to make this available to the commissioner every month and all his predecessors had accepted it. He also told Ram Kumar that Ram Kumar had to marry off his sisters for which this money would be useful.

What would you advise Ram Kumar to do. Alternatives—

1. To accept the commission as it was being done in the past and no specific favors were being asked for.
2. He should take the commission as he would require the money for the marriage of his sisters and convince himself that he will not allow this to influence his working.
3. He should refuse the commission and tell the Chief Engineer not to repeat it.
4. He should refuse the commission and take action against the Chief Engineer and also develop systems to control corruption.

Discussion

The first two alternatives are clearly not acceptable and amount to dishonesty. It does not matter if this was the tradition. Wrong practices should not be continued. Besides, it is not possible to take commission and then be fair and honest in your dealings. In fact, the Chief Engineer and his team would start dominating Ram Kumar and he would never be able to take action in cases of poor construction. Every person has some domestic problems but just because he has to arrange the marriage of his sisters does not mean that he should give up integrity. This action would be unethical.

Clearly he should refuse the commission. This will give him the moral authority to take action against corrupt practices. He should immediately develop systems in the organization to reduce corruption and take strict actions whenever any matter of corruption comes up before him. He should keep a close watch on the Chief Engineer after warning him and if any complaint comes to light he should initiate strong action against him. It is possible that the Chief Engineer will not cooperate with him and also instigate other officers against Ram Kumar. He may also plant stories in the media to discredit Ram Kumar but this should not deter Ram Kumar from his path of integrity and he should fight it out. It is also possible that the Chief Engineer may use political pressure to get Ram Kumar transferred. If this happens Ram Kumar should accept it but not allow such concerns to dilute his commitment to ethics and integrity.

Case 2

You are posted as Superintendent of Police in a district which is crime prone. You are determined to reduce crime and put the fear of law in the criminals. You find that the Station House Officers who are in-charge of the police stations do not register FIRs and are in collusion with criminals and mafias and this is the main reason for the increase in crime in the district. You start by inspecting each police station and monitoring the crime situations and holding the Station House Officers responsible. The public is very happy with your attitude and performance though some local politicians who have a nexus with criminals are not happy. One day about one month after your joining your personal assistant comes to you and gives you an envelope containing a lot of cash. You ask him from where this has come. He tells you that this is a regular tradition that every police station pays a fixed amount to the SP every month. He also tells you that all your predecessors have been accepting it.

What would you do?

1. Since this is a tradition and no direct favor is being asked you will accept the amount and go about doing your work as before. You will justify that you are not allowing it to interfere with your professional working.
2. You will refuse the money and tell the assistant to return it.
3. You will refuse the money and call a meeting of the Station House Officers and tell them that you do not accept such gratification and warn them that you would be closely supervising their work and take action if they are not able to control crime or there are complaints of corruption.

Discussion

This case study is similar to the first one and the answer is also the same. The tragedy is that this is a very common occurrence in the police department in the districts and one of the main reasons behind the SP not being able to control his police station in-charges.

Just because it is a tradition and no direct favor is being asked does not mean that an officer should compromise his integrity. In fact, most corrupt officers justify their behavior by saying that others are taking money or that it is a tradition or that just by their not taking the system will not get reformed. However, these justifications are an exercise in self delusion. The moment you accept this monthly payment you will have very little control over your police stations and never be able to control crime. Further, you will earn a bad reputation in the public also. The best course is to refuse it but there is always a danger that the personal assistant would pocket the money and not communicate any message to the Station House Officers. Therefore, it is essential to call a meeting of all SHOs and make it clear to them that all these traditions of corruption should end and henceforth you will be evaluating the officers on competence and honesty. You should also develop systems to monitor corruption and take strict action whenever anybody is found guilty of indulging in corrupt practices. It is true that they will not be happy and once again try to use political pressure to have you transferred but this is an occupational hazard which you must take in your stride.

Case 3

You are posted as a District Magistrate in a large district and have just successfully conducted the elections to the assembly. A strong local politician who has been elected has been inducted into the state cabinet and he comes on a visit to the district where the people accord him a huge welcome. He is supposed to be very close to the Chief Minister. He is very nice when you meet him and talks about how you should be fair and transparent and deliver public services. After he has gone one day your Superintendent of Police (SP) comes to you with a file and wants your approval. You realize that this is a proposal for taking action against almost a dozen people under the National Security Act where the DM has the powers to approve the proposal. You glance through the list of people against whom action is proposed and find that they are not criminals but normal citizens without any criminal record. In response to your query the SP confidentially briefs you that this list was given to him by the Minister with the specific direction that these people should be detained under the National Security Act. He confessed that these citizens were not criminals but active supporters of the main political opponent of the Minister. The SP himself was not in favor of taking this incorrect action but said that the minister was very powerful and had clearly said that the SP would need to do this if he wanted to continue in the district.

What would you advise the DM to do?

Discussion

The DM can simply approve the proposal without going into details of the grounds mentioned otherwise the minister would be annoyed and not only he but the SP would be in trouble. However, by taking this action he would be going against the basic ethics of a civil servant. This would mean that he is not being objective and impartial and using a stringent law like National Security Act to deprive citizens of their liberty without any justification. Such acts weaken the fabric of administration and are examples of very poor governance where instead of doing your duty towards the citizens you are bowing down to a political figure just to safeguard your own personal interest. The essence of ethics in public service is to always put your duty to the people, constitution and the law above your considerations of personal gain. You also acquire the reputation of being a weak officer and the politician would keep on making more and more demands to you. The best course of action is not to approve the proposal. The SP can always say that it was the DM who did not approve and so he is not at fault. The minister would be unhappy with the DM. The DM can brief the Home Secretary and Chief Secretary about the matter and also seek an appointment with the Chief Minister and brief him also. This would help to shield him against any action on the recommendation of the minister concerned. There will be a cold war with the minister but if the DM gets support from the top he should be able to survive in the district. Just to hang on to a posting one should not do wrong things as the commitment of the officers is towards the constitution and the rule of law. Also, once an officer acquires a reputation of firmness and integrity the politicians also do not pressurize him unduly to do illegal work. Everybody respects an officer who has unimpeachable integrity.

Case 4

Ramesh Singh is the Director of a government engineering college which has not been enjoying a very good reputation for academics and Ramesh is determined to change this. He analyses the situation in depth and also discusses with teachers and students to find out how to improve the quality of education in the institute. Ramesh finds that there is an acute shortage of teachers and the existing teachers are also not of the required level as most of them have been appointed on the recommendations of senior officers or politicians. Ramesh wants to change this by recruiting teachers purely on merit and holding them accountable for maintaining academic standards. He advertises for the posts of teachers and forms a committee of experts under his chairmanship to interview and select the best. However, as the interview date comes near Ramesh gets the information that many candidates are approaching the minister and there are also strong rumours of money being offered. Ramesh is confident that he will do a fair selection with the help of experts. However, a few days before the interview he is called by the minister and given an unsigned list of candidates with the direction that they should be selected. He tries to protest by saying that the selection would be on merit but the minister does not listen and also tells him that if he does not agree then it would be difficult for him to continue.

What course of action would you advise for Mr. Ramesh Singh?

1. Since the minister is the boss he should quietly agree and also safeguard his position and select the candidates as desired by the minister even if they are not worthy of it.
2. He should once again meet the minister and try to convince him that it is in the interest of the institution if the selection is done on merit.
3. He submits his resignation.
4. He approaches the senior officers and explains the situation to get their help and goes ahead with the selection on merit. If any candidate recommended by the minister does well then he would also select him.

Discussion

This kind of a pressure in recruitment is very common in government and many officers have to face this. If Ramesh goes by the first alternative and selects the candidates as per the desire of the minister he would be behaving in an unfair, unethical, partial and partisan manner which is not expected of a government officer. Moreover, these candidates would have most probably offered money and would not be of the required standards. The reputation of the college will go down further and it would be impossible to improve the quality of education in the college. Ramesh would be a failure.

The second alternative is worth trying. He should meet the minister and try to convince him at the same time assuring that if any candidate is reasonably good then he would adjust him. However, the minster in all probability would not agree.

Resigning amounts to escaping from the situation which is never advisable. A civil servant faces great challenges in his career and he has to stand-up to them otherwise he would be branded as weak and not having the character to carry out his duties.

The fourth alternative is the best as the officers of his departments like the Secretary or Director General would understand his view point and support him. It is possible that if all senior officers approach the minister then he would agree. Even if he does not then the director has support from the government for his actions and the minister would not be able to have him removed. Ramesh, after taking senior officers into confidence should go ahead and select the best possible candidates. This will enhance the reputation of the college and also Ramesh would be able to bring about the desired improvement in academic standards. Very often the politician tests the civil servant and if the latter is firm then the politician does not persist. Even if he does it is a battle worth fighting because it is in the interest of the citizens which is most important. One thing is important. Ramesh should never argue or talk rudely to the minister as this would put him in the wrong. It is important in civil service to achieve your objective with suitable use of diplomatic skills.

Case 5

You are Principal Secretary of the department of rural development and you find that work is suffering due to acute shortage of village level officers. You want to go ahead and recruit them. You find that there have been previous efforts to recruit these officers but have never succeeded due to allegations of corruption in the selection process. You go ahead by advertising the post and then appoint an independent consultant to carry out the exam in a fair manner through use of computer based OMR sheets. You also reduce the marks for interview so that there is less chance of favoritism. It is also decided that one copy of the OMR sheets shall be submitted for evaluation and one given to the candidate and third one kept in custody of the government. In this way you want to eliminate any chance of unfair practices. However, close to the exam the minister puts pressure on the secretary to do away with the third copy and only have two copies and allow several new exam centers which you had disallowed because of adverse reports from the district administration. You also hear vast sums of money are exchanging hands and realise that there is a chance of foul play if the third copy is not insisted upon. What would you do?

1. You will accept the direction of the minister and do away with the third copy and approve the dubious centers.
2. You will flatly refuse.

3. You will realise that it is not possible to conduct a fair exam and postpone the selection process.
4. You will form a committee to examine the issues and on the basis of the recommendation of the committee put up a note to the minister that any change would lead to allegations of corruption and should not be done.

Discussion

The first alternative is not advisable at all. You have information about likely malpractices in the exam and previous experience has been similar. Just by agreeing with the minister you would be creating an opportunity for unscrupulous elements hijacking the exam process. Unworthy candidates would be selected and later on there can be an enquiry where you may get implicated because unfair means would have been used. There should be no compromise on matters of integrity.

The third alternative is also not the right approach. By postponing the exam you will not be filling up the required posts and the work of rural development would be adversely affected. A civil servant has to deliver public services efficiently to the citizens and for this you need to fill up the vacant posts. Besides, it is never advisable to avoid or run away from a difficult situation.

The second and fourth alternative need to be taken together. The best course is to go ahead with a fair selection process so that you select the right person and ensure that the public money is utilized properly and good quality services provided to the citizens. However, it is never very advisable to bluntly oppose the minister as this would lead to a conflict situation and the minister would most probably get you transferred or do everything possible to make you uncomfortable. The fourth alternative should be the preferred one. You should discuss the matter in a committee of senior officers where views opposing the changes would come and should be put in the proceedings of the meeting and file put up to the minister suggesting that it would be incorrect to make these changes as a committee of senior officers have disagreed with this. No minister will pass a contrary order in writing and you will be able to carry out a fair transparent selection which will make sure that the benefits of government schemes reach the intended beneficiary.

Case 6

You are an executive engineer posted in the public works department and made in-charge of a major project costing about 1000 thousand crores. You realise that you have to ensure a high quality of work otherwise your own reputation and that of the department shall be damaged. You want to choose the best contractors through a fair tendering process. However, your Chief Engineer calls you and tells you that there are instructions from the top that certain contractors should be given the work. You insist that tendering has to be done in a transparent manner and it is not possible to ensure that any particular contractor succeeds in getting the contract. The Chief Engineer tells you that you should sit with the party to be favored and draw tender conditions in such a manner that only this party will qualify. You know that this contractor does not have the experience for such a large project and the quality of execution would not be of the required standards. There is every likelihood of there being time and cost over-runs.

What would you advise the Executive Engineer to do?

1. He accepts the oral direction of the Chief Engineer and prepares tender documents to favor a particular party as desired.
2. He refuses to do so and goes ahead with the tender process as per rules ensuring fairness and transparency.
3. He requests for a transfer from this project.
4. He will say that he will put up the matter before the tender committee which has representatives of finance department also and take a decision accordingly. He would then ensure that the committee recommends a fair and transparent tendering process and then go ahead accordingly after taking the approval of the Chief Engineer in writing.

Discussion

If he accepts the first alternative then he would be selecting the wrong contractor and behaving in a partial and partisan manner. The quality of the project would be adversely affected and charges of corruption are likely to be leveled against him thus this alternative is not at all advisable.

Once again the third alternative of requesting for a transfer does not serve any purpose and amounts to running away from your responsibility. Officers have to face situations and not avoid them as their duty is towards the common man whom they have to serve with honesty and integrity.

He has to carry out the tender process in a fair and transparent manner and select the best contractor. However, the Chief Engineer is his boss and he cannot openly disobey him. Moreover, the Chief Engineer says that instructions have come from the top. It is thus advisable for the Executive Engineer to adopt the fourth alternative and refer the matter to a committee where he can guide the deliberations. He can then put up the tender conditions finalized by the tender committee for approval to the Chief Engineer who would have no option but to approve it. In this way he will be able to do a fair tender and select the best possible contractor to carry out the project which involves huge public money. The duty of a civil servant is to see that public money is utilized properly and that there are no chances of money being siphoned off. In such matters the best things to do is never to accept oral orders but take them in writing. These days with the Right to Information Act making notings on files transparent no officer would like to give an illegal order. Also, it would help if the Executive Engineer briefs the secretary and other senior officers as it is possible that the Chief Engineer may be acting on his own and not as per instructions from the top as he claims.

Case 7

Krishna Kumar is the Chief Engineer of a development authority where a major project developing a park and tourist spot is being undertaken. It is a priority project and has the support of the minister and Chief Minister and is catching regular media attention. Your job is to supervise the project whereas the actual tendering and execution is to be done by the concerned Executive Engineer. It comes to your knowledge that tender guidelines are being violated to discourage competition and award contract to favored contractors on a higher rate than estimated. During your inspections these discrepancies come to light and you call the Executive Engineer and you direct him to follow the financial guidelines but he tells you that he has orders directly from higher up people to award contracts to certain contractors and that is why he is handling the tender process in a particular manner. Krishna Kumar is aware that this Executive Engineer is close to the minister but he has also seen some adverse comments appearing in the media. Krishna Kumar has only a few years left for retirement and does not want to incur the displeasure of the minister otherwise he may lose his post.

How should Krishna Kumar respond to this predicament?

1. Since the minister and other senior people are involved he should remain quiet as he is not directly responsible and just focus on timely completion of the project.
2. He should meet the Secretary and the minister and brief them about the matter and then act as per their directions.
3. He should pass an order in writing to the Executive Engineer to follow the government guidelines and say that he will be responsible for any discrepancy.
4. He should send a confidential report to the Secretary and the minister seeking orders in writing.
5. He should quietly give information to the media so that they may publish stories about a scam and hope that this will rectify things.

Discussion

The easiest thing for Krishna Kumar is to follow the first alternative but by doing so he is not carrying out his duties as a public servant. He may not be directly approving the tenders but supervision is his responsibility which means he has to see that there is no corruption or illegality in the process. Moreover, media may by itself start publishing stories about illegality which could lead to an inquiry where the Chief Engineer would not be able to escape responsibility. Once there is an inquiry no senior officer or minister helps anybody even if the subordinates have been working on their instructions. Each officer is responsible for his actions. Moreover, it is an intellectually dishonest act to see wrong things happening and keeping quiet. This is against basic morality that should be in a human being.

The fifth alternative is dangerous. Media is a double edged sword and an officer should never resort to playing up matters in the media. The Chief Engineer cannot escape his responsibility by leaking details to the media. Also, media reports could lead to an inquiry where he would also be in trouble and the project would also get delayed.

The second alternative is worth considering as he should brief his Secretary and minister about the facts and seek their instructions. However, if people at the top are also involved then this will not help and they will not support him. They may even say that he should allow the Executive Engineer to do his job as this project has to be completed on time and they have not heard any complaints about him. Oral discussion has no meaning in government.

The third alternative of issuing directions to the Executive Engineer to ensure that all financial rules are being followed should be done so that later on nobody should say that Krishna Kumar is in collusion with the Executive Engineer in his illegal acts. Along with this, he should also act as per the fourth alternative by sending a report to the seniors and also attaching a copy of his orders to the Executive Engineer. If things do not improve after this he is in a position to take action against the Executive Engineer and nobody would be able to interfere. It is possible that after sometime the minister may transfer him but no other action can be taken against him. At all times it is important not only to do the ethically right thing but also not allow anything wrong to be done if it comes to your knowledge. Further, it is a responsibility of the senior officer to design monitoring systems which will throw up an alarm the moment anything wrong or illegal is being done.

Case 8

You are the Secretary of the education department and you have analysed that one of the main causes of poor quality of education in government schools is teacher absenteeism. You also find that officers of education department are colluding with teachers in matters of transfers and postings and so have no control over them. Your minister insists that all transfers shall be done at his level and you find that the Director of education is by passing you and getting the lists approved by the minister even though he has full authority of transferring teachers and officers below the level of additional director at his level but he is informally obtaining directions from the ministers and issuing orders accordingly. You feel that if officers and teachers are posted according to political patronage then it would be difficult to improve the quality of education.

How would you handle the situation?

1. You may keep quiet and allow things to continue as they are as any interference will annoy the minister who may make life difficult for you.
2. You will call the director and tell him that all transfer proposals should come to you and you will scrutinize them in detail before taking the approval of minister.
3. You may brief the minister and request him not to interfere

in transfers as this would affect the working culture of the department.

4. You will tell the director to carry out the transfers at his level and not seek instructions from the minister.
5. You will design a scientific and transparent system of transferring teachers and officers laying down clear guidelines and insist that any deviation would need your approval and that the director would be personally responsible for acting as per the system designed.

Discussion

Political interference in transfers is extremely common and very often huge amount of money is exchanged in the process. Further when officers or teachers know that they have got their transfer through paying bribes, they would also act in a corrupt manner which would adversely affect public service delivery. The reality is that most civil servants follow the first alternative of keeping quiet so as not to earn the displeasure of the minister. However, this is an indication of weakness and is an unethical response. The job of the Secretary is to provide good quality education to all and this is not possible if officers and teachers earn their postings through corrupt means. Teachers will not teach and officers will not supervise them properly because they know that their future does not depend upon this as they have political connections. So, the Secretary cannot ignore the situation and must act.

The second, third and fourth alternatives will also not give any results. If you tell the director to use his powers as per delegation and carryout transfers at his level he would plead that he is helpless as the minister calls him and gives him transfer lists. If you request the minister not to interfere in transfers he would brush you aside. He may tell you that as a public representative he cannot say no to people meeting him and request him for the transfers. He will never accept that any money is being exchanged in the process. Telling the director to send the transfer list through you may help as you can carry out amendments to the list but the director may insist that the list is as per the directions of the minister and also on his own brief the minister who will be unhappy with you on this score.

The fifth alternative is the best. It is your duty to design a transparent system of transfers with clear guidelines. These days all transfers can be made online leaving very little room for discretion.

You can get this proposal approved by the Cabinet or Chief Minister. Thereafter, the director will not be able to deviate from the system as it would be transparent and anybody can question any arbitrary transfer. The minster will also have his hands bound.

It is the duty of a civil servant to design systems and methods of workings which reduce discretion and increase transparency and in this manner control corruption in the department. Technology should be used wherever possible.

Case 9

Prem Chandra is a bright and honest officer working under you and always carries his duties sincerely. One day the minister calls you and gives you an order to immediately suspend the concerned officer and even gives you the order in writing. You want to know the reason and the minister says that the Prem Chandra is an ill-behaved officer guilty of insubordination. You try and find out the facts and get to know that Prem Chandra has not been doing illegal acts on the directions of the minister and the latter is reacting to this.

How are you going to react to this?

1. You will carry out the orders of the minister and suspend Prem Chandra and start a departmental enquiry against him.
2. You will talk to the minister in private and say that Prem Chandra is an excellent officer and suspending him would give a wrong signal. Also to suspend somebody you need specific charges which are difficult to frame in this case. You will try to convince him.
3. You will send the file to the minister writing a strong note and suggest that the minister reconsider his orders.

Discussion

Prem Chandra has incurred the wrath of the minister because he has not carried out illegal orders. By suspending him you will set a very bad example for the department and lose your credibility by not supporting an honest and efficient officer. Such small things can badly damage the working of the department and you will not be able to make your officers work with honesty and sense of public service after this. Thus the first alternative is not acceptable.

The third alternative is the right one but it would annoy the minister as he would feel that you are not carrying out his orders. The second alternative is the preferred option. The Secretary should brief the minister in detail about Prem Chandra and also tell him that suspending him on flimsy grounds would create a bad precedent and antagonize all the officers of the department. You can also tell the minister that if Prem Chandra goes to Court he will get relief. Normally ministers are practical and if the facts and the correct situation are put up to them sincerely they would listen. It would be your duty to save an honest officer for acting with integrity. Since the minister has issued the orders in writing you can send the file to him after discussion with a polite note requesting him to reconsider his orders and diplomatically say that you have advised Prem Chandra not to be ill behaved with the minister. The minister would approve as this would help him not to lose face as it would appear that the minister himself has reconsidered his decision.

A senior officer must always support his subordinates if the latter is acting with integrity and efficiency. You cannot lead a department if you lose the respect of your team by sacrificing others for your personal advantage.

Case 10

You are posted as Superintendent of Police in a district known for criminal activity and you are taking a lot of steps to control crime and improve law and order. Accordingly you have selected the best sub-inspectors to hold charge as police station in-charge. One of you best sub-inspectors Yogendra is holding charge of a very sensitive police station and doing outstanding work. He has put the fear of God in the criminals and you are very happy with this work. One day information reaches you that there has been a case of gang rape of a lower caste woman and the woman has succumbed to her injuries in the hospital and the matter has been taken up by the media and opposition parties. You get to know that after the rape the girl with her parents had gone to lodge an FIR in the police station where Yogendra is in-charge but FIR was not registered. Only after the death of the girl FIR has been registered but no action taken. National media has taken up the issue and the government is also asking you to do the needful. However, you find that Yogendra did not register the FIR initially and is at fault but he is also an outstanding officer otherwise. Moreover, the accused belong to the same caste as the ruling party and so the government is also not very keen for action to be taken against them and Yogendra is also not exerting himself to arrest the accused.

In your opinion what is the best course of action for the SP.

Discussion

There has to be a policy of zero tolerance in matter relating to crime against women. The SP should immediately form a high level team and ensure that the accused persons are arrested at the earliest. Investigation should start immediately so that there is no delay in filing the charge sheet. The SP should not worry about the fact that the accused are connected to the ruling party as national media has taken up the issue and no government will put pressure on him to do otherwise. Even if media had not stepped in an officer has to do his duty. He has to treat everybody equal before law and not act in a partisan or politically aligned manner just for the sake of his career. Public service has to come before private gain. This is the essence of ethics and integrity. The SP should also regularly brief the media about action being taken otherwise media would flare up the issue to such an extent that it would go beyond his control.

The most important decision that the SP has to take is regarding the action to be taken against Yogendra who has so far performed very well. There should be no doubt in the mind of the SP. Irrespective of the past performance of Yogendra he has blundered in this very sensitive matter relating to offense against women. Yogendra should be immediately removed from the police station and placed under suspension and a departmental inquiry started against him. The SP may have to consider filing an FIR against Yogendra for being negligent to his duties. Unless he takes such strong action the whole case would boomerang on the SP and it is he who might get transferred and possibly suspended. It is his duty to take action against Yogendra for his lapses.

It is the duty of the public servant to ensure that there is no exploitation of women, weaker sections and other under privileged sections of society. This is the crux of good governance.

Case 11

You are the Chief Secretary of the state and implementing a very important scheme through which pension is being given to the women of the families below a certain level of income. More than 2000 crores of budget has been allocated for this scheme. Your Secretary in-charge of welfare department looking after this scheme is a very upright and dedicated officer and he is going into great detail to ensure that a correct list of beneficiaries is prepared. Detailed instructions and guidelines have been issued to the District Officers and village level general body meeting are being held to select the right person. Any complaint is being immediately inquired into. However, the local politicians and minister are unhappy as they want to have a hand in the selection of beneficiaries and want to use this as a system of giving patronage to their supporters who are otherwise not eligible to be included in the scheme. The secretary does not buckle under pressure and the aggrieved ministers prevail upon the Chief Minister to order his transfer and post a person of their choice. The CM directs you accordingly.

What should be your response?

1. Since the Chief Minister has given his mind you will go ahead and transfer the officer concerned.
2. You will try and talk to the ministers and make an effort to make them change their mind.
3. You will transfer the officer but post a new one of your choice who would also stand up for right action.
4. You will meet the Chief Minister and convince him that this transfer is not in the interest of the state and the program would suffer badly if there is a wrong selection of beneficiaries.

Discussion

The easiest thing to do for the Chief Secretary is to follow the first alternative. The Chief Minister and the ministers would be happy and there will be no tension for you. However, this would have the effect of derailing the pension scheme as the new officer whom the ministers want would adjust to the demands of the political people and prepare a list of beneficiaries which is not correct. This would mean that the objective of the scheme will not be fulfilled and public money wasted. A public servant has to hold the public funds in trust and see that he designs systems and processes so that money is spent for the benefit of the targeted people. Moreover, this will give rise to corruption because money will exchange hands for getting names included in the list. The citizen will not get the advantage of the scheme and this amounts to poor public service delivery which is the responsibility of the civil servant. It will also give a very wrong signal to the bureaucracy that it is of no use to work with integrity and for the benefit of the people and it is safer to bow down to political pressure. This would vitiate the work culture.

The Chief Secretary can talk to the ministers concerned and they could listen to him but will demand that the officer should adjust to their wishes. Hence the second alternative may not serve the purpose.

The third alternative is feasible and often resorted to in real life. An officer can be removed on the request of politicians but new officer should be of the choice of the Chief Secretary who can select an officer of equal ability and integrity so that the scheme does not suffer. However, the new person will take time to understand and the implementation on the scheme can get delayed. Moreover, the politicians who have tasted blood would start baying for the blood of the new officer also.

The best option is the fourth one. The Chief Secretary should personally brief the Chief Minister about the honest and correct working of the secretary and how it is in the interest of the scheme and the state that he continues. He can explain that wrong selection of beneficiaries would mean that the objective of the scheme would not be fulfilled and public money wasted. There would also be allegations of corruption whereby the government will not be able to claim much credit for implementing an important pension scheme. Once the facts are properly put forward the Chief Minister would agree and you will be able to get the scheme implemented efficiently and also give a proper signal to your team of officers.

Case 12

You are the Managing Director of a public sector corporation determined to turn around the fortunes of the loss making company. For this purpose you have created an excellent team of officers and your director of sales and marketing Mr. X is an outstanding professional who has created a brand image for the product of the company and you are confident that with him around you would be able to get results in less than a year. One day a lady employee whose working as a dispatch clerk in the sales division comes to you goes to the human resources head and complains against Mr. X. She cries and says that Mr. X has been making inappropriate advances and threatening her as she has been resisting. The HR head comes to you. You realise that this is serious but you also need Mr. X.

How would you handle the situation?

1. You would just ignore the situation and advise the HR head to hush up the matter.
2. You would tell the HR head to call the lady and convince her

to take back her complaint telling her that it is in her interest to keep quite.

3. You will advise the HR head to have a meeting with both and affect a compromise where the lady will withdraw her complaint and Mr. X will not bother her again.
4. You will immediately setup an inquiry committee as per the guidelines of the government in such matters and have the inquiry completed within 15 days and if Mr. X is guilty you will have him dismissed from service.

Discussion

This case study puts a dilemma before the MD. Mr. X is his best manager and he is in a position to turn the company around because of his ability and competence but at the same time harassment of women at the work place is an extremely serious matter and it would set up a very bad precedent for the future and damage the work culture of the organization if he ignores the complaint. The first alternative is just not acceptable. Once the matter has come to the knowledge of the MD he cannot ignore it. If he ignores then it would amount to collusion with Mr. X in his wrong behavior.

The second and third alternatives are also not the right ones. Harassment of woman employees is a very serious matter and no effort should be made get the matter closed without proper action. The best course of action is the last one whereby an immediate inquiry should be ordered in the matter to give a report in the shortest possible time and if charges against Mr. X are substantiated then action for his dismissal should be taken. It is true that work may suffer and the MD may not be able to turn around the corporation as fast as he wanted to but in a situation like this an officer must listen to his conscience and also do the right thing as per law. The protection of safety of women employees is a far bigger goal than making the organization profitable. Moreover, if such incidents are allowed then they will damage the work culture and ultimately adversely impact the efficiency of the organization. No officer or manager is such that you tolerate his wrong acts in the interest of performance. Nobody is indispensable. Mr. X will go and you can always get another manager who may be equally competent. Moreover, as a leader you will get the respect of your team if you set the right examples.

Case 13

You have been promoted to the investigation wing in income tax and it is your duty to identify chronic defaulters, collect evidence against them and carry out raids so that the right amount to income tax and penalty is collected from them. You acquire a reputation of being very honest and strict and all your raids have been very successful as many big fish have been caught. You are due for promotion and are expecting it any time. However, one day your superior calls you and gives you an unsigned list of people and asks you to immediately conduct raids against them. When you see the list you find that these are political people against whom income tax has no file or information of being tax defaulters. When you point this out your superior tells you that this list has come from the top political level and is being monitored. Your boss also quietly indicates that you are due for promotion and should not do anything at the moment to annoy the political masters.

How would you respond?

Alternatives—

1. Realizing that this list has come from the political bosses through your superior you will carry out the instructions and raid the people on the list.
2. You will flatly refuse to do so and walk away.
3. You will investigate the matter and once you find that there is no reason to raid these people you will put up a report in writing suggesting that such action is not warranted under law.

Discussion

It is a duty of the income tax officer to collect maximum tax which is used for the development of the country and this officer has been doing a very good job. However, he has been acting fairly and only carrying out raids against major willful defaulters and tax evaders. To carry out raids against innocent people just because the political party in power wants it amounts to unethical conduct. You would be harassing innocent people and working against the dictates of the law and your conscience. It is true that if you agree you will get promoted and have a smooth career to the top but for personal gain it is not correct or moral to carry out acts not warranted by law. Hence the first alternative is not acceptable.

The best thing is to refuse but if you do so with arrogance and in anger your superior and the political bosses will start gunning for you and make your life miserable and damage your career.

The third alternative is the best. You do the right thing but on the basis of evidence collected and on the papers that you have and giving it in writing. The superiors would not be able to overrule you and even the political bosses remain quiet even though they may be unhappy with you and not consider you for favored assignments in the future. There is always some sacrifice to be made if you want to be firm on the path of ethical conduct and duty towards the constitution and the citizen. Besides, if an officer has a reputation of being forthright, straight forward, ethical and moral then normally the superiors do not pressurize him to do anything wrong. He has to take a stand once and then his reputation will manage his future career.

Case 14

A chemical industry is located on the banks of river Ganges and has been known to discharge effluents into the river leading to contamination of river water and destroying aquatic life. You are Secretary in the department of environment in the state and are making all efforts to control pollution of the rivers. You immediately send your team and force the industry to install an effluent treatment plant so that the discharge from the factory is treated fully before entering the river. The industry complies and your officers give you a report that the treatment plant is working satisfactorily. One day a report appears in the newspapers that thousands of fish have been found dead and floating on the river near this plant. You are convinced that this is because of the discharge of toxic material into the river by the industry. Your officers give you report supporting the industry. You are convinced that they are giving false report but are not able to take action as everything seems to be correct on paper.

How would you resolve this situation?

Discussion

River water pollution is a major issue and the rivers are dying because of this. Even the holy Ganga water has become unfit for drinking or bathing. It is thus of the greatest importance for the health of the citizens and aquatic life that strong action is taken to control pollution of rivers. Discharge from industry into the river is a major cause of this pollution and it is now imperative as per law for all such units to install effluent treatment plants to treat the toxic material before discharge. However, there is a cost to running these treatment plants and so industry tries to avoid doing so and is often in collusion with the local officers of the environment department. Whenever the officers visits the plant the industrialist runs the treatment unit for some time and the officers record this in their inspection notes. The very fact that thousands of fish have died clearly points to contamination of water by the discharge from this chemical industry. Your local officers are involved in collusive corruption with the industrialist and so have given you an incorrect report.

You have to immediately set up another team including experts to visit the spot, check the water quality and conduct an inquiry and give their report. Once you get a report confirming the pollution of the river by the industry you must take strongest possible action against the industry under law by ordering its closure and lodging an FIR against them. However, you must act against your officers also by placing them under suspension and conducting a departmental inquiry. You will also take steps to develop systems of monitoring and use technology for this purpose to see that these kinds of incidents do not happen in the future. Real time monitoring is possible through use of technology. It is also better to see that such industries which discharge toxic material are not located near the river and are shifted. A civil servant must have total commitment to conservation of the environment.

Case 15

You are posted as the District Development Officer and a major scheme has been launched for rural employment by the government. Targets have been issued. You have been working very hard to actually generate employment for the people. At the end of the month reports have to be sent and your subordinate puts up a report showing 100% completion of target. You are aware that this report is false and point it out but your subordinate who is an old and experience hand tells you that if a report showing less than 100% achievement is sent it will be viewed adversely at the top and all officers of the district would suffer. You do not listen to his advice and get the figures corrected to give a true picture and send the information to the state headquarters. You are surprised when you get a letter from the Secretary asking for your explanation for not being able to fulfill the target when all others have done so. You find that your district is the only one showing less than 100% performance.

How would you react?

Alternatives—

1. You will discuss with your subordinate and suggest that he may amend the report and then send a fresh report to the government showing 100% fulfillment of target.
2. You will send an explanation that things will improve and from the next month send 100% completion reports as advised initially by your subordinate.
3. You will send a detailed explanation indicating the work done by you and how you have given authentic figures and also suggest that physical verification may be done by state headquarters in your district and others also. You will continue to give correct figures in the future also.

Discussion

In government many officers are adept at the fine art of always giving figures which show that the targets have been fulfilled. Your subordinate belongs to this category. You did not listen to his advice and have come to grief as your performance has been viewed adversely by the state government. Other districts have evidently sent reports which do not give the real picture but show fulfillment of the targets. Your subordinate can indicate to you that he can make a case that some data has been left out and you can give a fresh report. In this ways you can easily salvage your position but this is not correct as giving incorrect information leads to poor service delivery and improper utilization of public money and it's clearly an unethical practice. Carrying the same logic further the second alternative is also not the right one.

The best course of action is the third one where you give a detailed explanation to the government listing out the work done by you and also requesting for verification to be done by the state headquarter in all districts to find out the real level of implementation. You can indicate the steps taken by you to implement the program correctly and also the systems you have developed to monitor it. If you feel that the targets are excessive you can politely point this out and request for more realistic targets to be framed. In all probability the government would accept your request and when later on evaluation of the scheme is done it would be found that the data of your district is genuine whereas many others have given false data.

Giving false reports about government programs is a widely prevalent disease and most officers fall into this trap as they find it convenient. However, this is the main reason why the actual benefits of the schemes do not reach the real beneficiaries and there is always a chance of corruption because instead of doing real work the focus of everyone is just on fulfilling targets.

Case 16

You are the District Magistrate of an important district on the bank of the river Ganges. There are a lot of tanneries on the banks of the river employing thousands of people and are the backbone of the leather industry in your district which generates a lot of value as exports. The industry is important for the economy. However, reports reach you that toxic waste from the tanneries is regularly flowing into the river causing a high degree of pollution making the water totally unfit for any kind of use. It is also the policy of the government to see that there is no pollution of the river Ganga. It is also the policy of government to encourage industrialization. You carry out an inspection with your team of officers and find that there is a common effluent treatment plant but that is not working due to poor maintenance and also as more and more tanneries are coming up the quantity of discharge is more than what the treatment plant can handle. Your engineers tell you that it will cost 400 crores to set up a new plant and as per the polluter pay principle the tanneries should contribute to this. However, the tanneries are not in a financial position to do so and the government is not able to make that much budget available.

As an administrator how would you go about handling this situation?

Discussion

A public servant has to take all aspects of a situation into consideration while trying to solve a problem. Ideal solutions are rarely possible in the real world. However, it is important that the District Magistrate does not allow things to continue as they are because pollution of river has to be stopped under all conditions. One option for you is to order the closure of the tanneries but this would lead to large scale unemployment and adversely affect the leather industry which is very important from the point of view of exports. The other option is to carry out a survey of the tanneries and allow only that number of tanneries which have a discharge that can be handled by the existing plant and close down the tanneries that have come up after the plant has been set up. Once again this will create problems as it would be difficult to say which tanneries have come up first and which later there will always be scope of corruption at the lower level in making such a list. A civil servant has to see that any policy he makes should not create room for corrupt practices. Setting up a new plant is a good idea but it would be difficult to make the tanneries pay for it. The government is also not willing to spend the entire amount and there are Supreme Court directions that the polluter must pay. One compromise solution could be to share the cost between the government and the industry and the entire maintenance to be done by a professional body the cost of which shall be borne by the tanneries. The District Magistrate has to have several meetings at the government level and with the tanneries to make both parties accept this formula. However, even if a new plant comes up there is every chance that the maintenance would not be very good and more tanneries will come up to increase the discharge and the same situation will get repeated. Besides, any time the treatment plant is not functioning properly the discharge will go into the river. The District Magistrate can consider a solution where he allots land away from the river to the industry and motivates them to shift allowing them to make commercial use of the existing land so that they also gain financially. If he is able to do so then this would be the best solution under the circumstances.

Public servants have to behave in a professional and efficient manner and should always involve all concerned before taking a decision. They should use the participatory method of leadership to deliver results. It is important for a civil servant to be not only honest but also deliver outcomes and be result-oriented.

Case 17

Yogesh Sharma has been appointed Executive Director of an industrial unit which has not been doing well and his job is to turn it around. He recruits a good team of managers and monitors their performance vigorously and starts getting results. This industrial unit discharges toxic liquid waste into a canal from where it goes to the river. An effluent treatment plant has been installed to take care of this and the pollution department has given its approval. However, Yogesh finds that this plant is not working most of the time and the operations manager informs that running the plant is costly and so it is better to keep it shut so that the company is able to turn around fast by generating more profits. He also says that the toxic waste is not being discharged into the river but sent underground. Yogesh protests but the operations manager reminds him of the targets for profits given by the Chairman and the Managing Director of the company who has also indicated that the job of Yogesh and operations manager is linked to their meeting the targets of production and profits. Yogesh agrees with his advice and keeps quiet. One day he reads in the papers that people on the surrounding villages are suffering from physical deformities as a result of drinking contaminated water which has been polluted by the discharge of his industry. Yogesh sends a team to verify this and finds the news to be correct. His conscience pricks him but he is worried about making losses and losing his job.

What should Yogesh do?

Discussion

The easiest way out for Yogesh is to keep quiet as per the advice of the operations manager and keep the effluent treatment plant shut and let the discharge go underground to pollute the ground water and continue to make profits which will be appreciated by his superiors and he will continue in his job. He also knows that the pollution department can be managed through payments of bribes and they will never report that these diseases are a result of the discharge from this industrial unit. This is the easy way out but most unethical when just for personal gain you are damaging the health and lives of so many citizens. There should be no dilemma here. Yogesh has to see that the treatment plan functions and no toxic water is discharged underground. The cost will go up but Yogesh can inform his top management about that the entire situation and it is likely that they will also listen to reason. Further, if Yogesh is a capable leader then he should find other ways of making the unit profitable. Unethical means are not justified under any condition. If at the end of it all the management is unhappy with him and removes him he should accept it as this would not be the end of the world. Values are more important than short term gains. In fact, Yogesh should go one step further and use corporate social responsibility fund to give medical attention and care to the people who have been affected. Any administrator or manager must put human beings before any other goal and should always look at the larger picture rather than small selfish advantages.

Case 18

You have been appointed as an independent director in company ABC limited. You know that as per the company law you have to behave in an independent manner and see that the company carries out all legal compliances and follows the principles of ethics and corporate governance. The Chairman of the company treats you with a lot of respect and allows you to discuss freely on most subjects that come up before the board. However, it comes to your knowledge that a lot of matters are getting decided without being put up to the board and money is being siphoned off from ABC Limited to the companies of the son and relatives of the chairman. The auditor is also involved and not reporting these transactions to the board as he is supposed to do under the company law.

How should you react?

Discussion

The company law has mandated a minimum number of independent directors with the intention of ensuring that they know about unethical or illegal practices in the company. You have to act as the watch dog and cannot get away by saying that all these matters have not come up before the board and hence you are not responsible. It is your duty to raise these issues and by not doing so you are not acting as per the law and guilty of criminal collusion. One option is for you to immediately resign but this will not help and you will not also be true to your conscience for not acting on something illegal which has come to your notice. Tolerating illegal or unjust acts or by getting yourself transferred or resigning you do not absolve yourself from the consequences of these acts. As an independent director you can have a meeting of all the independent directors where the Chairman and Managing Director are not invited and raise these issues. Then together the matter should be brought to the notice of the board and the auditor should be asked to conduct a detailed and fair audit and submit his report. Once the matter is raised before the board it would not be possible for the Chairman or the auditors to hide things. The truth will come out and you can immediately take action to put an end to these practices and also initiate disciplinary or legal action wherever possible. The auditors stand to lose their professional certificate by indulging in such activities and so have no option but to put up the correct picture once they are pressurized to do so. Your responsibility is towards the shareholders funds and the law of the land. You cannot keep your eyes shut and have to act.

Case 19

You are posted as District Magistrate in a district which has a major cement manufacturing plant which is giving lot of employment to local people and also supporting several small scale ancillary units. You have a very competent Superintendent of Police who is young and dashing and committed to control crime. One day the general manager of the plant approaches you and looks very upset and informs you that his company is planning to shut the factory because of undue interference by the local MLA and his supporters who are constantly extracting money from the factory and want contracts to be given only to their people. You try to assure him and realise that if the factory shuts down it will give a bad name to the district and the State and reflect poorly on the performance of the district administration. You speak to the SP and a joint team is sent to the spot to resolve the matter. However, after 15 days the general manager comes to you and says that there is no improvement and the factory will be shut down within 15 days. You and the SP call the officers of the team you had deputed for the task and they say that since the MLA is very powerful and close to the Chief Minister it is not possible to take any action against him.

What should the DM and SP do?

Alternatives—

1. You both will also keep quiet as annoying the MLA could jeopardize you career and you may be transferred.
2. You will try and talk to the MLA to convince him not to harass the management of the factory.
3. You will intervene personally and take action against the criminal elements and ensure the security of the factory.

Can you think of any other action to be taken?

Discussion

The first alternative is the simplest but it amounts to dereliction of duty and by allowing criminals to go scot free because of political pressure you would be forcing the factory to shut down causing large scale unemployment and giving a bad name to the State which has been trying to attract new investors. Looking at the sensitivity of the situation the DM and SP can call the MLA and prevail upon him to leave the factory alone. However, the MLA is not likely to agree to this and even protest by saying that his people are not indulging in criminal acts and instead pour out his grievances against the management of the factory. The best course of action is the third one because it is your duty to enforce the rule of law and also in the interest of the development of the State to see that the factory should not close down and cause unemployment. A public servant has to be professional and result oriented in his working. It is unethical to be aware of illegal activities and remaining quiet about it. However, as the MLA is powerful this may lead to your transfer from the district.

In such situations the best thing to do is to brief the seniors. You and the SP should go to the State head quarters and meet the Home Secretary and Chief Secretary and get their approval for your proposed action. You can also give a report in writing. If advised to do so by senior officers you can call on the Chief Minister and brief him. Once the Chief Minister gives his approval you can take the strongest possible action and no harm will come to you. A civil servant must take tough decisions but not behave like a bull in a china shop. He cannot ignore the social and political environment and has to handle situations in a strategic manner so that the objective will be achieved without any problem for him. Use of common sense and basic intelligence is very necessary.

Case 20

You are a young officer posted to a district and the District Magistrate tells you a lot of stories about how he has handled difficult law and order situations. You are very impressed. However, when you talk to other officers in the district you find that they have a very low opinion about the DM and have no respect for him but are scared of him. You find out that the DM has a style of working in which whenever there is a law and order problem in the district he does not go to the spot himself and in fact goes on a tour to some other part of the district and returns later in the day. If the situation has been tackled properly he takes all the credit and writes to the government accordingly. However, if there has been an issue like lathi-charge or firing has been resorted to by the police then he immediately blames his subordinates and writes to the government to take action against them. You wonder whether this is the right way of handling the situation.

Discussion

The District Magistrate may be getting appreciation from his superiors and possibly good media coverage but is disliked by his team. He takes the credit if things go well but blames his subordinates if anything goes wrong. This is a very poor quality in a leader. A civil servant has to show exemplary leadership qualities if he wants to motivate and inspire his team members and mould all the officers into a cohesive unit with the right team spirit. Goals and objectives are achieved only if a leader is able to give the proper direction to his team and gains their respect. An officer like this District Magistrate would never succeed as his team members would not support him and be very careful about taking decisions. They would develop a tendency to avoid decision making, not taking initiative and never reporting the facts or correct situation to the DM. A public servant has to be professionally competent and effectively deliver results to the people. You as a young officer should never follow the working style of the DM. It is unethical not to support your team and put the blame on them for everything just to serve your personal interests.

Case 21

You are posted as General Manager of a public sector company and are looking after its manufacturing plant. You find that the plant is not running efficiently and production targets are not being met because of frequent break downs. You setup a committee to examine the reasons and find that one of the main factors is poor quality of spare parts being used which have a very small life and frequently breakdown. You also find out that the substandard spare parts are being purchased because of the policy of inviting tenders and giving the order to the person who offers the lowest price. Further you get the information that most of the suppliers are linked to your senior engineers who always recommend them and never complain about quality. There is a lot of corruption in the plant. You decide to handle the problem but are warned by your administrative officer that the unions are in the control of the senior engineers and they always use the unions to create trouble for any General Manager who tries to curb their corrupt practices.

What would be your response to the situation?

Discussion

It is your duty as the General Manager to ensure that production targets are met and the public sector company makes profits otherwise public money would unnecessarily be spent in trying to keep an inefficient and corruption prone company afloat. However, most of your senior engineers are using public resources for their personal gain which is immoral and unethical but difficult to control as they would all gang up against the General Manager and make his life miserable. If the General Manager takes no action then he would be failing in his duty as a public servant and also not be able to perform successfully. He cannot avoid his responsibility just because he is afraid to take on the entrenched vested interests. He should collect the data and confront the engineers about the poor quality of spare parts leading to breakdowns. Through discussion with them he should convince them that there should be a system of calculating the economic life of each spare part and see if the spares being bought give that economic life. You should devise a system where responsibilities of the materials manager, inventory manager and production engineer is specified and they are held accountable against them. You can setup an audit team to continuously carry out an internal audit of the operations so that such problems are regularly thrown up. Regarding the unions the General Manager should personally develop an understanding with them by holding talks and regularly solving all genuine problems of the labor. In this way he will get the support of the majority of the labor and it would be difficult for any union to instigate them. If some union does go on strike it should be dealt with an iron hand. Not all officers or labour are corrupt. He should also take action against some of the most corrupt engineers and employees. If the GM is seen as honest and committed and as a good leader then most of the employees and the officers will begin to support him. The result would be the performance of the company would improve and the General Manager would get praise for his action from his seniors. Difficult situations confront a civil servant daily but he should never run away from them and tackle them by using his administrative and leadership skills.

Case 22

Mr. X is very capable officer who has been posted as District Magistrate in a remote district. He is making a lot of effort to bring about economic development of the district and give good governance. One day he goes on an inspection of the district hospital. The medical officer in charge is showing him around and explaining the steps that he has taken to improve the working of the hospital. Mr. X finds that the standard of hygiene and cleanliness is quite satisfactory and he generally feels that things are under control. However, just as Mr. X is about to leave the hospital some people approach him and complain that despite the government policy of providing free medicines this hospital is not providing them any medicine and the doctors are recommending that patients buy medicines from outside. The medical officer in charge starts defending his doctors and claims that these people are complaining due to ulterior motives. He takes Mr. X to the store room and shows him that all required medicines are available. Mr. X is not convinced and feels that there is something wrong. He also notices that just outside the hospital gate there are a lot of chemist shops and in front of every shop there is a large crowd. Mr. X is convinced that the complaint was genuine.

How should Mr. X handle the situation?

Discussion

Mr. X can believe the doctors and do nothing. However, enough indication has been given to him that there are malpractices going on regarding giving of medicines to the patients. Mr. X as a responsible public servant must take action because government is spending so much money to supply free medicines to the patients but they are not getting the benefit.

One option is that Mr. X should start shouting at the doctors at the time of inspection itself and accuse them of corruption and warn them to be careful in the future. However, this may not solve the problem. Things may improve for a while but then go back to the earlier situation since it appears that a large number of people like doctors, chemists, storekeeper and even the medical officer in charge are involved. Besides a District Magistrate should not lose his temper in public and if he accuses the doctors of corruption without evidence they may get together and start protesting against him. The reality is that the doctors and other departmental officer have very strong associations which immediately spring to the support of their members.

The best course of action is to take measures after collecting evidence. Mr. X should get a confidential enquiry conducted by using methods like sending some people to pretend as patients to find out the truth. It is most likely that he will find that there is a big racket in the supply of medicines. Government is sending medicines to the hospitals but they are finding their way to the shops of the chemists outside. Whenever a doctor prescribes a medicine the store tells the patient that it is not available and they can purchase it from outside. Mr. X will find that a lot of people are involved in this. He then has to take action against all concerned and write to the government against the doctors. However, his work does not end with this. He must design a system to ensure that such things do not happen in the future. A public servant has to ensure that public services are delivered properly and the benefits of the government schemes, which involve a lot of public funds, reach the people.

Case 23

You have been posted as District Officer recently and have taken a meeting of the citizens to find out the main problems of the district. It comes out that one of the main concerns of the people is the poor quality of primary education in government schools. You inspect a few schools and find that the children have not attained any learning competence. A student of Class V is not able to read the books prescribed for Class II and same is the situation in arithmetic. You also find that there is very high percentage of teacher absenteeism. You launch a drive for checking the attendance of the teachers and suspend all those found absent. This causes a lot of agitation amongst teachers and you get pressure from the state headquarters also to repeal their suspension. You also find that this action of yours has not led to any improvement in the quality of the schools.

As an administrator how should you respond to the situation?

Discussion

You have done the right thing by calling a meeting of various groups of citizens to understand the problems of the district. The best way in which a public servant can serve the people is by taking them into confidence, understanding their problems and resolving them. It is very important to improve the quality of government schools otherwise the children when they grow up will be unemployable. You have taken the right step again by inspecting the school and finding out the poor quality of learning and negligence of teachers. There is no better method in administration than to actually visit the spot to assess the situation and you have done so. Your idea of carrying out a surprise inspection is also a good one any by suspending a large number of teachers you are sending a strong message. However, your action has agitated the teachers and such large scale suspension has brought in pressure from state headquarters. Moreover now the situation in the schools is even worse as there is a shortage of teachers and no learning is taking place.

Your responsibility as a public servant is to take a comprehensive view of the situation and bring about improvement in the quality of school education. Organizing a campaign for checking teacher attendance is a good idea but instead of suspending you could have issued a strong warning to all those found absent. Then after a few months you could repeat the exercise and now suspend those found absent. This time the percentage of absenteeism would be less and so your action would not agitate the teachers or the State headquarters to that extent. However, your responsibility does not end here and you have to sit down with the teachers and other stakeholders and develop a system which will ensure that actual learning takes place in the classroom and wherever required you can take the help of the education department at the State headquarters. By taking the teachers into confidence you can motivate them to be present in the schools and actually teach. A public servant can always take strict action but often that alone does not give results and so he has to involve all concerned and develop systems to change things for the better in a sustainable manner. You will be surprised to see how people respond positively if they are taken into confidence and allowed to participate in the process of change.

Case 24

You have retired from a very senior position in a public sector company and now a large private sector multinational has taken you on the board as an independent director. You are aware that your role is to ensure high standards of corporate governance and see that all laws and regulation are complied with in a transparent and fair manner. The chairman and management of the company give you lot of respect and importance and you develop good friendship with them. However, it now comes to your knowledge that the company is following unfair labour practices. They are making the labour work for about twelve hours instead of eight and not giving them any safety equipment even though many of them are working in hazardous conditions. You also find that the company is discharging toxic waste which is causing health problems in nearby villages and is against the environmental laws. You are worried that you raise the matter then the chairman would be unhappy and it would lead to bitterness.

You wonder how you should react?

Alternatives—

1. You ignore the information that has come to you and keep quiet and continue to participate in the board discussions on other issues and maintain good relations with the management.
2. You tender your resignation.
3. You raise the matter in the board and ask for a report and are satisfied if the report comes in the favor of the management.
4. You do not rely on the report of the management and insist on a committee of experts to carry out a through audit of labor and environment related practices of the company and on the basis of the report take all steps to rectify the situation.

Discussion

Even though the chairman and management have become your friends and give you lot of respect you cannot ignore the information that has come to you as it is your duty as an independent director to see that labor laws and regulations as well as environmental laws are followed. By ignoring you will become a partner in the illegal practices of the management and no longer remain an independent director.

Resignation is not a bad move as you should not continue to be a part of an organization which is indulging in unfair and illegal acts. However, even though you are absolved of all responsibility the problems remain. You are a person with a conscience and ethical background and cannot feel happy if unjust things are going on.

It would be advisable to raise the matter before the board but the management can easily come up with the report in their favor and then you would have nothing to say. Hence, after raising the matter you should insist upon external agency or committee to enquire in this matter. This would certainly lead to a correct report coming. Thereafter you can insist on corrective action and also fix responsibility on officers who have been responsible for illegal acts. It is the duty of an independent director to see that all laws are complied with by the company.

Case 25

You are posted as Secretary Industries to the State government which has been loudly proclaiming that they have implemented a lot of reforms concerned with the ease of doing business and have achieved a good ranking in comparison to other states. Through advertisements in print and electronic media you are requesting potential investors to invest in the state. One day you get a reference from a colleague of yours to meet with an industrialist who is having some problems. He has been trying to contact you but your personal assistant is not allowing him to get through to you. You give time. On the appointed day the person comes and apologises for coming a little late as it took him a lot of time to get through the pass office at the gate and then trying to locate your office. You ask him not to worry and listen to his problem but in between there are a lot of calls coming on your mobile which you are answering. When the industrialist finishes speaking you tell him that this is a problem which can be sorted out by your junior officer and he should go and meet him. The industrialist tries to say that he has tried to meet the junior officer without much success and requests you to help. You tell him that he should not waste your time and go to the junior officer. With these words you dismiss the industrialist who goes out feeling very dissatisfied.

Do you think the Secretary Industry has handled the situation correctly?

Discussion

Every where there is talk of ease of doing business to attract private investment to bring about the industrial development of the state and country. As Secretary Industry you are responsible and accountable to bring new investment in the State. However, even though you proclaim through advertisements that you have taken steps to make the life of a businessmen easy and are requesting for fresh investment. The reality at the ground level is different. In this case an Industrialist has a genuine problem but your response to him has made him feel unwelcome and is not in the interest of getting fresh investment in the State. Firstly the Industrialist has not been able to contact you as your PA would probably have not connected the phone to you and given him the cold shoulder. You meet him only after your colleague speaks to you. This is not correct as an essential quality of a public servant is accessibility. Even after giving time you have not made any arrangements and the visitor has to waste a lot of time to reach your office. It is because of these problems that the citizens are wary of approaching senior government officers. While meeting him you do not give your full attention to him and keep attending to mobile calls. This would have definitely given a very wrong signal to the industrialist. It is important that a public servant must give his full attention to the citizen who has come to him with a grievance. Finally you tell him to approach your junior officer who has not been helpful to the Industrialist. You should have attended to his problem at your level and made all efforts to resolve it. If required you should have spoken on the phone to the junior officer and instructed him to take action within a time frame. If you had done this the Industrialist would have gone away satisfied with a positive image about your department and he would have made investment in the state. By your indifferent and negative behavior you have put him off and this is the opposite of having a climate of ease of doing business. A public servant must be responsive to the people and his behavior should show empathy and concern. Arrogance is never the right approach. If you continue to behave like this you are not likely to succeed in your job as Secretary Industries.

CASE STUDIES ON OTHER TOPICS OF THE SYLLABUS

Case 26

Sometime back a major industrialist had suggested that harassment bribes should be legalized. A famous economist had initially put forward this idea. The concept was that a major problem in India is that even for the smallest legitimate work bribe has to be paid to officials at various levels to get the work done. This not only takes time but leads to considerable harassment of the people. The suggestion was that for every clearance or license a certain amount should be fixed as facilitation fees which could be capped at ₹ 5000 or 10000 and this should be given to the concerned officials that they do not delay the work. Many people agreed with this suggestion but many others were very critical of it.

In addition, it was also suggested that there should be an amendment in the prevention of corruption act and only the bribe taker should be punished and not the bribe giver. This would encourage people to lodge complaints in the event of a bribe being taken from them and it would be in the interest of the bribe giver to get the concerned official caught. This would lead to reduction in the demand for the bribes.

Question: How would you react to the above suggestion?

Discussion

This is about an ethical dilemma. The industry is frustrated that nothing in government moves easily without payment of bribe and so a suggestion has come to legalize bribe by calling it facilitation charges and giving this to the concerned officials so that they do not delay decisions or harass the applicants. This could fulfill the objective of faster economic development but it is not ethical. There should be zero tolerance for corruption rather than trying to legalize it. Corruption is an unethical, illegal and immoral act and should not be accepted by the government or the society under any conditions. Moreover, just by fixing a certain amount of facilitation fees will never lead to eradication of corruption. First of all, how the limit would be decided. Secondly, a corrupt person is always greedy for more money and would not be satisfied with a fixed amount coming to him. He will ask for more and there would be no change in the situation. A society which accepts and institutionalizes corruption would only lead to a very unethical working environment and ultimate increase in the level of corruption.

The second suggestion about bribe giver being taken out of the prevention of corruption act is also not acceptable. Bribe giving is as unethical as bribe taking. In fact, most business people and others are often willing to give bribes for certain decisions from government especially in matters where their proposal is not strictly acceptable. A bribe giver, if he is able to get his work done, would never complain against the bribe taker. Such a situation of a complaint being lodged would arise only if there is a disagreement between the bribe giver and the bribe taker. Unethical acts cannot be condoned. Thus none of the above two suggestions can be called ethical and should not be accepted.

Case 27

A very young and dashing officer of the Indian Forest Service has been posted as the Field Director of a national park and he is doing outstanding work. He has introduced a lot of technology through which he is able to identify cases of poaching of wild animals and illicit felling of trees. As a result the number of tigers and other species in the park has gone up and the jungle is being saved from the wild life and timber mafia. However, this mafia is closely involved with important political figures who try to control the officers by threatening them and their family but this officer is a man of integrity and courage and does not bend down. Finally, the mafia use their political connections and pay a handsome amount as bribe to the high level politicians and get this officer transferred. He is replaced by Mr. Ramesh Kumar, another young and active officer. He also wants to control poaching and illegal cutting of forests but he is told that if he does so he will meet the same fate as his predecessor. He decides to keep quiet and maintain status quo in the interest of his career.

If you had been in place of Ramesh Kumar what would you have done and do you agree with his approach?

Discussion

To preserve the environment it is essential we conserve our forest and the diversity of wild life species. National parks have been created for this purpose to protect the flora and fauna. The first officer did his job with integrity and his conduct was ethical and moral. He did not bend down to threats and continued to take action against poachers and jungle mafia. The result was that wild life and the jungle was conserved and developed. The officer was doing his job successfully. However, it often happens that criminals have political connections and are willing to pay large amounts of money to have honest officers removed from such postings. They succeed in getting him transferred but the new officer Mr. Ramesh Kumar also wants to take action against illegal activities. However, he is threatened and told that he will also be transferred. In the interest of continuing on this prestigious post he succumbs to the pressures and decides to let the mafia continue with their illegal activities. This would definitely lead a situation where he continues on his post for a long time and also be in the good books of politicians and earn illegal money as well. However, it would lead to complete destruction of the national park. The action of Ramesh is not that of a man of integrity. He has shown a weakness of character and is more concerned about his personal gain rather than doing his duty properly with a sense of public service. If every officer starts acting firmly as per the law and with total integrity then there is a limit to which the nexus between the mafia and the politicians can succeed. The criminal elements succeed only because many officers are willing to compromise their integrity and become part of the corrupt system

Case 28

In the Himalayan ranges there are a lot of eco sensitive zones. A study done by glaciologists and other geological experts has pointed out that the Himalayas are a relatively young mountain system which is not yet stabilized and his prone to earthquakes, landslides and flash floods. The government is keen to tap the mountain river to set up a hydroelectric project which will contribute to the development of the area and provide employment to people also. The local politicians and also local people are in support of this. The government has asked Mr. Kailash, District Magistrate to give his report in the matter. Kailash is convinced that this kind of a project can lead to a major disaster causing loss of lives and property at a future date but he has been presurrized by his seniors to give his approval.

Question: How should Mr. Kailash Kumar react in this situation?

Discussion

This is again a case of a classic ethical dilemma—development vs. environment. The District Magistrate has reports from experts which says that allowing a hydro-project on the river could lead to disturbances in the mountain systems leading to a major disaster in the future. However, the senior officers and the politicians in the government are in favor of the project as they say that this would lead to substantial economic development of the area. It would generate electricity and also employment. The District Magistrate should in fact ask for a major risk assessment study to be done by a committee of experts which should go into all aspects of the situation and give their view whether such a project is sustainable in an eco-sensitive area of the Himalayan ranges. It would be against the ethics as a public servant to give blanket approval for the project unless a high power technical committee give its clearance and also all aspects of risk management are taken care of by the project authority. It is possible that senior officers and politicians may not like his approach but he should give his report in writing so that even if he is removed from his post the paper remains on the file and will have to be attended to at the senior level in the government. Officers are expected to have a clear vision and not look at the short term goals but at the long term impact of development projects.

Case 29

You are appointed as Transport Commissioner in the state and find that the department is a very corrupt one. The regional transport officers are known to take bribes for almost every activity like getting a driver's license, road worthy certificate, registration of vehicles or allowing of buses and private transports on certain routes. You also find that every transport office in the state has middlemen or touts sitting near the office who take money on behalf of the officers to get the work done. You find that it is almost impossible for any citizen to get any work done without going through these touts and paying money. You are also aware that these officers have the support of top level politicians.

Questions: How would you as an officer respond to this situation?

Discussion

It is your duty as the Transport Commissioner to take steps to eliminate corruption which causes of a lot of harassment to the ordinary citizen and also is giving a very bad name to your department. However, just by telling people to improve and not indulge in corruption will not solve the problem. Besides, efforts will be made to get you shifted from that post. You have to first of all identify certain major cases of corruption, suspend the concerned officers and hold inquiries against them and on the basis of the inquiry report take firm action against them. This will send the right message. However, this is not enough. You have to introduce technology and develop systems which would eliminate the need to go to touts and interface between officers and citizens. For example, you can have a system where registration of vehicles is done online as also the payment of road taxes. Similarly, you can have technology introduced in the driving tests whereby an automatic score is generated which would determine whether a driving license is to be issued or not. It should not depend on the discretion of the concerned officer. Once the systems are made they will be appreciated by the people and it would be very difficult for anybody to try and get them changed or get you removed from that post. This is not an isolated case in government. In most departments such situations exist. The duty of an officer is to provide quality public service without any corruption. He has to build systems to make this happen and introduce technology wherever possible. The interaction between the citizens and the officers should be at a minimum and discretion should be removed to the maximum possible extent. This is the way to good and ethical governance.

Case 30

You are the Chief Executive of a Metro project being executed in the capital city of a State. The alignment of the Metro goes through crowded streets. The project cost does not allow you to go underground as this is very costly. A lot of encroachment exists and to construct this Metro many shops and buildings will have to be demolished including some buildings belonging to government departments. People are trying to obstruct this project which is for the public good by staging agitations and also threatening to go to the courts to get stay order. Many of these illegal shops and houses have got electricity connections and also have ration cards issued to them and claim to be carrying on business for several years at the same place. You are aware that if even one person obtains a stay order from the court the project would get delayed by several years leading to escalation in costs.

How would you resolve this dilemma?

Discussion

This kind of a situation is very common in implementing major development projects. It is important that such projects which give a lot of benefit to the citizens should be implemented. It is also vital that these projects are completed on time otherwise the costs go up and become difficult to finance the project. This also often leads to lower quality standard of work. Encroachers have no right and can be forcibly evicted but the problem is that the authorities have allowed them to exist for several years and even given them legal facilities like electricity connection or ration card. On the basis of this they can claim relief from the court. Further, many constructions are legal and belong to government departments. The best course of action in such a situation is to negotiate with the people and convince them of the benefit of the project. They will have to be allotted land at a different place and also awarded compensation so that they can construct fresh houses or shops. It may seen unethical to compensate illegal houses or shops but the fact remains that they have been existing for several years due to collusion with government officers and so there is no option but to incentivize them to move to a different location. The compensation would have to be a part of the cost. Regarding government buildings new buildings will have to be constructed by the Metro project. For example, if there is an office building of the police department which has to be demolished then a new building has to constructed by the authorities.

In the above manner you can construct the Metro on time with the cooperation of all concerned. It is important for a public servant to deliver a result on time and for this some time he has to adopt a practical approach rather than go strictly by the rule book. Legally you could demolish the illegal buildings but it would create human problems as well as create a lot of opposition to the project which would ultimately lead to failure on your part. It is important to take a balanced view of a situation and always take into account the human aspects of a situations.

Case 31

You have become the Director of Technical education in your State and find that the quality of education is not satisfactory. The main reason is that every year a lot of undeserving colleges are getting affiliated to the university and you are told that there is lot of corruption in this. You start a technical audit to try and improve quality of education but you find that there is not much that you can do about the existing colleges and also that these colleges are owned by some very powerful people. However, you find that every year new colleges are coming up for affiliation. You resolve to be very strict in giving approval this year. When you chair the committee for affiliation you find that the officers who had been sent to conduct inspection have given inaccurate reports and you are told by the people that a lot of money had exchanged hands. You ask for more detailed information and find that the office is unwilling to provide this information. You postpone the meeting and give a check list of details that you want given under the signature of the three senior-most officers of your department. A few days after this the officer who is in charge of affiliations comes to you and requests you to give your approval to all the fifty pending cases and tells you that at least rupees five lakhs per case would be given to you.

How would you react to the above situation?

Discussion

As the Director of technical education it is your duty to improve the quality of education and as chairman of the approval committee it is your right to ask for all relevant information. You should be clear that this concerns the life of students and if undeserving colleges are approved then they will spoil the life of young boys and girls. Your suspicion regarding corruption has been found to be correct as the concerned officer is promising money to you. As an ethical public servant you must refuse the illegal money being offered to you and carry out a very strict scrutiny of all the applications. You should change the inspection team also preferably going for third party inspections to get all the relevant information. You should also reconstitute the approval committee and bring in technical experts to have a fair evaluation of the applications.

Now that you know that there is corruption in the department you have to take action against the concerned officers and at least have them removed or transferred from the department at the earliest and bring in fresh officers who are known for their integrity. It is also important that you develop systems for all activities in your department to minimize if not eliminate the chance of corruption in future. You should also make public the performance parameters of existing colleges so that the students can choose rationally. Colleges offering poor quality education will not get students and be forced to close down.

Case 32

Rahul Singh, IAS is appointed as Secretary of secondary education in a backward state of India. Rahul finds that the state has a large population and the school leaving board exam has more than 20 lakh students appearing. The surprising thing is that more than 80 percent students are passing the exams and some surveys by media agencies have shown that even the toppers are not having basic knowledge about their subjects. Rahul holds discussions with all concerned and realizes that the root cause for this is the large scale cheating taking place in the examination centers. The teachers, parents, students, managers and officers are all involved in this racket. In fact he finds that managers of private schools use a lot of political influences to get their school declared as an examination center because they will earn a lot of money by allowing cheating. Rahul is told by his officers that a lot of influential people including officers and politicians are involved and it is almost impossible to control cheating and that this would be opposed by majority of the people. He is advised to let things go on as they are.

What would you advise Rahul to do?

Discussion

Cheating in examinations has become an organized racket particularly in the backward states of the Country. All stake holders are involved in this including the parents and teachers. Mass scale cheating takes place in the examination and this is the main cause for the poor quality of education. The result is that we have young boys and girls who do not acquire any knowledge and pass exams by cheating making them unemployable. This leads to poverty as well as law and order problems as many of these students take to crime. The talent of the youth goes in a deviant direction instead of contributing to the development of the nation. Rahul should not listen to the advice of his team members to allow the existing situation to continue. He should, first of all, take his minister and senior officers into confidence and convince the political executive that controlling cheating in an examination would ultimately give a lot of credit to the government. Once he gets the political will behind him he must use his leadership qualities to convince his team members and get them committed to the goal of eliminating cheating in the exams. He should first of all get the examination centers selected purely on merit. There after close circuit cameras. should be installed in as many centers as possible. A very strict system of invigilation should be put in place and no crowd be allowed to assemble within 500 meters of the centers. The District Magistrate and the Superintendent of Police should be fully involved in the process and their team should constantly inspect the examination centers on the exam day. A strict system of evaluation should be put in place. Rahul should personally monitor on a regular basis to coordinate all activities. In this way he will certainly be able to curb cheating and also earn an excellent reputation for himself. He would also be doing his duty as a public servant in an ethical manner and his action would be an example of integrity, transparency, objectivity and effectiveness in governance.

Case 33

A major pandemic has hit the country and a lot of people are becoming ill and need urgent hospitalization and intensive care. There are directions that testing for the disease should be increased to find out the exact number of people getting infected so that proper treatment is given to them. You are the District Magistrate of a District where the numbers of cases are going up on a regular basis. The Chief Minister is unhappy and has asked for your explanation for this phenomenon. You know that the reason has been that some people from outside the state have come to your district and are the cause behind this spurt in the cases. Your team advises you to go slow on the testing and also under report the actual cases so that the State headquarters are satisfied and your district does not earn a bad name.

How would you respond to the situation?

Discussion

It is your responsibility to handle the pandemic in an efficient manner and reduce the number of infections as well as the number of deaths due to the infection. The cases are going up and the State headquarters is evidently unhappy with this situation. However, it would be absolutely unethical for you to listen to the advice of your team and reduce the testing or under report the actual number of infections. You should immediately take strong steps to control the pandemic. Containment zones should be identified and a strict lockdown imposed in these areas. The medical facilities should be strengthened and more beds made available in intensive care units and ventilators and essential medicines made available. In fact the testing should be increased and the correct figure reported and contact tracing and tracking done. You should personally monitor the situations on a regular basis. All this would certainly lead to a reduction in the number of cases and the fatalities. You may send your explanation to the Chief Minister giving reasons for the increase in the number of cases and outline your action plan for controlling the spread of the pandemic in your District and you can assure him that you will be able to handle the situation. It never pays to hide the truth or misreport facts or give wrong data. You should always have the correct position before you so that you can manage it. The important thing is the prompt and effective action that you are taking to handle the situation. It is good governance that is important and not the unethical manner or hiding the factual situation.

Case 34

You are a Director of a very important medical college and are proud of your team of doctors who are amongst the best in the country. In particular, a doctor in cardiology is of national and international fame and the reputation of your institute is enhanced by his presence. However, one day you get a notice from the nurses association who want to go on strike unless this doctor is removed. You find out that one of the nurses has been complaining of sexual harassment against the doctor saying that he keeps calling her into his room, sending indecent text messages and also tries to touch her physically. When the nurse did not respond the doctor has started scolding her and threatening to take action against her. You call the doctor and talk to him but he denies all allegations but the nurse shows you the text messages sent by the doctor and other nurses and employees testify that the doctor's behavior towards this nurse had not been normal.

As a Director it is your responsibility to maintain the work culture and the reputation of the institute, how would you respond to the situation?

Discussion

The reputation of the institute is of the greatest importance and as a director it is your responsibility to maintain it. It is a fact that if this cardiologist is removed from his job then it will have an adverse impact on the institute. At the same time, the complaint of sexual harassment is an extremely serious matter and cannot be ignored. Ultimately, this will also damage the reputation of the institute and also adversely impact the work culture and work ethic and gender ethic. As a director you cannot try for a compromise. Such situations have to be dealt with firmly. There are clear Vishaka guidelines issued after Supreme Court judgment about how to handle cases of sexual harassment in an organization. You should strictly follow the guidelines and set up an independent inquiry committee to enquire and submit the report within 15 days after giving due opportunity of being heard to both the parties and evaluating the evidence. After 15 days if you get a report that the complaint is correct. There is no option for you but to take action against the doctor including removal from the service of the institute. This will mean that ethical practices are being followed in the institute and in the long run lead to greater efficiency.

Case 35

Conducting elections is a major responsibility of the district administration which has to ensure free and fair elections without violence or disturbance of law and order. The District Magistrate and his team work as officers of the election commission during the period of the elections. Elections to the assembly have been announced and the District Magistrate has started preparations for the elections. One day he gets a call from the office of a senior minister who says that the local candidates of the party will meet the DM as they have some problems and request him to sort out the issues. You give time to these candidates but are surprised by their demands. They want certain specific officers to be posted on election duty in their constituency and in particular booths. You tell them that there is a software according to which duties are allotted but they are not convinced and pressurize you to handle things in a manner so that their request is granted. They also give you a list of polling booths where they want additional police to be deployed and another list of booths where they want only a home guard to be put on duty because in the latter booths they are in a strong position while in the former they are weak. They also asked you to take action under preventive sections against a list of people which you find are close to the candidates of the opposition parties. They tell you that their party is going to come back in power and they will look after your interests if you agree with them. Your feedback also tells you that the ruling party is likely to retain power.

What kind of action would you like to take in the matter?

Discussion

It is the duty of DM to conduct free and fair elections which is so important for democracy in the country. Even though the DM may be having the feedback that the ruling party is going to come back in power and he realizes that if he complies with the request of the party candidates he will be in the good books of the ruling party which will be a great help to his career. On the contrary if he does not agree then these people will carry a grudge against him and at a later date transfer him and also take vindictive action against him. However, he cannot deviate from the ethical path. He has to conduct elections in an absolutely fair manner. He cannot agree to any request of the candidates of the ruling party. He must carry out all his duties in a transparent manner as per the guidelines of the election commission and not bow down to any kind of political pressure. Even if this means that he suffers at a later date he should not worry about the consequences and do his duty as per the rule of law. The duty of polling officers has to be done confidentially and in an impartial manner so that officers belonging to one caste or community are not posted to the same booth and that no candidate has knowledge of which officer is being posted to which booth. In fact even the pooling officers get to know their destination on the poling day. There is now a software approved by election commission for this purpose and should be used. Similarly, the categorization of booths as sensitive should be done by the District Magistrate and his police counterpart on the basis of their objective assessment. Under no condition should provisions of preventive sections of the criminal procedure code be used against the candidate or supporters of a particular party in order to favor another party. Conducting elections is a sacred duty and the future of democracy depends upon it and the officer must be aware of his immense responsibility.

Case 36

You are the Chief Development officer of a District and you find that one of the major problems of the area is rapid depletion of its ground water reserves due to over exploitation for the purpose of agriculture. Every year more and more blocks are becoming critical. At this rate the entire District could become barren after some time leading to loss of income for the farmers and enhanced poverty. One of the main reasons is that water guzzling crops are being grown and secondly because of free power and water the farmers are over exploiting the limited water resources. There is a ban imposed on constructions of new tubewells but this is being violated by the powerful farmer lobby with political connection. You are advised by your subordinates not to disturb the vested interests as this would lead to a powerful political backlash. You are told that you will be in the district only for a couple of years and should not do anything which could ultimately harm your career.

As the Chief Development Officer what would be the right approach for you?

Discussion

Your job is to develop the District and it is your ethical duty to honestly take all steps to bring about overall development of the District. Depletion of ground water is a serious problem which will lead to impoverishment of the farmers and the families living in the District besides creating environmental issues. This could also lead to diseases amongst animals and human beings. You must coordinate with all the concerned departments and prepare a detailed action plan. You can send a project to the State Government for funding. It is possible that the State Government may not respond. In that case you must pool the funds of various schemes and achieve your objective by convergence. You should also visit all the villages along with your team of officers and hold meetings with the farmers. You should make them aware of the seriousness of the problems and convince them not to grow water guzzling crops, nor dig any new tubewells, use sprinkler or drip irrigation to irrigate your farm and follow all necessary ecological and environmental safe guards. An officer should be able to convince the farmers and once he is able to do that more than half the battle is won. An officer must involve the citizens in any scheme or project he takes up which may require the citizens to change their existing ways of thinking or acting. There after he should build a team to handle the project and monitor it regularly at his level to see that results come. He can brief the media also and if he gets good coverage in the media then he will not face any political interference. He should set a goal of not allowing any further reduction in ground water and bringing up the water table in the District in a specified time frame.

Case37

You are posted as Director in the environment department of the state government and are concerned about the fact that there is no concrete action plan to tackle air and water pollution in the state. The latest report put up by Government of India shows that five major cities of your state are in the top 20 of the most polluted cities of the state. You raise this point in a meeting at the higher levels of Government but are told that there is no allocation in the budget and also this does not appear to be a priority with the Government. You are very concerned about the problem and want to do something immediately to address the issue because you are aware of the fact that this high level of air pollution is leading to severe health issues for the citizens and even leading to a reduction in their life spans.

What would be your approach?

Discussion

It is clear that two basic principles of ethics are involved in this. The first is your duty as a public servant to provide a clean and disease free environment to the citizens of the state. The second is your commitment to your job where you are expected to give your best and be efficient and effective and give results in the responsibilities entrusted to you. You have not got an encouraging response from your seniors who feel that this is not a priority with the Government and there is a problem of funds. This should not deter you. Difficult situations should bring out the best in a public servant and his job is to resolve problems. He should prepare a presentation showing the high levels of air pollution and the impact that this is having on the health and life of the citizens. You should also prepare an action plan with the time frame and required budgetary resources to tackle the menace. Then you should take time from senior officers and the political executive including the Chief Minister to give a presentation of the situation. If the issue is presented well you will find understanding and support coming from the other side. Funds to a certain extent will be made available but there are a lot of non-financial aspects of the problem also which can be attended to by immediate instruction from the government like phasing out of old transport vehicles. Then you can also converge funds of various departments to help you in solving the problems. You should be able to convince the political executive that it is politically also very important that this problem is resolved otherwise it will give a bad name to the State. Once the action plan is approved and funds allotted you should monitor it on a regular basis to ensure results to the people of the State. You will face opposition from many departments like industries and transport. You have to use your communication skills to overcome them.

Case 38

Most of us are living in cities and daily face some problems like garbage not being removed, water supply not being available or street lights not functioning or sewer overflowing etc. Citizens are greatly concerned about these issues and are unhappy that they do not know where to make a complaint and how to get a response. More often than not the citizens are unhappy that their problems are not attended to on priority. Mr. Ankur Kumar is posted as Municipal Commissioner of city X and finds that the citizens have a lot of problems with the Municipal Corporation which are not being resolved to their satisfaction. You also find that despite this instruction the staff is lazy and indisciplined and often do not take any action on complaints for a long time.

How should Ankur Kumar manage the situation?

Discussion

In a situation like this there are two things that Ankur Kumar should do. He should use technology to get a grip on the problems of the people and also communicate with his team to change their negative attitude towards their work and grievances of the people. Ankur as a Municipal Commissioner is duty bound to provide redress to the citizens in a time bound manner. Ankur could start by having a free frank discussion with his team members and firmly tell them that it is your conviction that problems of citizens should be accorded the highest priority. You should also listen to the problems of your team in terms of human and financial resources and prepare a plan to solve these problems. Then you motivate your team with the promise of rewards and punishment depending upon the promptness and efficiency with which they resolve their problems of the people. Then you can use technology and build an app through which the citizens can directly register their complaint. You can also develop a call center where people can lodge their grievances using their mobile or even through email. Ankur may also develop a Citizen Charter and put it on your website and also on all the ward offices showing which officer is accountable of what kind of problem and the procedure for redressal of grievances. Ankur Kumar will personally have to monitor to see that all grievances are sorted out in a time bound manner and that he also has a system through which the public can get a feedback on their complaints. In this manner, Ankur will be able to provide satisfaction to the people and deliver public service in an efficient manner.

Case 39

The moment Vinay Kumar took over as Secretary in the department of Rural Development he found that he had been summoned by the honorable High Court in two matters relating to contempt of court of its decisions regarding promotion of certain officers of the department. Vinay hurriedly called for the files found that the honorable court had issued specific orders for promotion of two officers several months back and these have not been complied with. Vinay takes legal opinion which advices him to comply with the orders immediately. He issues orders in compliance and present himself before the court and is exonerated from the charge of contempt. Later on, Vinay reviews the promotion policy of the department and is aghast to find that the seniority lists of officers have not been finalized. For more than fifteen years no meeting of the department promotion committee has taken place and as a result officers are suffering and feeling de-motivated. On closure scrutiny Vinay finds that there is a racket in the department involving lower level secretariat employees who are deliberately not promoting officers in the proper manner and encouraging some of them to approach the courts and get orders which these employees do not put up to the secretary and wait for contempt of court proceedings to start thereby forcing compliance. A lot of money is exchanged hands in the process.

What would you advise Mr. Vinay Kumar to do?

Discussion

These kind of unethical practices are quiet common in the Secretariat in matters relating to establishment issues of officers like promotion. Vinay Kumar must act to break the unholy nexus between his secretariat employees and some officers. To do this he must set up a team under his chairmanship to review all the seniority lists and finalize them after taking objections from the people. Thereafter, any matters relating to seniority pending in the courts should be contested and resolved. After this as per the guidelines of the Government he should convene the departmental promotion committee meetings and bring all promotions up to date. This would greatly motivate his field officers and they shall work with more enthusiasm and energy. Once all promotion processes are regularized there would be no need for any officer to go the court to seek orders for his promotion and the nexus operating in the secretariat would become in-operational. He should not rest at this. He should identify the secretariat employees who have been indulging in these unethical practices and initiate departmental action against them and also get them transferred. For future he should also design a system where any order of the honorable court is put up before him personally on the date it is received and he should personally monitor action taken in consequence of this order. Establishment issues are of great importance to Government employees and officers and it is unfortunate that certain Secretariat employees take advantage of this situation to harass the officers and make money in the bargain. Strictest possible action is required in these matters.

Case 40

Mr. Ranveer Singh has been appointed as the General Manger of a public sector manufacturing unit known for its disturbed industrial relations due to the presence of militant trade unions. Mr. Ranveer Singh's predecessor had been physically attacked inside the factory by four anti-social elements in the labour and their services had been terminated. However, just before the GM was transferred the labour unions met him and apologized for the conduct of the four employees and took advantage of the emotional farewell moment to get orders for taking these four people back in work. After Ranveer joins the labor unions meet him and ask him to issue the orders for re-appointment of these four laborers telling him that his predecessor had already issued the orders on file. You find that their statement is correct but your officers including the Personnel Manager and Chief Engineer advise you against doing so as they tell you that these four are known anti-social elements and attempt at physical assault on the earlier GM was a serious matter which if condoned would lead to increasing in-discipline in the factory which already suffers due to the militancy of the unions. Ranveer realizes the situation that if he has to run the factory he must control the unions. He refuses to reinstate these four workers. The labour unions start threatening that they would go on a strike. They prepare a list of about fifteen demands and give to him saying that if action on these demands is not taken within fifteen days they would go on indefinite strike.

Should Ranveer Singh accept the demands of the union or take some other course of action. What would you advise him to do?

Discussion

It is clear that this public sector unit like many others is suffering due to union trouble because of which the workers are not doing their duties properly and creating a lot of indiscipline. The result of this is that the production capacity of the plant is not being properly utilized leading to losses for the company. If Ranveer succumbs to the pressure of the unions and reinstates the four workers and also concedes some of the demands of the unions which are *prima facie* not acceptable then this would mean that unions will get an upper hand and start dominating him. The atmosphere in the plant would be vitiated and even your senior officers will lose respect for you. The unions will realise that you are having a weak backbone and character and not allow you to do any new thing to improve the functioning of the plant and constantly give you the threat of strike to make you concede their demands. This simply means that you will be an ineffective general manager and the poor performance of your company will continue. You will not be doing justice to public money or to the responsibility entrusted upon you by the government. Therefore, Ranveer can start by calling the unions for several rounds of talks and try and convince them to withdraw the strike notice. In all probability, they will not agree. Ranveer should then make all arrangements to handle the strike and let them go ahead. He should then handle the strike with an iron hand which may include issuing termination slips to some employees indulging in violence and also take the support of the police and the local administration to get the prominent leaders arrested. If he shows this kind of intent ultimately the unions will buckle down and withdraw the strike unconditionally. Once this is done Ranveer should reach-out to the workers and labour unions in a pro-active manner and develop a system of resolving their grievances on a monthly basis by holding regular talks with the unions and also giving time to each employee to meet him if he had any problems. In this way he will gain a lot of goodwill and there would be no labour disturbance and the plant would run efficiently. It is the ethical duty of Ranveer to see that resources are used properly and efficiently for the benefit of the citizens of the state.

Case 41

You have been posted as District Magistrate recently and have started touring the district and implementing Government programs in the best possible manner. During your inspections you find that in several places the buildings and the roads constructed are of a very poor quality which shows that Government money is not being utilized properly and that there is a lot of corruption. You start taking steps to control the malpractices and soon there is a lot of appreciation in the society to the way you are working and the quality of the implementation of Government schemes has improved considerably. The media is also praising you. However, there is a small weekly newspaper which has very little circulation but a lot of nuisance value has been making adverse comments about you in this paper. You try to find out the reason and are told that the editor of this paper was one of the beneficiaries of the corruption in the building of roads before your tenure. The way you acted has hurt his interests. The editor comes to you one day asking for a lot of financial support in the form of advertisements. You refuse by saying that the paper has very little circulation. The paper resorts to yellow journalism and starts writing pieces to damage your reputation and character and all of them are examples of fake reporting.

How would you responds to this situation?

Discussion

It inevitably happens that when an officer behaves in a dashing and effective manner and takes action against corrupt practices he disturbs the existing *status quo* and the vested interests. These people gang up against him and want to defame him. False complaints are made and also political influence is used to try and get such an officer transferred. One of the main agents of this kind of action are the local newspapers which exists not to serve the cause of giving news but only to make money by trying to blackmail senior officers. These journalists are often involved in all kinds of activities to get money and especially they take out scanty newspapers just to get advertisement from the Government which are their main source of revenue. If denied, they resort to blackmailing the officers by publishing false news. This is totally unethical conduct on the part of such journalists. It is not that all journalists are like this. Most of them are very professional and dedicated but a small minority does indulge in all kinds of unethical practices. You have started doing good work in the district and nothing should distract you from your purpose of bringing about effective delivery of public services. In fact the citizens always support an officer who is honest and delivers results. One option before you is to completely ignore the negative reporting against you. This is very often the best option as the moment you start reacting this becomes the topic of gossip all over the place and even those who have never read that newspaper would become aware of the new items and create an unnecessary controversy.

The second option is to use your powers to get the premises of the newspaper inspected and you will find that the guidelines of the Government are not being followed and you can initiate action by suspending the license of the newspaper and also by lodging a first information report (FIR) with the police. If the newspaper has been coming out with stories which are causing genuine damage to you then this kind of action can be resorted to.

A third alternative is to go to the court and file a suit of defamation. However, cases in the courts often take an unduly long time and also this has the potential of creating a major controversy which would be in your interest to avoid.

A fourth alternative could be to just stop giving advertisements to this newspaper and tell others also not to patronize this paper. The moment the financial squeeze is applied the newspaper would be facing great difficulties to continue publication. This perhaps is the best course of action if the negative reports are persisting. However, if only a few news items have been published then it is best to ignore them. The public always knows about your good work and will not be swayed by such yellow journalism.

A good officer doing ethical work will never find it easy. He will face opposition from all angles but he must never give up and continue to work with integrity and honesty and fulfill the purpose for which he has joined the service that is to deliver results for the people and ensure their welfare.

Case 42

You have been posted as Secretary of the housing department and you find that this department is in fact being run by the builders lobby. Most of your officers are virtually in the pay of these builders and turning a blind eye to their corrupt practices. Some builders are doing their work as per the rules and guidelines and spending the money taken from the customers on projects itself but there are many others who are illegally siphoning off the money into their personal accounts or projects and as a result delaying the completion of the projects leading to escalation in cost which they are demanding from the helpless citizens. You also find that the construction is a poor quality and many of the rules and guidelines of the housing and urban development act are being violated. In fact even the requirement of green areas or widths of roads or other common facilities are not being adhered to. You want to correct this situation but are aware that the builder mafia has a very close nexus with powerful officers, politicians and other sections of society.

Would you accept the situation as it is or take steps to remedy it at the personal cost of getting transferred or even incurring the displeasure of the political master?

Discussion

Once again the choice is between doing nothing to change a situation where corruption is rampant and actually taking the lead to change things for the better interest of the citizens who want to own a house and are being exploited in the current system. You must review the situation with your officers to devise a strategy and an action plan to tackle the irregularities taking place. You can then call a meeting of the builders and share your views with them asking them to cooperate otherwise legal action would be taken against them. You also design a system of customer grievance redressal whereby any citizen wanting a house and having problems with builders can lodge a complaint which can be attended. Many builders would change their way of working and start taking action as per rules once they realized that you are honest and incorruptible and mean business. However, some and especially those who enjoy political patronage will refuse to comply and start making complaints against you with the intention of getting you transferred from their post. The Housing Secretary has to face the builders' mafia but any officer who wants to change the corrupt practices in any department will find that the people involved in the organized racket of corruption would start opposing him and try to get him removed. In this case he should get the colonies inspected by a team of officers and initiate action wherever there is violation of the rules. He should also take action against some of his corrupt officers without whom such large scale disregard for Government rules and guidelines cannot take place. He should force the builders to have a system and any money taken from homebuyers should be kept in a separate escrow account so that it cannot be siphoned off and utilized to complete the project with all the promised services within time. If the builder is not providing any common facility despite having promised then he should use the powers given to you under various acts to discipline the builders. It is likely that you will face a lot of stiff resistance but ultimately you will see that customers get their houses on time and without paying extra and so provide a lot of satisfaction to the ordinary citizens of the state.

Case 43

This is a real case and I have used the real names. Please read the case and answer the related questions. The case of Satyendra Dubey has attracted widespread attention from the media and public for the tragic end to a noble whistle-blowing incident. Satyendra Dubey was employed with the NHAI (National Highway Authority of India) as an assistant project manager. He was employed in the prestigious golden quadrilateral project in a segment in Jharkhand. Dubey was known to be strict with quality, had high professional integrity, and did not condone the waste of public resources and laxity on the part of contractors.

Having seen many irregularities and poor quality of work, he apprised the authorities of NHAI about these incidents. No action was forthcoming because it was alleged that the officials from NHAI were hand in glove with the contractors in the irregularities being committed.

Having exhausted the normal channels to initiate action against the irregularities, Dubey wrote directly to the Prime Minister of India at whose initiative such a massive project was initiated. He had specially requested that his name should be kept confidential. Despite this request, it was alleged that Dubey's letter was circulated to many concerned departments from where his name was leaked to the road mafia.

On 27th November 2003, Dubey was returning from Varanasi after attending a wedding. He had reached the Gaya railway station at 3 am. He had expected his car to come but as the car was not there, he hired a rickshaw to go home. His body was later found by the side of the road.

This is a case of a whistle blower suffering for coming out with the truth. Discuss the case keeping in mind the role of whistle blower and how they should be protected. Also do you think Satyendra Dubey did the right thing or he should have kept quiet?

Discussion

Satyendra Dubey was a whistle blower whose identity should have been kept confidential. This is the basic requirement of protection to whistle blowers who are people working in an organization and see acts of corruption around them and complain to higher authorities. The advantage of this is that the top management gets to know what is happening at the lower level so that they can take measures to control corruption and irregularities. The Whistle Blower Act of 2011 and Whistle Blower Protection Act 2014 also contain these provisions. There are guidelines issued regarding protection of whistle blowers in corporate undertakings and Government organizations, however the fear of retaliation and victimization of whistle blowers is still very much present. The identity of Satyendra Dubey was made public and naturally this led to enmity with those indulging in corruption who planned and got him murdered. Disclosing his identity was an unethical and improper act.

We must give credit to Satyendra Dubey for being a man of honesty, integrity and total commitment to his organization. It is not as if only he became aware of the corrupt practices. Others would be knowing about it also but they either choose to remain quiet about it or they joined in the unethical practices. You will be surprised to know that most people belong to this category and Satyendra Dubey was a rarity. He felt very deeply about the situation and when his seniors did not respond he wrote directly to the Prime Minister. He could not allow public resources to be wasted. We must honor and commend such people of integrity but unless the system protects the people would stop coming forward with the truth.

Case 44

Some gold coming from abroad illegally has been intercepted and confiscated by the customs authority which is investigating the case and the National Investigating Agency has also been asked to conduct an enquiry. As the officer in-charge of customs you find that this is a major racket in which very senior officer of the Government of the State and influential people are involved. You take steps to build the case against the culprits including officers of your own department who may be involved in it. You also develop systems using technology to see that this kind of thing does not happen in the future. However, you get pressure from senior level in the Union Government to try and implicate senior politicians of the State ruling party. You know that they are not involved as per your investigations but there is pressure from the top.

How should you as custom officer respond to the situation?

Discussion

As the custom officer it is your duty to see that smuggling does not take place and you should take very strict action in the matter. Gold has been confiscated and a lot of senior officers and people of influence are involved. You should not hesitate to take action against anybody no matter how important or senior that person is. However, because of the situation the matter becomes extremely sensitive and has political implications also. This calls for a very detailed and thorough inquiry so that no innocent person suffers and no person who is involved is able to get away with it. You should not buckle down to any pressure from the top which wants you implicate certain political people. However, you should not hesitate to take action against them if they are involved. Thus, you must conduct a very thorough investigation and find out all those people who are directly or indirectly involved and there is evidence against them and take action at the earliest. You should be careful not to disclose any details of the investigation to the media before the inquiry is complete. This kind of situation is often faced by officers of the Indian revenue service (income tax and customs) and the way out of the ethical dilemma is to be absolutely fair, transparent, correct, impartial and objective in your investigation.

Case 45

A prominent businessman of the district where you are posted as DM has always maintained very good relations with the officers. The moment you join the District he calls on you and you find him to be a very pleasant and dignified looking person. You keep getting invited to all social and cultural functions. He also is in the habit of inviting senior officers for dinner to his house and almost all officers attend his functions however, within a couple of months you realise that even though he goes around as a religious person doing a lot of social service and charity he in fact indulges in black marketing of essential goods and commodities. He has a petrol pump where the petrol gets adulterated. Moreover his movie hall does not pay the entertainment tax properly. You start taking action against these activities. One day the businessman invites you for a dinner to his house saying that he has called many other senior officers also and it will be an honor for him if you attend.

This situation presents a dilemma before you. How would you react to the situation?

Discussion

These kind of situations crop up quiet often and the dilemma that you are facing is not uncommon. The businessman is one of the most respected people of the district and he spends a lot of his money in social work and charity. However, you have definite information about his being involved in anti-social, illegal activities. If you as District Magistrate attend his dinner it gives him a sense of legitimacy in the eyes of the people. In fact he maintains such good relations with senior officers of the District to have a cover for his illegal activities. There would be psychological pressure on you to attend the dinner as other officers are going and all through this person has been very decent and courteous in his behavior towards you. Your not going would send a major signal. Civil servants have to be very careful about their social relations as many people who indulge in illegal activities maintain good social contacts with their administration so that the needle of suspicion does not fall upon them. It may appear to be a small issue but has very large implications. If you mix socially with such people you will not be able to take action against them and your subordinates will also never act against such people. Therefore, the best course of action for you is to politely refuse the invitation by giving some excuse and in future also avoid social interaction with him. You should also initiate action with respect to all illegal activities that this person is indulging in. It is important to point that very often such people invite you to functions and then click photographs with you which can be used against you at a later date. Thus it is important to maintain a distance from such people.

Case 46

You are Secretary in-charge of rural development and implementing a lot of government schemes for both individual beneficiaries and community projects. There are large targets to be met for the individual beneficiary schemes which depend upon on loans being given by banks and subsidy by the government. You hold a review meeting with your officers and find that the progress is very slow. On questioning, your officers tell you that the problem is with the banks who are not cooperating in sanctioning loans. Banks come under the purview of Government of India and are not directly under the state government. However, many of these programmes are part of government of India initiatives. You call a meeting of the bankers and motivate them to fulfill targets and also take up the matter at the state level banker's committee where senior officers in the bank and the Government sit together and deliberate. There is improvement in loan sanctioning but all of a sudden you start getting complaints that the banks are taking bribes to sanction loans. You want to put an end to this but your officers advise you to let things be as any action on your part like filling a criminal complaint would immediately derail the schemes as banks would slow down or even stop sanctioning loans. Your officers say that it is better to overlook the complaints of corruption.

How would you balance the conflict between allowing corruption or not being able to meet the targets?

Discussion

In most schemes related to rural development the banks have a major role to play as all the schemes have a loan and a subsidy component. Banks are not directly under the control of the state government yet their cooperation and support is essentials for the success of these schemes. There are mechanisms for coordination between the banks and Government like the state level and district level bankers committee meetings. In this case you have used this channel to motivate the banks and the performance of your district has improved but allegations of corruption are coming in a big way. You have the option of complaining against the banks to higher levels of Government as also lodging an FIR or criminal complaint with the police. It is important for you to ensure that there is no corruption in Government project. However, it is true that the moment you take some action the banks would stop cooperating and you may not be able to meet your targets which will affect your performance appraisal. Similar activities must be going on in other districts but the officers there are allowing the banks to charge commission but are firm about meeting targets and as a result your performance in comparison to them would suffer and people higher up in the Government will not appreciate it. This is a very difficult situation of an ethical dilemma. Each person could have his own way of handling this but once there is knowledge of corruption it cannot be ignored also. The best method would be to take action in a few cases where specific complaints have come to you and not go for a general action against all which would cause a disruption. In fact taking action against a few sends the rights signals and others also would fall in line. You may not be able to eliminate corruption which is always difficult but you will certainly be able to control it. Your objective is to meet your targets as well as ensure that there is no rampant corruption or that no specific complaint of corruption goes unattended.

Case 47

You are Superintendent of Police in a district where a major criminal gang is operating under the leadership of "X" who is a known mafia leader. You have been trying to take action against this gang for several months and have being filing numerous criminal cases against X and his gang. You find that X has links in your police department also and he is getting all the information as a result of which it is becoming difficult to arrest him. X has been arrested twice in the past but has always managed to be out on bail and continue his criminal activities. You mount a lot of pressure on X and his gang and as a result of this one day X surrenders in the court. You seek police remand which is granted by the court. You are aware of the fact that X has enough money and muscle power and will manage bail once again. You decide to kill him in an encounter. You give directions to your subordinates and they kill him saying that X escaped from police custody and when he was chased he managed to get weapons from somewhere and started firing on the police force which fired back in self defense killing X. There is a lot of uproar about this encounter in the media and even certain members of the public are supporting him on caste grounds and asking for an enquiry against you.

Do you think Superintendent of Police acted in the right manner.

Discussion

It is the duty of the SP to take action in the strongest possible manner allowed by law against criminals. X is a criminal who is becoming a nuisance for the people of the district and action against him is definitely required. You have rightly filed several cases against him and also done the right thing by approaching the court and taking X in police custody. However, the constitution and the law do not allow the police to kill anyone without due process of trial. The right thing as per law would be for the SP to investigate the charges and file a strong charge sheet in the court so that the court directs strongest possible punishment against X. The SP cannot take the law into his own hands. A genuine encounter is permissible but cold blooded murder is not.

However, there is another side to this. The criminal justice system has not been able to deliver with the result that very often criminals escape without any legal action against them and cause further problems for the citizens. In such situations sometimes the police does resort to encounters to eliminate the menace. However, this is not legal and if the court orders an inquiry then the SP can land himself in trouble. There have been cases where criminal actions have been taken against the police officers in similar situations. The ultimate solution, of course is to speed up and make affective the criminal justice system.

Case 48

X and Y are DM and SP of a district which has a large jail where a lot of major criminals are in custody. X and Y find that a lot of criminal activities are taking place in the district and on inquiry it is found that most of these crimes are being committed by the criminals inside the jail using their mobile phones illegally and secretly. X and Y go on a surprise inspection to the jail and are shocked to find that leading criminals are leading a life of luxury inside the jail where they are getting whatever want for eating and drinking and mobile phones are readily available to them and in fact they have access to arms also. X and Y confiscate all the mobiles and arms and issue strict directions to the jail officers to treat these criminals as they should be treated and not allow any luxury. However, the jailor tells you that they are scared for their life and it may not possible for them to control so many dreaded criminals.

How should X and Y respond to the situations?

Discussion

This is a type of situation which does take place in reality. The dreaded criminals are so strong that they threaten the jail officers and their families and as a result are able to get mobiles and any other facility that they demand. The jail officers do not act for fear of life and the criminals continue their criminal activity without any restraint within the jail premises. X and Y have done the right thing by going on a surprise inspection and confiscating all the mobiles and arms and directing that these criminals be treated as prisoners. However, the jail officers will never be able to manage the situation and after a few months the same condition will be repeated and mobiles and other luxury items will find their way into the jail. X and Y will have to take up the matter with higher up authorities in the government and get these major criminals shifted out of their district jail and sent to far away districts and also lodged in separate jails. They should also provide security to the jailors and have a system of regular inspection of a jail by Magistrates and police officers. It is also important to break the financial support that these criminals might be getting and suitable action in this direction should be taken by X and Y. Continuous vigil would be required to see that the situation is kept under control.

Case 49

You are in the Government as officer looking after tourism and a study has shown that the best way to employ more people is by focusing on the tourism sector which has the largest impact on reducing unemployment. In your State there is a city which is known for its historical and heritage monuments which attracts a lot of domestic and foreign tourists. You are told that there is a lot more potential for growth in tourism revenue if we can have attractions for the tourists to spend more time in the city. One suggestion is that if building of Casinos is allowed then more tourists will flock to the city and spend more time and money leading to greater employment and prosperity. You agree with the suggestion and sanction the building of Casinos. However, almost immediately there are a lot of protests from opposition parties and members of the public who feel that the Casinos amount to legalizing gambling and it implies that Government is allowing immoral activities. You have an ethical dilemma.

What are your views about it?

Discussion

This is a very interesting dilemma but it is not unusual to face such situations in Government. As an example most States get major share of revenue from excise which means basically from the sale of liquor. Every year there is a higher target for excise revenue which means that people are being encouraged to imbibe more alcohol. This is opposed by many people who advocate prohibition or at least do not like the idea of the Government earning revenue out of liquor sales. Yet most States continue with this policy as they need funds for the development of the State. In this case opening of Casinos would lead to more employment and more income for the people as well as the State which could spend it on development activities. There are moral arguments against allowing gambling but then a lot of tourism revenue comes from activities like people drinking alcohol. Nobody will be forced to visit the Casinos. The location of Casinos can be far from the City and definitely not near any educational institutions or residential colony. Further there can be restriction on entry allowing only adults to visit the Casinos. The activities of the Casinos should also be regulated so that they remain a source of revenue but do not become dens of vice. One has to be pragmatic in such situations and not apply moral principles without thinking.

Case 50

Suresh has been a brilliant officer with an outstanding record. He is known for his honesty and integrity. Unfortunately he approves the project with all the good intentions which later on becomes the subject of a CBI enquiry. Just because his signature is there on the file, which he has done with the intention of prompt disposal of work and ensuring greater development of the State, he has been questioned and to his horror he finds that he has been implicated in the case on the charge of criminal conspiracy and cheating. He has to contest the case in the Court where this is likely to go on for several years and the lawyers are asking for huge amount of money on each date to argue the case. He has to defend himself in his individual capacity as the Government does not support you in a criminal matter. You have been an extremely honest officer and do not have the resources to fight the case. One businessman comes to you and offers to handle your legal expenses and does not ask for any favor in return. Suresh hesitates as he has never accepted anything from anyone. Suresh asks for your advice.

What advice would you give to him?

Discussion

This kind of situation is tragic but has happened in real life. Sometimes honest officers with good intentions approve proposals on trust and if the proposal becomes the subject matter of the CBI enquiry then anybody who has signed on the file becomes liable for criminal action. He then has to defend himself in the Court which takes an agonisingly long time and will cost a lot of money. You have to take the services of a lawyer and will have to go for a good lawyer because if your case is not argued properly then you can get convicted for no fault of yours. Unfortunately, good lawyers come at an exorbitantly high price. Normally they charge for each date. No honest officer can afford the fees charged by these lawyers. If he does not hire them he can go to jail which would damage his personal and professional life forever. Therefore, he must contest the case in the best possible manner and should hire the best lawyer. The businessman is offering Suresh the money required for hiring a lawyer. Taking money is strictly not ethical but the circumstances of this case are such that he either allows his life to be ruined or accepts the money offered. There could be different views on this but if he has no other source of income then the best course of action is to accept the offer so that he wins the case and redeem himself. It is like firing in self defense and killing somebody. Suresh could accept the offer but not make it a habit. He should continue to be honest in his working and never take money again from anybody. He would be favorably inclined towards the businessman in future but should not do anything which is grossly illegal or improper to help him. In fact he should make this clear at the time of accepting the offer itself.